January Crystal

HISTORICAL NOTES
by ELIZABETH DRIVER

The *Five Roses Cook Book*, as it has always been known, is the longest-running recipe collection from a Canadian flour company. Lake of the Woods Milling Company produced its first culinary manual in 1913 and consumers can still order a Five Roses cookbook via the address on the flour package. The 21st edition (reprinted here) was published in 1967,* Canada's centennial year, and is a direct descendant of the 1932 version.

Every decade or so, the company redesigned the cover and revised the contents. Earlier covers were a plain dark blue (1932) or dark red (1938), or featured five rose blossoms against a vivid blue background (1950s), but the photographic still-life that was introduced in 1967 and that decorated editions up to the 24th struck a bold, new note. The white utensils in a white setting were a perfect foil for the red roses and the red lettering on the flour bag, but the all-white image also symbolized the colour and purity of the flour and brought to mind a thoroughly modern kitchen.

The stylish design of the cover seemed to signal a change in the contents, but the recipes and cooking techniques were mostly familiar ones carried forward from the earlier version of the book, for example: the same Basic Sweet Dough for preparing such sticky delights as Butterscotch Rolls and Chelsea Bun; Bran Muffins, Tea Biscuits, and other favourite quick breads; a special section for Christmas Cakes; a huge selection of cookies and bars, including Chinese Chews and Date Squares; Prize Butter Tarts (leading the Tarts section); Ribbon, Checkerboard, and Rolled fancy sandwiches; Creamed Salmon on toast and Macaroni and Cheese for lunch time; Jellied Cabbage Salad; and Corn Relish. In 1975, the text still began with Depression-Era instructions for How to Take Out the Printing from Cotton Flour Bags! A few new recipes made their first appearance—Prize Pizza (Canadians remain attached to this convenience food), Hawaiian-style Turkey Casserole (pineapple as a flavouring no longer has the same allure), and Barbecued Short Ribs (the fashion for grilled food continues). And there was a significant innovation at the end of the text—a new chapter of sophisticated "Foreign Fare." Dishes such as Crêpes Suzettes, Lasagne, Fondue Bourguignonne, Melon Soup (Dong Gwah Jong), Sukiyaki, and Swedish Meat Balls brought the world to Canada's tables. Yet, this version of the Five Roses cookbook is more a symbol of the enduring traditions of Canadian cuisine up to 1975 than a break with the past. More profound change would come in 1980, when the editors of the 25th edition dropped directions for bleaching flour bags, introduced metric measurements and microwave ovens, and integrated the "foreign" recipes into the main text as part of the standard Canadian repertoire.

* *The 21st edition is undated, but one owner reported acquiring her copy in 1967.*

Fourth printing, 2008

The publisher acknowledges Carol Ann Shipman for securing the permissions to reproduce
this edition.

Special thanks to Sheila Clark for providing her copy of the book.
Special thanks to Stephanie Cunningham for providing a copy of the book with a pristine cover.

Whitecap Books is known for its expertise in the cookbook market, and has produced
some of the most innovative and familiar titles found in kitchens across North America.

Printed in Canada

Library and Archives Canada Cataloguing in Publication
Five roses: a guide to good cooking/historical notes by Elizabeth Driver

(Classic Canadian cookbook series)
ISBN 1-55285-458-2
ISBN 978-1-55285-458-7

1. Cookery. I. Series
TX715.F575 2003   641.5   C2003–910176–2

The publisher acknowledges the financial support of the Government of Canada through
the Book Publishing Industry Development Program (BPIDP) and the Province of British Columbia
through the Book Publishing Tax Credit.

Please note that the ingredients, methods and cooking times listed in this book are
consistent with the kitchen appliances and techniques that were in use in 1967.
Current equipment and supplies may produce different results that are inconsistent
with contemporary food safety theories.

A GUIDE TO GOOD COOKING

For well over half a century the Five Roses Guide to Good Cooking has been Canada's most popular cookbook. Prized as a practical, down to earth recipe book, it is the day to day friend of thousands of Canadian homemakers.

This exciting new 21st Edition contains the best of previous editions and a host of new and interesting recipes. Every recipe has been approved and thoroughly tested in the famous Five Roses Kitchens. We guarantee that they will work perfectly in your kitchen.

This book has been specially designed for today's busy homemakers. The attractive new cover has a plastic finish—wipes clean instantly. New, easy to read type has been used throughout, and the layout of the sections has been planned for your convenience. There are handy cross references for compatible recipes matching, for example, cakes with icings, meats with sauces. The familiar spiral binding allows the book to lie flat while in use, while the many helpful hints and instruction charts make it a joy to work with.

No wonder the Five Roses Guide to Good Cooking has become a popular gift for the new bride. It is this tradition of service to homemakers which has made Five Roses Flour Canada's most respected name in baking.

TWENTY-FIRST EDITION

Published and Copyrighted by

LAKE OF THE WOODS MILLING COMPANY, LIMITED

Montreal, Winnipeg

Pre-Sifted Flour

To-day, Canada's best baking flours are so perfectly milled that they are termed pre-sifted. To the homemaker, this means that the laborious and messy step of sifting is no longer necessary.

Five Roses All-Purpose Flour is a pre-sifted flour—cloud-soft and light—sifted through the finest of silk screens to give you an exacting uniformity and fineness of texture once achieved only by sifting in your own home.

All recipes in this book are based on Pre-Sifted Flour and require no sifting.

How to Measure

Recipes calling for pre-sifted flour

Spoon flour lightly into a dry measuring cup (see page 7) and level off with a flat knife or spatula. DO NOT SCOOP OR POUR FLOUR from bag or container. Some people still have a personal preference to sift, even when using pre-sifted flour. If you would like to do so, measure as above, then sift.

Other recipes calling for flour to be sifted

Some of your recipes may specify that the flour should be sifted. You may use pre-sifted flour, following the recipe exactly, sifting where indicated. If you prefer the convenience of not sifting, measure as for pre-sifted flour (above) then remove 2 tablespoons of flour per cup called for in the recipe.

Note: When you select not to sift, your dry ingredients are added by stirring them with the flour until well blended.

We appreciate the fact that from time to time certain problems may arise with regard to home cooking and baking. For this reason we are pleased to remind you that our Five Roses Kitchens will always be most pleased to help you. Address all inquiries to:

PAULINE HARVEY, *Director*
FIVE ROSES KITCHENS
BOX 6089
MONTREAL, P.Q.

CONTENTS

INTRODUCTION

It must be borne in mind that all the recipes in this book have been developed for use with pre-sifted FIVE ROSES ALL PURPOSE FLOUR. They are not designed for use with flours of inferior quality and are absolutely unsuited for so-called SPECIAL or PASTRY FLOURS.

You will find all recipes are based on products available across Canada, however, in some Provinces, can sizes and jars will vary. In these instances, the size nearest that asked for may be used.

How to Take Out the Printing from Cotton Flour Bags

1. Remove all excess flour from bag.
2. Wet the bag in warm water.
3. Spread out on a flat surface and soap all lettering well with laundry soap or detergent.
4. Soak in the following solution for 1 hour.

   2 quarts warm water
   1 cup bleach

   This solution is enough for two 100 lb. bags or four 50 lb. bags at one time.
5. Remove bag from solution and wash in washing machine. If washing is done by hand, the material should be rinsed first in warm water, preferably by agitating with a stick, to remove excess bleaching solution. Although not unduly strong, the solution may affect the skin if hands are exposed to it.

Note: Best results will be obtained if the solution is made up fresh for each occasion. A slight indication of lettering may be noticeable in some cases, but will mostly disappear when exposed to sunlight. Should it be necessary to repeat the operation, give only 15 minute treatments as excessive exposure to bleach will weaken the fabric.

Care of Flour

Always store flour in a dry place. The ideal temperature is 70°F. or under. Flour will lose its strength if kept in a hot place. As flour absorbs odours quickly, always store it away from anything which has a strong odour, such as onions, paint, turpentine, etc. If flour is stored in a cold place during the winter months, a sufficient quantity for each baking should be placed where it can be warmed to room temperature before mixing into dough or batter.

How to Plan Well-Balanced Meals

Good nutrition consists of eating the right foods at the right time and in the right quantities. Following a few basic rules gives you the key to simplified meal planning and wise shopping.

Canada's Food Rules

The following foods should be eaten every day.

1. **MILK:** children: 1 pint to 1 quart
   adults: ½ to 1 pint
2. **FRUIT:** one serving of citrus fruit or tomatoes, or their juices, and one serving of other fruit.

3. **VEGETABLES:** one serving of potatoes and two servings of other vegetables, preferably leafy, green or yellow and frequently raw.

4. **CEREALS AND BREAD:** one serving of whole grain cereal and at least 4 slices of bread (whole wheat, brown or white) with butter or fortified margarine.

5. **MEAT AND FISH:** one serving of meat, fish, poultry or meat alternates, such as beans, peas, nuts, eggs or cheese. In addition, use eggs and cheese at least three times a week each. Use liver occasionally.

6. A fish liver oil, as a source of vitamin D, should be given to children and expectant mothers and may be advisable for other adults.

How to Measure Correctly

Successful cooking begins with exact measuring. All measuring should be done with standard measuring cups and spoons. Check to see that they are in good shape. If cups or spoons are warped, they will not measure accurately. Buy only those that are marked "standard" or "accurate".

Liquids.

Use a standard glass measuring cup. Place on level surface and fill to mark. Bend down and check measure at eye level. If using a measuring spoon, dip spoon into liquid; lift out carefully as spoon should be so full that it won't hold another drop.

Dry ingredients.

Use standard measuring spoons and nested measuring cups. Cup sets should measure 1 cup, ½ cup, ⅓ cup and ¼ cup. Fill to overflowing by spooning and then level off, using straight edge of knife or metal spatula. Do not pack except for brown sugar. Pack brown sugar firmly in cup so that it will keep the cup shape when turned out. Lightly pack bread crumbs.

Butter, shortening or lard.

Use one of two methods. Press firmly into fractional cup or measuring spoon so no air holes are left; level off and scoop out. Or, partially fill a measuring cup with water leaving space for amount of shortening to be measured. Add shortening until water level moves up to the 1 cup mark, then drain off water. For example, if ¼ cup shortening is desired, pour ¾ cup cold water into cup, add shortening until water reaches top, then drain off water.

Chunky foods.

Use a large standard glass measuring cup and pack lightly.

How to measure moulds and bowls.

Measure the amount of water required to fill them. Mark size on bottom. Most are measured according to American measures — i.e. a 1 quart bowl or mould will hold 4 cups.

How to measure baking pans.

Measure pans across the top from inside rim to inside rim, using a ruler.

Table of Kitchen Measures
(All Measurements Are Level)

A few grains	= less than ⅛ teaspoon	1 cup	= 16 tablespoons
A dash	= 2 to 3 drops or a few grains	8 fluid ounces	= 1 cup
1 saltspoon	= ¼ teaspoon	1 Imperial pint	= 2½ cups
1 tablespoon	= 3 teaspoons	1 Imperial quart	= 5 cups

1 Imperial gallon = 4 Imperial quarts

FRACTIONS OF CUPS

⅞ cup = 14 tablespoons	½ cup = 8 tablespoons
¾ cup = 12 tablespoons	⅓ cup = 5⅓ tablespoons
⅔ cup = 10⅔ tablespoons	¼ cup = 4 tablespoons

⅛ cup = 2 tablespoons

TABLE OF FOOD EQUIVALENTS

Note: The equivalents are **approximate** and serve only as a guide for your convenience.

Ingredient	Amount	Equivalent
Almonds (shelled)	8 oz.	1½ cups
(blanched)	8 oz.	1¾ cups ground
Apples	1 medium	1 cup sliced
Bread crumbs	3 to 4 slices	1 cup dry bread crumbs
	1 slice	½ to ¾ cup soft bread crumbs
Butter	1 lb.	2 cups
Cheese	4 oz.	1 cup grated
Chocolate (unsweetened)	1 lb.	16 squares
	1 square	1 oz.
Citron peel (diced)	4 oz.	¾ cup
Cocoa	1 lb.	5 cups
Coconut (shredded)	7 oz. pkg.	3¼ cups
Crackers, graham	15	1 cup fine crumbs
Crackers, soda	22	1 cup fine crumbs
Cream, whipping	1 cup	2 cups whipped
Currants	1 lb.	3 cups
Dates	14 oz. pkg.	2½ cups
Dry beans	1 cup	2½ cups cooked
Eggs, whole	1 cup	4 to 6 medium
whites	1 cup	8 to 10 medium
yolks	1 cup	10 to 14 medium
Flour, all-purpose	1 lb.	3½ cups
graham	1 lb.	4⅓ cups
rye, wholewheat	1 lb.	4¼ cups
Gelatin	¼ oz. envelope	2½ teaspoons (equivalent to 1 tablespoon in recipe)
Lard	1 lb.	2⅓ cups
Lemon	1	3 tablespoons juice
		2⅓ tablespoons grated rind
Macaroni, spaghetti, noodles	½ lb.	4 cups cooked
Oats, Quick	1 lb.	5¾ cups
Instant	1 lb.	6½ cups
Orange	1	⅓ cup juice
		2½ tablespoons grated rind
Onion	1 medium	½ cup chopped
Pecans (shelled)	4 oz. pkg.	1¼ cups **or** 1 cup chopped
Raisins, seedless	1 lb.	3 cups
seeded	1 lb.	2½ cups
Rice, long grain	1 cup	3½ cups cooked
pre-cooked	1 cup	2 cups cooked
Shortening	1 lb.	2⅓ cups
Suet	½ lb.	1½ cups chopped
Sugar, brown	1 lb.	2⅓ cups
fruit	1 lb.	2½ cups
granulated	1 lb.	2¼ cups
icing	1 lb.	4½ cups sifted
Walnuts, pieces	8 oz. pkg.	2 cups chopped

GENERAL COOKING TERMS

Bake — To cook by dry heat, usually in an oven. When applied to meat, it is called "roast".

Baste — To moisten food while baking by pouring liquid or fat over it.

Batter — A mixture of flour, liquid and other ingredients that can be beaten or stirred.

Beat — To mix with an over-and-over motion, either by spoon, rotary beater or electric beater.

Blanch — To immerse foods briefly in boiling water, usually followed by a quick cooling in cold water. Used to whiten or remove skins and for vegetables that are to be frozen.

Blend — To combine two or more ingredients so that each loses its identity.

Boil — To heat until bubbles constantly break on the surface.

Braise — To simmer in a covered dish in a small amount of liquid.

Broil — To cook under direct heat or over hot coals.

Caramelize — To heat dry sugar or foods containing sugar until light brown and of a caramel flavour.

Chill — To place in refrigerator or other cold place until cold.

Combine — To mix ingredients together.

Cream — To work foods until soft and fluffy. Usually applied to shortening, butter or other fat and sugar.

Dough — A mixture of liquid and flour that is stiff enough to be handled or kneaded.

Dredge — To coat completely with flour or other mixture.

Dust — To sprinkle lightly as with flour or sugar.

Eviscerate — To remove internal organs of fish or poultry.

Flake — To break into small pieces, usually with a fork.

Fold — To combine a solid ingredient with a delicate substance such as beaten egg white with a folding motion rather than beating to avoid loss of air.

Glaze — To coat with syrup, thin icing, jam or jelly.

Grate — To rub a food against a grater to form small particles.

Grind — To put food through a food chopper.

Knead — To manipulate with a pressing motion plus folding and stretching. Usually applied to bread dough.

Lard — To place strips of fat into or on top of lean meat or fish.

Marinate — To let stand in a marinade (usually a mixture of oil, lemon juice or vinegar and seasonings).

Mince — To chop very fine.

Mix — To combine ingredients.

Poach — To cook slowly in hot liquid to cover.

Purée — The thick pulp with juice obtained by putting food through a colander, sieve, food mill or blender.

Sauté — To cook in a skillet in a small amount of fat.

Scald — To heat just below the boiling point. Also means to pour boiling water over food or dip food briefly in boiling water.

Score — To cut lightly so as to mark the surface of the food with lines.

Sear — To brown the surface of foods quickly.

Simmer — To cook just below boiling point so that tiny bubbles form on bottom or sides of pan.

Steam — To cook over, not in, boiling water.

Stir — To mix ingredients with a circular motion using a spoon or other utensil.

Whip — To beat rapidly with wire whisk or beater to incorporate air and make a substance light and fluffy.

MIXING

The method used for putting ingredients together is important in cookery. Rules for mixing, given with each type of recipe, should be followed carefully.

To Stir. Mix by using a circular motion — widening the circles until ingredients are blended.

To Beat. Turn ingredients over and over with a brisk whipping or stirring motion, either with spoon or beater, and thus making mixture smooth and enclosing air.

To Whip. Incorporate air or produce expansion as in whipping cream or egg whites by beating rapidly.

To Fold. This method is an important one and is used to add new ingredients to a mixture that has been beaten until light. Cut down through mixture with rubber spatula, spoon, whisk or fork; go across bottom of bowl, up and over, close to surface. Repeat until ingredients are just blended. Cutting and folding prevents the escape of air or gases that have already been introduced into mixture.

To Cut in. This method is used to mix shortening with dry ingredients so as to leave the shortening in small particles. Use two knives or pastry blender.

WHEN BEATING EGGS

Well-beaten egg — one which has been whipped until foamy and slightly thickened.

Well-beaten yolk — one whipped until thick and lemon coloured.

Well-beaten white — one whipped until firm peaks form when beater is lifted out. Never beat until peaks are dry and over-stiff.

TABLE OF SUBSTITUTIONS

Ingredient	Amount	Substitute
Baking powder (phosphate or tartrate type)	1½ teaspoons	1 teaspoon double acting baking powder
	1 teaspoon	½ teaspoon baking soda plus 1 teaspoon cream of tartar
Butter	1 cup	1 cup margarine **or** 1 cup shortening **or** ⅞ cup lard plus ½ teaspoon salt
Chocolate	1 square unsweetened	3 tablespoons cocoa plus 1 tablespoon shortening or butter
Cream	1 cup light cream	⅞ cup milk plus 3 tablespoons butter
	1 cup heavy cream	¾ cup milk plus ⅓ cup butter
Eggs	1 whole egg	2 egg yolks
Flour (for thickener)	1 tablespoon	½ tablespoon cornstarch **or** 2 teaspoons quick-cooking tapioca
Flour	1 cup all-purpose	1 cup plus 2 tablespoons cake flour
	1 cup cake flour	⅞ cup all-purpose flour
Meat Stock	1 cup	1 bouillon cube dissolved in 1 cup hot water **or** 1 cup consomme
Milk	1 cup whole milk	1 cup skim milk plus 2 tablespoons butter **or** ½ cup evaporated milk plus ½ cup water
	1 cup sour milk	1 tablespoon lemon juice or white vinegar plus fresh whole milk to make 1 cup **or** 1 cup buttermilk

BAKING

Correct temperature is the secret of nearly all successful cooking. Many foods which have been well-mixed are spoiled in the oven. When the home oven is not equipped with a thermostat, a portable oven thermometer should be used. These are available in most hardware and department stores at a reasonable price.

THERMOMETERS

Oven thermometer — useful to have, especially if home oven is not equipped with a thermostat or to use as a cross check.

Candy thermometer — useful for making candies, jams and jellies. Not essential to have but very handy.

Deep frying thermometer — useful for deep fat frying. If a lot of deep fat frying is done without an electric deep fat fryer, this thermometer should be used.

Meat thermometer — useful for roasting meats and poultry. Is not essential but does serve as a guide to better roasting.

TEMPERATURE CHART

Very slow oven - - - - - - - - -	250° to 300°F.
Slow oven - - - - - - - - - - -	300° to 325°F.
Moderate oven - - - - - - - - - -	325° to 375°F.
Moderately hot oven - - - - - - -	375° to 400°F.
Hot oven - - - - - - - - - - -	400° to 450°F.
Very hot oven - - - - - - - - -	450° to 500°F.

To Test Oven Temperatures Without A Thermometer

Sprinkle a small amount of flour in a pan and place in a heated oven, leave 5 minutes.

If flour is a delicate brown	— oven is slow	— 250° to 325°F.
If flour is a golden brown	— oven is moderate	— 325° to 400°F.
If flour is a deep brown	— oven is hot	— 400° to 450°F.
If flour is a deep dark brown	— oven is very hot	— 450° to 500°F.

BAKING TIMES AT PREHEATED OVEN TEMPERATURES

Note: This is an **approximate** guide. Follow baking times and temperatures given in individual recipes.

	Temperature (°F.)	Time (minutes)		Temperature (°F.)	Time (minutes)
Yeast Breads and Quick Breads			**Cookies**		
Bread - loaves	375° to 450°	30	Drop cookies	350°	8 to 12
- rolls	350° to 450°	15 to 20	Macaroons	350°	8 to 10
Coffee cake	375° to 400°	20 to 25	Meringues	250°	60, then dry 1 hour
Corn Bread	375° to 400°	30			
Fruit and Nut			Pressed	350°	10 to 12
Bread	350°	60	Refrigerator		
Muffins	400°	30	(sliced)	350°	8 to 10
Popovers	450°	15	Rolled	375°	8 to 10
	then 350°	15 to 20			
Tea Biscuits	450°	12 to 15	**Pastry**		
Cakes			Pie shells		
Angel Food	375°	30	- single crust		
Butter cakes			without filling	450°	10 to 12
- layer	350°	25 to 30	- double crust	450°	10
- square	350°	50 to 60		then 350°	30 to 40
Cake mixes	350°	30 to 35			
Chiffon cake	325°	60	Tart shells		
Cupcakes	350°	20 to 25	without filling	450°	10 to 15
Fruit cake	275° to 300°	1½ to 4 hours	Turnovers	450°	10
Gingerbread	325° to 350°	50 to 60		then 375°	30
Jelly Roll	325°	15	Puff pastry	450° to 500°	10
Pound cake	325°	1 to 1¼ hours		then 350°	10
Sponge cake	325°	60	Cream puffs		
Upside-down			and éclairs	425°	30
cake	350°	50		then 325°	10 to 15

A GUIDE TO HIGH ALTITUDE ADJUSTMENTS IN BAKING*
Cakes

Adjustment	3000 ft. above sea level	5000 ft. above sea level	7000 ft. above sea level
Increase liquid: for each cup, add —	1 to 2 tablespoons	2 to 3 tablespoons	3 to 4 tablespoons
Reduce baking powder: for each teaspoon, decrease —	⅛ teaspoon	⅛ to ¼ teaspoon	¼ to ½ teaspoon
Reduce sugar: for each cup, decrease —	—	—	1 to 2 tablespoons
Increase flour: for each cup, add —	—	—	1 to 2 tablespoons

*This is merely a guide and it may be necessary to experiment a few times with each recipe to discover the best proportions. When two amounts are given, always start with the small adjustment. A 10 to 15 degree increase in baking temperature at high altitudes may give better results with cup cakes and layer cakes. Recipes requiring baking soda may need a slight reduction in that leavening.

Angel, sponge or chiffon cakes.
These will require less beating but number of eggs may have to be increased. For every 5000 ft. altitude increase, increase baking temperature by 10 or 15 degrees.

Rich cakes.
It is sometimes necessary to reduce the shortening by 1 or 2 tablespoons.

Yeast Breads.
Little adjustment is needed. However, the rising time may be reduced. Oven temperature should be increased by 10 or 15 degrees. Bake loaves at a higher temperature (425°F.) for first 15 minutes and then reduce temperature to the temperature called for in the recipe for remainder of baking time.

Cookies.
No changes are necessary.

Pastry.
No changes are necessary.

Candy, Jams, Jellies.
Water boils at 212°F. at sea level but at 4000 ft. above sea level it will boil at 204°F. Thus candies, jams and jellies will cook faster and will need constant watching.

Deep Fat Frying.
Fry at 350°F. to 360°F. instead of 375°F.

KITCHEN HINTS

To sour milk, combine 1 tablespoon lemon juice or white vinegar with fresh whole milk to make 1 cup.

To keep scalding milk from scorching, rinse the pan with hot water before using.

To keep cut fruits from discolouring, (such as bananas, peaches, pears or apples) sprinkle with lemon or pineapple juice.

To prevent deep-dish fruit pies from bubbling over, place a pyrex custard cup upside down in centre of dish. Add fruit and top with crust. Cup also lifts pastry so that it won't get soggy.

To moisten brown sugar which has already hardened, place apple slices in container with sugar and cover tightly.

To divide an egg, beat slightly and measure with a tablespoon.

To make dish washing easier, rinse egg or flour coated utensils with cold water before washing.

To tint coconut, place a small amount of shredded coconut in a glass jar. Add a few drops of food colouring. Cover jar and shake until coconut is coloured.

To whip evaporated milk, place can of milk in freezer unit until partially frozen. Pour contents into a very cold bowl, add 1 tablespoon lemon juice to ⅔ cup milk and whip as cream.

To coat chicken or meat, measure flour and seasonings into paper bag. Add a few pieces at a time and shake to coat. Use remaining seasoned flour to thicken gravy.

To remove odours from jars and bottles, pour a solution of water and baking soda into them and let stand for several hours.

YEAST BREADS

Baking yeast breads is surprisingly easy and such a simple task! No other type of baking can give you such a wonderful sense of personal satisfaction. You can feel the real thrill of creative cooking when that rich aroma of home made bread fills your kitchen.

A perfect loaf of bread is plump with a rounded top and straight sides. It has a tender, golden brown crust which may be crisp, or it may be shiny and soft from having been brushed with melted butter. The grain is fine and even, with slightly elongated cells; the crumb should feel moist and elastic to the touch.

The secret of good bread making is to select your ingredients with care and to master a few simple skills. Don't let the long list of ingredients frighten you.

INGREDIENTS

Flour—Flour is the chief ingredient in all breads. Wheat flour is superior to all other flours for bread making because it contains certain proteins which unite to form gluten when mixed with liquid. Gluten is the substance which gives the dough its elastic quality so that it can expand and hold within it the gas bubble formed by the yeast. Although bread flour is used by commercial bakers, the flour used for making bread in the home is all-purpose flour. FIVE ROSES ALL-PURPOSE FLOUR contains enough gluten to make delicious, light rolls and breads each time. A continuous quality control programme ensures that FIVE ROSES ALL-PURPOSE FLOUR will give you the same, uniform, dependable, baking results. Because FIVE ROSES ALL-PURPOSE FLOUR is "pre-sifted" it is not necessary to sift before measuring. FIVE ROSES ALL-PURPOSE FLOUR is enriched flour and therefore has the essential iron and vitamin value of whole wheat flour.

Most bread recipes state an approximate quantity of flour. Add only enough to make the dough handle easily. **Too much flour** will make a heavy dough which will not rise properly. **Too little flour** will make a soft dough, coarser in texture and more likely to collapse during rising or baking.

FIVE ROSES DARK RYE FLOUR, FIVE ROSES WHOLE WHEAT FLOUR and FIVE ROSES GRAHAM FLOUR are used in making specialty breads, usually in combination with all-purpose flour.

Yeast—Yeast is the leavening agent used in bread making. It is a tiny living plant which transforms the dough by fermentation into the delicious porous structure which we call bread. It may be purchased in two forms—active dry yeast and compressed yeast.

> **Active Dry Yeast** is in the form of tiny brown granules or pellets. It stays fresh for several months. However, always check the expiry date on the back of the envelope before using. The yeast requires softening in lukewarm water

(95°F.). All yeast recipes in this book are based on this type of yeast as it is the most common type available.

Compressed Yeast is in the form of a cake and is often called fresh yeast. It is very perishable and must be refrigerated. It is greyish-tan in colour, should be firm and springy to the touch and should break easily without undue crumbling. When stale, it turns brown and develops a strong "off" odour. To substitute for active dry yeast, use one yeast cake for each envelope of dry yeast. Soften in lukewarm water but do not add sugar to the water.

Sugar—Sugar is food for the yeast and works with yeast to form the carbon dioxide gas which causes the dough to rise. It also adds flavour and aids in browning the crust. Too much sugar, however, can retard the action of yeast.

Salt—Salt helps control the rate of rising and contributes to the flavour.

Fat—Fat makes the bread tender, helps to increase its volume and improves the keeping quality and flavour. Shortening, lard, vegetable oils, margarine and butter are all suitable fats when used in reliable recipes calling for them.

Liquid—Liquid binds the other ingredients together. Those most commonly used are water or milk. Occasionally fruit juices may be used for special flavours. Bread and rolls made with all water have a wheaty flavour and crisp crust, while those made with milk have a more velvety grain and a creamy white crumb. All liquids should be lukewarm. Fresh milk must be scalded to destroy undesirable micro-organisms which might interfere with the yeast action.

STEPS IN MAKING BREAD

There are 3 basic methods in making bread:

1. **Straight Dough Method:** This is the most familiar method of making bread. The mixing is done in a continuous operation. After the yeast has been softened in lukewarm water and sugar, it is added to the liquid, sugar, salt and shortening. The flour is then added to make a soft dough that can be kneaded. The rising time will depend on the amount of yeast. Different recipes vary in the amount of yeast and therefore will vary in rising time. Most of the yeast recipes in this cook book are prepared by this method.

2. **Sponge Method:** One of the oldest methods of making bread. The mixing is done in two operations. First, a sponge is made by dissolving the yeast and some sugar in lukewarm water and then combining this mixture with half of the flour. The batter is allowed to rise until bubbly and spongelike. The other ingredients are added with enough flour to make a dough that can be kneaded. The dough is then kneaded and finished in the same way as for the Straight Dough Method.

3. **Batter Method:** A quick and easy way to bake with yeast. The ingredients are merely mixed together to form a batter rather than a dough and is allowed to rise in the bowl or baking pan. It requires no kneading or shaping. When ready to bake, the batter will look moist and somewhat rough with small air bubbles just under the surface. An open texture is characteristic. Casserole breads and yeast coffee cakes are often made this way. Kugelhoft (page 26) is typical of this method.

Temperature—Temperature plays an important part in bread baking. **Too much** heat can kill the yeast. **Too little** can slow it down. For best results, dissolve active dry yeast in lukewarm water (95°F.). To test, drop a little on your wrist. It should feel neither warm nor cold. Before combining hot ingredients to softened yeast, they should be cooled to lukewarm.

MIXING

Mixing — Measure flour accurately by spooning it into measuring cup. Level off with small spatula or flat knife. Many recipes state to stir half the flour into the yeast mixture first, beating with a spoon until almost smooth. The remaining flour is then added gradually, using only enough to prevent dough from sticking to bowl or hands. At this point, the dough is often too heavy to be mixed with a spoon and it is easier to use your hands. An approximate amount of flour is given in the recipes because the flour's absorptive properties vary with temperature and humidity.

KNEADING

Kneading — Kneading develops the gluten which in turn develops good grain and texture. As you knead, you can feel the dough changing from a rough, uneven texture to a smooth elastic ball. Turn dough onto a lightly   floured board, canvas or table top. Keep a supply of flour handy as you may require extra as you knead. The amount needed is determined by the amount the dough will absorb. Flour hands lightly and press dough into a slightly flat ball. Fold dough over on itself towards you then push it lightly with a sort of rocking motion, with the heel of the hand, away from you. Make a quarter turn and repeat the process rhythmically until the surface of the dough feels satiny and smooth. This usually requires from 8 to 10 minutes of kneading.

RISING

Rising—Round dough into a smooth ball and place in a lightly greased bowl that is large enough to let it double in bulk without overflowing. Turn dough over to grease top. Cover with a clean linen towel to prevent a crust from forming. Let rise in a warm place (80-85°F.) free from draft until double in bulk. Temperature is important as the yeast works best at these temperatures. The rising time can vary depending on temperature, amount of yeast, type of flour used and recipe. The times given in the recipes are approximate, and are a useful guide to tell you when to test the dough. **To test whether dough has doubled in bulk**—press two fingers into it. If dents remain, then dough is ready.

WHERE TO LET THE DOUGH RISE

If room is not warm enough, we suggest one of the following:

1. Set bowl in a cupboard beside a pan of hot water. Add more hot water occasionally to keep temperature up.

2. Set bowl in a cold oven. Place a pan of hot water on the shelf beneath it. Add more hot water occasionally to keep temperature up.

3. Set bowl on broiler rack with hot water in broiler pan. Add more hot water occasionally to keep temperature up.

4. Place near stove or radiator but never directly on either.

In cold weather, warm the bowl before putting in the dough.

Punching down
— When dough is ready, punch down by plunging fist into dough, then fold edges toward the centre until dough is original size. If second rising is indicated on recipe, place folded edges down

in bowl; cover and let rise again. Second rising is usually shorter in time.

SHAPING

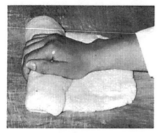

Shaping the loaves
— Divide dough into as many portions as there are to be loaves. Knead each part lightly to make a smooth ball. A resting period at this point makes the dough easier to handle. Cover with a towel and let rest 10 minutes. Flatten each ball and roll to a rectangle of uniform thickness. Shape with hands if necessary. Roll dough towards you as for a jelly roll. Press gently with heel of hand to seal each roll. Seal final seam. Seal ends of loaf by pressing side of hand down on ends. Gently fold sealed ends of loaf under.

Letting loaves rise __

Place each loaf seam side down in a greased loaf pan. Size of pan will vary with recipe. Do not work corners of the roll into corners of pan. Cover loaves with a clean towel and set in a warm place until double in bulk.

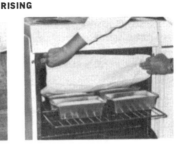

Baking__ When loaves are double in bulk, the surface should be smooth and moist in appearance with no dry areas or cracks. Place loaves evenly spaced in a pre-heated oven. Temperature of oven and cooking time will vary with individual recipe.

To test if loaves are done __ When bread is done, it shrinks slightly from the sides of the pan and has a golden brown crust. The loaf should sound hollow when lightly tapped on the bottom.

Cooling the loaves—Remove bread from pans as soon as it comes from the oven. Let cool on cooling rack, uncovered and away from drafts. If a soft crust is preferred, brush tops of hot baked loaf with melted butter.

Storing—When completely cooled, wrap in waxed paper and store in well ventilated bread box or in refrigerator.

Freezing—Wrap completely cooled bread in moisture-vapor-proof freezer wrapper. Make sure wrapping is airtight. Store in freezer. Bread will hold its freshness for several weeks in freezer.

STANDARD BREAD

1 pkg. active dry yeast	2 tablespoons shortening
½ cup lukewarm water	2 tablespoons salt
1 teaspoon sugar	2 cups water
2 cups milk	10-12 cups Five Roses All-purpose
¼ cup sugar	Flour

Sprinkle the yeast in ½ cup lukewarm water with 1 teaspoon sugar; let stand 10 minutes, then stir. Scald milk; add sugar, shortening and salt. Stir until shortening melts; add water and cool to lukewarm. Add yeast to cooled milk mixture. Stir in 6 cups of the Five Roses Flour and beat with a spoon until almost smooth. Add remaining 6 to 7 cups of flour gradually, mixing it in thoroughly and using just enough flour to prevent sticking to either the board or the hands. Turn dough out on lightly floured board and knead it until smooth and satiny (about 8 to 10 minutes). Shape into a smooth ball and place in a greased bowl, turn ball of dough over in bowl to grease surface. Cover, and let rise in a warm place (80 to 85°F.) until double in bulk (about 1 hour). Punch down, let rise again until double in bulk (about ¾ hour). Punch down again and turn out on a lightly floured board. Divide into 4 equal portions and round into balls; cover and let rest 10 minutes. Mould into loaves, place in greased 8½″ x 4½″ x 2½″ loaf pans. Cover and let rise in a warm place until double in bulk (about 1 hour). Bake at 400°F. for 30 to 40 minutes.

Yield: 4 loaves.

VARIATIONS

Three Hour White Bread: Follow Standard Bread recipe. Use 2 packages of active dry yeast and dissolve in 1 cup lukewarm water. Reduce the 2 cups water called for in the recipe to 1½ cups. Omit second rising.

Whole Wheat Bread: Follow Standard Bread recipe but use half Five Roses All-purpose Flour and half Five Roses Whole Wheat Flour.

Rye Bread: Follow Standard Bread recipe but use brown sugar in place of white sugar. Add 6 cups of Five Roses All-purpose Flour and then add 5 cups Five Roses Dark Rye Flour. Add more all-purpose, if necessary, to make a dough stiff enough to knead.

Raisin Bread: Follow Standard Bread recipe but increase sugar to 1 cup. Add 3 cups raisins just before second half of flour is added.

Currant Bread: Follow Standard Bread recipe and add 1 cup clean dried currants just before second half of flour is added.

Cheese Bread: Follow Standard Bread recipe and add 1½ cups grated Cheddar cheese mixing it in with the last of the flour to be added.

FRENCH BREAD

1½ tablespoons shortening	4 cups Five Roses All-purpose Flour
1 tablespoon sugar	2 teaspoons salt
1¼ cups boiling water	Cornmeal
¼ cup lukewarm water	1 egg white, slightly beaten
1 pkg. active dry yeast	

Combine shortening, sugar and boiling water; cool to lukewarm. Sprinkle yeast over lukewarm water, let stand for 10 minutes; stir until dissolved and add to first mixture. Stir salt and Five Roses Flour together in large bowl. Make a well in

Top Left:
BOHEMIAN BRAID
page 22

Bottom Left:
STANDARD BREAD
page 18

Centre Right:
FRENCH BREAD
page 18

Top Right:
BOWKNOTS
page 25

centre and add liquid mixture; mix well. Turn out dough on lightly floured board; knead until smooth and elastic. Place in greased bowl, turn to grease top. Cover with a clean cloth, let rise in a warm place (80-85°F.) until double in bulk—about 2 hours. Punch down dough; divide in two. Pat each half into rectangle on lightly floured board. Form each rectangle into French loaf by rolling dough towards you, then rolling and pressing into desired tapered shape. Place loaves on greased baking sheet that has been sprinkled with cornmeal. Cover and let rise in warm place to just less than double in bulk—about 1 hour. Brush with slightly beaten egg white. Cut ¼″ diagonal slits across top of loaves with razor blade or sharp knife. Place a shallow pan of boiling water on bottom rack of oven when pre-heating oven. Bake 15 minutes at 400°F.; remove pan of water from oven and brush bread again with egg white; bake 30 minutes longer at 350°F.

Yield: 2 loaves.

CRACKED WHEAT BREAD

¼ cup sugar	2 tablespoons molasses
½ cup lukewarm water	5 cups hot water
1 pkg. active dry yeast	10-12 cups Five Roses All-purpose
1 tablespoon salt	Flour
4 tablespoons melted shortening	3 cups Ogilvie Cracked Wheat

Dissolve 1 teaspoon of the sugar in ½ cup of lukewarm water; add the yeast and let stand 10 minutes, then stir. Dissolve remaining sugar, salt, shortening and molasses in 5 cups hot water and cool to lukewarm. Add yeast mixture and stir. Combine the Five Roses Flour and Cracked Wheat; add to yeast mixture, working in the flour until stiff enough to knead without sticking to the hands. Add extra flour if needed. Knead on floured board until dough is smooth (about 10 minutes). Shape into two smooth balls and place in two greased bowls; turn balls of dough over in bowls to grease surface. Cover and let rise in a warm place (80 to 85°F.) until double in bulk (about 1¼ hours). Punch down, let rise again until double in bulk (about 1 hour); punch down again and turn out on lightly floured board. Divide dough into 4 equal portions and round up into balls; cover and let rest 10 minutes. Mould into loaves and place in greased 9″ x 5″ x 3″ loaf pans. Cover and let rise until double in bulk (about 1 hour). Bake at 400°F. for 50 to 60 minutes.

Yield: 4 loaves.

VITA-B BREAD

1 cup Ogilvie Vita-B Cereal	1 teaspoon sugar
4 cups water	½ cup lukewarm water
2 tablespoons shortening	1 pkg. active dry yeast
¾ cup molasses	10-12 cups Five Roses All-purpose
1 tablespoon salt	Flour

Combine Vita-B and water; bring to boil, stirring constantly. Remove from heat and add shortening, molasses and salt; cool to lukewarm. Dissolve sugar in ½ cup lukewarm water; add yeast and let stand 10 minutes, then stir. Add softened yeast to Vita-B mixture. Stir in 5 cups Five Roses Flour and beat thoroughly. Add remaining flour, mixing it in thoroughly by spoon and hand, and using just enough flour to prevent sticking to either bowl or the hands. Turn out on floured board and knead until smooth (about 30 minutes). Shape into a smooth ball and place in a greased bowl, turn ball of dough over in bowl to grease surface. **Cover and let rise in a warm place (80° to 85°F.) until double in bulk (about 1¾ hours). Punch down and let rise again until double in bulk (about 1½ hours); punch down again.** Turn out on floured board and divide into 4 equal parts; shape into balls, cover and let rest 10 minutes. Shape into loaves, place in greased 8½″ x 4½″ x 2½″ loaf pans; brush tops with melted butter or shortening. Cover and let rise in a warm place until double in bulk (about 1 hour). Bake at 350°F., 1 to 1½ hours.

Yield: 4 loaves.

Note: This dough is very stiff and takes longer to knead than other breads.

Things To Do With Bread

BUTTERED CRUMBS

Melt 1½ tablespoons butter; add ⅓ cup stale bread crumbs. Mix over low heat until butter is distributed. Use on scalloped dishes, macaroni and cheese, etc.

CROUTONS

Spread leftover slices of bread sparingly with butter. Cut in ½″ squares, oblongs or rounds. Place in a shallow baking pan and bake in a moderate oven (350°F.) 10 to 15 minutes or until golden brown. If desired, sprinkle with grated cheese before baking. Serve with soup.

TOASTED BREAD BOXES (Croustades)

Cut unsliced bread in 2½″ thick slices. Trim off the crusts and cut out the middle portion, to within ½″ of bottom, leaving square boxes open at the top. Brush sides, top and bottom with melted butter. Place on a baking sheet and bake in a moderate oven (375°F.) 12 to 15 minutes or until golden brown. Use as you would for patty shells.

MELBA TOAST

Remove crusts from very thin slices of day-old bread. Cut into desired shapes and place on a baking sheet. Bake in a moderate oven (350°F.) 12 to 15 minutes or until lightly browned.

CINNAMON TOAST

Cream together ¼ cup butter, 3 tablespoons sugar (brown or white) and ½ teaspoon cinnamon. Spread mixture over hot toast. Place under broiler until bubbly.

GARLIC BREAD

Slice loaf of French Bread (preferably 1-day old) to within ¼″ of bottom crust. Spread Garlic Spread on one side of each slice, being careful not to break slices. Wrap in aluminum foil and heat in a hot oven (425°F.) 30 to 40 minutes. Break off slices and serve immediately.

TO FRESHEN STALE BREAD OR ROLLS

Sprinkle inside of paper bag with cold water. Place bread or rolls (not more than 6 rolls or 6 slices) in bag. Twist top of bag to close tightly. Heat in a moderate oven (375°F.) 15 to 20 minutes. Serve at once.

ROLLS AND FANCY BREADS

BASIC SWEET DOUGH FOR SWEET ROLLS AND FANCY BREADS

2 pkgs. active dry yeast	½ cup sugar
1 cup lukewarm water	1 teaspoon salt
2 teaspoons sugar	6 cups Five Roses All-purpose Flour
1 cup milk	2 eggs, beaten
¼ cup butter	1 teaspoon grated lemon rind

Sprinkle yeast into lukewarm water, add 2 teaspoons sugar; let stand for 10 minutes, then stir. Scald milk; add butter, sugar and salt. Cool to lukewarm and add softened yeast; mix together. Add half the Five Roses Flour to make a thick batter; beat well. Add eggs and lemon rind; beat well. Stir in remaining flour, using only enough to make a soft dough that does not stick to hands or bowl. Turn out on a lightly floured board and knead until smooth and satiny—about 10 minutes. Place in a greased bowl; turn dough over to grease top. Cover and let rise in a warm place until double in size—about 1½ hours. Punch down and knead lightly. Shape into rolls or bread or one of the following variations. Place in greased pans, cover and let rise in a warm place until double in size—about 1 hour. Bake at 375°F. 15 to 20 minutes for rolls; 35 to 40 minutes for bread.

Yield: 3 dozen rolls or 2 sweet breads.

SWEDISH TEA RING

Make Sweet Dough as directed. To shape: divide the dough in half. Roll each half out to a rectangular sheet about ½" thick and three times as long as wide. If desired, save one half for another variation. Brush with melted butter and spread with brown sugar and cinnamon. Roll up as for jelly roll, pressing down edges to seal. Shape into a ring and place on a greased cookie sheet. With scissors, cut through ring almost to inside edge, in slices about 1" thick. Turn or twist each slice on its side. Brush with melted butter. Let rise in a warm place until double in bulk. Bake at 375°F. 30 to 35 minutes. Frost with Confectioner's Frosting (page 54) and sprinkle with chopped nuts.

BOHEMIAN BRAID

Make Sweet Dough as directed. To shape: divide half the dough into 9 portions. Roll each portion into a long roll. Braid 4 rolls loosely and place on a greased baking sheet. Then braid 3 rolls and place on top of the first braid. Twist last 2 portions together and place on top. Repeat with second portion of dough or use for one of the other variations. Cover and let rise in warm place until double in bulk. Bake at 375°F., 40 to 45 minutes. Frost with Confectioner's Frosting (page 54) and sprinkle with chopped nuts.

CINNAMON BUNS

Make Sweet Dough as directed, adding 2 teaspoons cinnamon with first half of Five Roses Flour and adding 1 cup currants or seedless raisins with second half of flour. To shape: divide dough into equal portions and shape each into a smooth ball. Place close together on lightly greased cake pan. Brush tops with melted butter. Cover and let rise in a warm place until double in bulk. Bake in a moderate oven (375°F.) for 10 minutes; reduce temperature to 350°F. and continue baking 15 to 20 minutes longer or until browned. While warm, frost with Confectioner's Frosting (page 54) and decorate with glacé cherries.

HOT CROSS BUNS

Make as for Cinnamon Buns. When half risen, cut two gashes at right angles across tops of buns. Let rise until double in bulk. Bake as for Cinnamon Buns. When warm, fill gashes with Confectioner's Frosting.

BUTTERSCOTCH PECAN ROLLS

Make Sweet Dough as directed. To shape: roll gently into a rectangle ¼" thick, 15" wide, 18" long. Combine ½ cup brown sugar, ¼ cup melted butter and 1 teaspoon cinnamon; spread over dough. Roll up as for jelly roll, pressing down last edge firmly. Cut in slices, 1" thick. Grease bottom and sides of two 9" or 10" square pans. Combine ½ cup melted butter, ¾ cup brown sugar and ¾ cup pecans; spread evenly over bottom of pans. Arrange rolls, cut side down on filling, leaving space for expansion. Cover and let rise in a warm place until double in bulk—about 1 hour. Bake in a moderate oven (350°F.) 25 to 30 minutes or until golden brown. Remove from pans all at once and cool bottom side up.

YEAST DOUGHNUTS

Make Sweet Dough as directed. Omit grated lemon rind but add ½ teaspoon nutmeg with first half of Five Roses Flour. To shape: roll dough ½" thick on lightly floured board. Cut with floured doughnut cutter. Place on a greased baking sheet; cover and let rise in a warm place until double in bulk. Heat 1 quart vegetable oil to 375°F. in a deep fryer or saucepan. Cook doughnuts, a few at a time, until golden brown on bottom; turn to do other side. Takes about 2 to 3 minutes on each side. Drain on absorbent paper. When cool, roll in icing or granulated sugar.

Yield: 4 dozen.

BRIOCHE

½ teaspoon sugar	¼ cup sugar
½ cup lukewarm water	3 egg yolks
1 pkg. active dry yeast	¼ teaspoon lemon rind
½ cup milk	3 cups Five Roses All-purpose Flour
⅓ cup butter	

Dissolve ½ teaspoon sugar in ½ cup lukewarm water; add yeast and let stand 10 to 15 minutes, then stir. Scald milk, add butter and ¼ cup sugar; stir until butter is dissolved and cool to lukewarm. Add softened yeast to the lukewarm milk. Stir in egg yolks, lemon rind and 1½ cups Five Roses Flour. Beat thoroughly for 10 minutes with a wooden spoon or electric mixer. Add the remaining flour; mix well. Grab the dough and throw it on a hard surface. Keep slapping or throwing the dough this way until it begins to pull away from your hands—takes about 10 to 15 minutes. Place the dough in a greased bowl and turn to grease the top. Cover and let rise in a warm place (80 to 85°F.) until double in bulk—about 2 hours. Punch down the dough, cover and refrigerate overnight or a minimum of 4 hours. Divide the chilled dough into ¼ cup portions. Shape each portion into a smooth ball, working only with 4 or 5 at a time and keeping the remainder in the refrigerator. Place brioches into well greased muffin pans. Cover lightly with waxed paper and let rise in a warm place until double in bulk—about 2 hours. Brush tops carefully with melted butter and bake in a moderate oven (375°F.) 15 to 20 minutes.

Yield: 18 to 20 brioches.

REFRIGERATOR ROLLS

1½ cups scalded milk	2 eggs, well-beaten
2 pkgs. active dry yeast	5 cups Five Roses All-purpose Flour
⅓ cup sugar	⅓ cup melted butter
2 teaspoons salt	

Scald milk and cool to lukewarm. Sprinkle yeast in ½ cup of the lukewarm milk and 2 teaspoons of the measured sugar; let stand for 10 minutes and stir. Add remaining milk, sugar, salt, eggs and 3 cups of Five Roses Flour. Beat vigorously until well blended. Add melted butter and beat well. Stir in remaining flour, using just enough to make a soft dough. Turn out on lightly floured board and knead until smooth and elastic. Quickly shape into a ball. Place in a greased bowl and turn to grease top. Cover and place in refrigerator until ready to use. Remove the required amount from refrigerator, as needed. Let stand until dough warms to room temperature (about 3 to 4 hours). Then shape into rolls. Place in greased muffin pans (or close together on greased cookie sheet). Cover and let rise in warm place (80 to 85°F.) until double in bulk—about 1½ to 2 hours. Bake at 400°F., 10 to 12 minutes.

Yield: 3 dozen medium-size rolls.

Note: Dough will keep up to one week in refrigerator. Cover with waxed paper and a damp cloth. Dough may require occasional punching to keep it down.

STANDARD ROLLS

2 pkgs. active dry yeast	¼ cup sugar
1 cup lukewarm water	⅓ cup shortening
2 teaspoons sugar	8 cups Five Roses All-purpose Flour
2 cups milk	Melted butter or margarine
1 tablespoon salt	

Sprinkle yeast in lukewarm water with 2 teaspoons sugar; let stand 10 minutes, then stir. Scald milk and combine with salt, ¼ cup sugar and shortening; stir until shortening is dissolved. Cool to lukewarm; add softened yeast. Add half the Five Roses Flour and beat with wooden spoon or mixer until smooth. Stir in remaining flour using just enough to make a soft dough and prevent sticking to hands or bowl. Use more if necessary. Turn out on lightly floured board; cover with a clean towel and let rest 10 minutes. Knead until smooth and elastic. Shape into a smooth ball and place in a greased bowl; turn dough over to grease surface. Cover and let rise in a warm place (80 to 85°F.) until double in bulk—about 1½ hours. Punch down and divide into equal portions. Shape as desired (see below) and place on a greased pan; brush tops with melted butter. Cover and let rise in a warm place until double in bulk—about 1 hour. Bake in a moderate oven (375°F.) 15 to 20 minutes.

Yield: 4 dozen rolls.

WHOLE WHEAT ROLLS

Use half Five Roses All-purpose Flour and half Five Roses Whole Wheat Flour.

METHOD OF SHAPING ROLLS:

Plain Rolls—Shape dough into smooth round balls of equal size. For crusty rolls, place 1″ apart on greased baking sheet. For tall soft rolls, place close together so that they touch.

Cloverleaf Rolls—Shape dough into small round balls—about the size of a walnut. Dip each ball into melted butter and place 3 balls in each section of a greased muffin pan. Size of balls will depend on size of muffin pans.

Crescents—Roll dough into a circular shape about ¼" thick. Cut in equal pie-shaped pieces. Brush with melted butter and roll up each piece, beginning at wide end. Curve slightly to form a crescent, tucking ends under. Place on greased baking sheet.

Parkerhouse Rolls—Roll dough ¼" thick. Cut with floured 2" round cookie cutter. Make a crease across each round, a little off centre, with back of knife. Brush with melted butter. Fold over at crease so that wider half is on top; press edges together. Place 1" apart on greased baking sheet; brush with melted butter.

Finger Rolls—Shape dough into smooth round balls. Roll each ball with palm of hand to desired thickness, keeping them smooth and uniform in size. Place 1" apart on greased baking sheet.

Bowknots—Divide dough in half and roll into rectangle, ¾" thick, 18" long and 6" wide. Cut into strips, 6" long and ¾" wide. Roll each strip slightly. Tie each strip into a knot and place on greased baking sheet. Brush with melted butter.

Fan Tans—Divide dough in six and roll each part into rectangles 9" x 5" x ¼" thick. Brush with melted butter. Cut each rectangle into five 1" strips. Stack strips in piles of 5, buttered side up. Cut each pile into 6 equal pieces. Place cut side down in greased muffin pans.

CHRISTMAS STOLLEN

1 pkg. active dry yeast	¼ cup chopped candied orange peel
¼ cup lukewarm water	1 cup seedless raisins
¾ cup scalded milk, cooled	1 tablespoon grated lemon rind
¼ cup sugar	3-3½ cups Five Roses All-purpose
1 teaspoon salt	Flour
1 egg	2 tablespoons melted butter
¼ cup butter	¾ cup icing sugar
¼ cup slivered blanched almonds	1 tablespoon milk
¼ cup chopped walnuts	Candied cherries (optional)
¼ cup chopped candied lemon peel	Sliced blanched almonds (optional)

Sprinkle yeast in lukewarm water with ½ teaspoon of the measured sugar; let stand 10 minutes, then stir. Stir in lukewarm milk, sugar, salt, egg, butter, slivered almonds, nuts, lemon peel, orange peel, raisins, lemon rind and 1½ cups Five Roses Flour. Beat with wooden spoon until smooth. Mix in enough remaining flour to handle easily. Turn out onto lightly floured board; knead until smooth and elastic—about 10 to 15 minutes. Put in greased bowl; brush top with a little of the melted butter. Cover with a towel and let rise in a warm place (80 to 85°F.) until double in bulk—about 2 hours. Punch down and roll or pat dough into a 12" x 8" oval. Spread with 1 tablespoon melted butter. Fold in half lengthwise and shape into a crescent. Press edges firmly to hold together and place on greased cookie sheet. Brush top with remaining melted butter. Let rise in a warm place until double in bulk—about 35 to 45 minutes. Bake at 375°F. 25 to 30 minutes or until golden brown. Frost while warm with Confectioner's Frosting (page 54). Decorate with candied cherries and slivered almonds, if desired.

Yield: 1 stollen. If desired, shape crescent smaller to make 2 stollens.

KUGELHOFT

1 pkg. active dry yeast
2 teaspoons sugar
¼ cup lukewarm water
¾ cup scalded milk
¾ cup butter
¾ cup sugar
4 eggs

3½ cups Five Roses All-purpose Flour
1 teaspoon salt
1 cup sultana raisins
½ cup slivered, blanched almonds
1 tablespoon grated lemon rind
½ cup ground almonds

Sprinkle yeast with 2 teaspoons sugar into lukewarm water; let stand 10 minutes, then stir. Cool milk to lukewarm and add to softened yeast. Cream butter and sugar until light in large bowl of electric mixer. Add eggs, one at a time, beating well after each. Add the yeast mixture and stir until blended. Stir Five Roses Flour and salt together; add to batter and beat at medium speed until smooth. Stir in raisins, slivered almonds and lemon rind. Cover and let rise in warm place (80-85°F.) until double in bulk (about 2½-3 hours). Meanwhile, butter a 10-cup mould and sprinkle with ground almonds, turning pan so that bottom and sides will be covered. When batter is light, punch down and turn into prepared mould. Cover and let rise in a warm place until the batter comes to about 1″ of the top of the mould (about 1½-2 hours). Bake in a moderate oven (350°F.) 50 to 60 minutes or until cake tester comes out clean. Let cool in pan, then turn out.

CRUSTY ROLLS

2 cups boiling water
2 tablespoons sugar
2 teaspoons salt
2 pkgs. active dry yeast

4 tablespoons shortening
6-7 cups Five Roses All-purpose Flour
2 egg whites, stiffly beaten
Cornmeal

Combine boiling water, sugar and salt in large bowl; cool to lukewarm. Sprinkle yeast over cooled water mixture; let stand 10 minutes, then stir. Add shortening and 1 cup Five Roses Flour; beat until smooth. Fold in stiffly beaten egg whites. Add enough of the remaining flour to make a soft dough. Turn out onto lightly floured board and knead until smooth and satiny—about 5 minutes. Place dough in lightly greased bowl, turn to grease top. Cover and let rise in warm place (80 to 85°F.) until double in bulk (about 1½ hours). Punch down dough and divide into 28 equal portions; let rest 10 minutes. Shape into rolls; place 2″ apart on a greased baking sheet which has been sprinkled with cornmeal. Let rise until double in bulk (about 30 minutes). Bake in a hot oven (450°F.) 15 to 20 minutes. Place a large pan filled with boiling water on bottom rack of oven during baking.

Yield: 28 rolls.

We appreciate the fact that from time to time certain problems may arise with regard to home cooking and baking. For this reason we are pleased to remind you that our Five Roses Kitchens will always be most pleased to help you. Address all inquiries to:

PAULINE HARVEY, Director
FIVE ROSES KITCHENS
BOX 6089
MONTREAL, P.Q.

QUICK BREADS

Quick breads are easy and quick to make. They are leavened with baking powder, baking soda, steam or air, rather than yeast. Quick breads include certain loaf breads, tea biscuits, scones, muffins, popovers, dumplings, waffles, pancakes and quick coffee cakes. Quick breads are almost always served hot and with plenty of butter. The one exception are nut breads — their flavour improves if stored at least a day. A crack down the centre of a nut loaf is typical.

DATE BREAD

1 teaspoon baking soda
1 cup boiling water
1 cup chopped dates
1 egg
1 cup brown sugar
1 cup chopped nuts

1 teaspoon vanilla
½ teaspoon salt
1½ cups Five Roses All-purpose
    Flour
1 tablespoon melted butter

Dissolve baking soda in boiling water and pour over dates; let cool. Beat egg; gradually add brown sugar, beating well after each addition. Add to cooled date mixture and mix well. Stir in chopped nuts, vanilla, salt and Five Roses Flour. Add melted butter and mix well. Pour into greased 8½″ x 4½″ x 2½″ loaf pan and bake in a moderate oven (350°F.) 50 to 60 minutes.

ORANGE NUT LOAF

1¾ cups Five Roses All-purpose
    Flour
1½ teaspoons baking powder
1 teaspoon salt
¼ cup butter

¾ cup sugar
2 eggs
2 teaspoons orange rind
½ cup milk
½ cup chopped nutmeats

Glaze

2 teaspoons orange juice

1 tablespoon sugar

Stir Five Roses Flour, baking powder and salt together. Cream butter; add sugar gradually, beating between additions. Beat in eggs, one at a time; add orange rind. Add dry ingredients alternately with milk, mixing well after each addition; fold in nuts. Pour into a greased 8½″ x 4½″ x 2½″ loaf pan. Bake in a moderate oven (350°F.) 50-60 minutes. Cool ten minutes; mix orange juice and sugar together for glaze and spread on loaf with pastry brush. Return loaf to oven for 1 minute. Cool 10 minutes before removing from pan; cool on rack.

Note: If desired, the nutmeats may be increased to ¾ cup.

BANANA NUT LOAF

1½ cups Five Roses All-purpose
    Flour
2 teaspoons baking powder
¼ teaspoon baking soda
1 teaspoon salt

¼ cup sugar
½ cup chopped walnuts
2 eggs, beaten
⅓ cup corn syrup
1 cup mashed ripe banana

Stir dry ingredients together in a large bowl. Stir in nuts. Mix remaining ingredients together in another bowl. Make a well in the centre of the dry ingredients, pour in liquid, stir only until flour is moistened. Spoon into a greased loaf pan (8½" x 4½" x 2½"). Bake at 350°F. 55 to 60 minutes.

Store 6 hours or overnight before cutting.

LEMON LOAF

½ cup shortening
1 cup sugar
2 eggs
Grated rind of 1 lemon

1½ cups Five Roses All-purpose
    Flour
½ teaspoon salt
1 teaspoon baking powder
½ cup milk

Glaze
Juice of half a lemon

¼ cup sugar

Cream shortening; beat in sugar gradually. Add eggs, beating well; stir in rind. Mix Five Roses Flour, salt and baking powder together. Blend in dry ingredients alternately with milk; mixing well. Bake in a greased 8½" x 4½" x 2½" loaf pan in a moderate oven (350°F.) 50-60 minutes. Remove from oven. Mix lemon juice and sugar and spread over top immediately. Let cool 10 minutes; remove from pan and cool completely before slicing.

CRANBERRY CASSEROLE BREAD

2 cups Five Roses All-purpose Flour
¾ cup sugar
2 teaspoons baking powder
½ teaspoon baking soda
1 teaspoon salt
¼ cup shortening

¾ cup orange juice
1 tablespoon grated orange rind
2 eggs, well-beaten
1 cup coarsely chopped cranberries
½ cup chopped glacé green cherries

Stir Five Roses Flour, sugar, baking powder, baking soda and salt together. Cut in shortening until mixture resembles coarse cornmeal. Combine orange juice and grated rind with well-beaten eggs. Pour all at once into dry ingredients, mixing just enough to dampen. Dust chopped cranberries and cherries with a tablespoon of flour; carefully fold into batter. Spoon into a well greased 1½ quart casserole. Bake in a moderate oven (350°F.) about 1 hour or until toothpick inserted in centre comes out clean. Cool in casserole 10 minutes, then remove. Store over night for easy slicing. Frost with Confectioner's Frosting (page 54) or serve slices with butter. Delicious when toasted under broiler.

APRICOT BREAD

2 cups Five Roses All-purpose Flour
3 teaspoons baking powder
1 teaspoon salt
1 cup sugar
½ cup chopped nuts

1 cup chopped dried apricots
2 eggs, well-beaten
1 cup milk
2 tablespoons vegetable oil

Stir Five Roses Flour, baking powder and salt together in a large mixing bowl. Add sugar, nuts and apricots; mix well. Combine well-beaten eggs, milk and vegetable oil and add to flour mixture; mix just until blended. Pour batter into a greased 9″ x 5″ x 3″ loaf pan and allow to stand 10 minutes. Bake in a moderate oven (350°F.) 50 to 60 minutes.

COFFEE CAKES

Is there anything more delicious than a good coffee cake? Try these favourites next time you have company. SERVE warm, plain or with butter.

PRIZE COFFEE CAKE

⅔ cup sugar
2 tablespoons shortening
1 egg, beaten
½ teaspoon salt

2 teaspoons baking powder
1¼ cups Five Roses All-purpose
  Flour
⅔ cup milk
1 teaspoon vanilla

Topping

1 teaspoon cinnamon
1 cup chopped nuts

¼ cup brown sugar
¼ cup white sugar

Combine all ingredients for topping. Grease and flour an 8″ square cake pan. Blend sugar and shortening together. Stir in beaten egg. Mix salt, baking powder and Five Roses Flour together. Add vanilla to milk and add to batter alternately with dry ingredients. Spread a little of batter into prepared pan; sprinkle half of topping on top. Cover with remaining batter and sprinkle with remaining topping. Bake in a moderate oven (350°F.) 25 to 30 minutes. Allow cake to sit at room temperature in pan on cooling rack for 10 to 15 minutes before serving. Cut pieces from pan.

SPICE 'N' COFFEE CAKE

1 cup Five Roses All-purpose Flour
1 cup brown sugar
¼ teaspoon salt
½ teaspoon cinnamon
⅛ teaspoon mace
¼ teaspoon nutmeg

1½ teaspoons dry instant coffee
¼ cup butter or margarine
1 egg
1 cup commercial sour cream
1 teaspoon baking soda
½ cup chopped walnuts

Combine Five Roses Flour, brown sugar, salt, cinnamon, mace, nutmeg and instant coffee. Cut in butter until mixture is the size of large peas. Beat egg, stir in sour cream and baking soda. Pour all at once into dry ingredients, mixing just enough to dampen. Spread into a greased and floured 9″ square cake pan. Sprinkle top with nuts. Bake in a moderate oven (350°F.) 40 to 45 minutes or until done. Serve warm or cold. Cut in squares.

APPLE COFFEE CAKE

1½ cups Five Roses All-purpose
 Flour
1½ teaspoons baking powder
¾ teaspoon salt
⅓ cup butter

1 cup sugar
2 eggs
1 cup commercial sour cream
½ teaspoon baking soda

Topping

1 medium-size apple
1 tablespoon lemon juice

⅓ cup brown sugar
¾ teaspoon cinnamon

Prepare topping first. Wash and core apple but do not peel. Slice apple very thin and sprinkle with lemon juice; cover and set aside. Combine brown sugar and cinnamon. Stir Five Roses Flour, baking powder and salt together. Cream butter; add sugar gradually, beating well. Beat in eggs. Combine baking soda with sour cream and add to batter alternately with dry ingredients, blending well. Pour batter into a greased and floured 9″ square cake pan. Sprinkle with ⅓ of brown sugar-cinnamon mixture. Place apple slices on top and cover with remaining topping. Bake in a moderate oven (325°F.) 50 to 60 minutes. Serve warm.

MUFFINS

Muffins are truly delicious quick breads. They are popular, appetizing, economical and quickly made — good for any meal or snack!

The Secret of Good Muffins is to stir the batter until the flour is just dampened. The batter should be lumpy. Overmixing causes tunnels and a tough texture.

Perfect Muffins are light and tender, with rough, shiny golden crusts.

To Reheat Muffins, wrap in foil and heat in a hot oven (400°F.) 15 to 20 minutes.

MUFFINS

2 cups Five Roses All-purpose Flour
3 teaspoons baking powder
1 teaspoon salt
2 tablespoons sugar

2 eggs, well-beaten
1 cup milk
¼ cup melted butter

Stir the Five Roses Flour, baking powder, salt and sugar together. Combine beaten eggs, milk and melted butter; add all-at-once to dry ingredients. Stir quickly until ingredients are just mixed and batter is lumpy in appearance. Fill greased muffin pans ⅔ full and bake in a hot (400°F.) oven, 15 to 20 minutes.

Yield: 10 to 12 medium-size muffins.

MUFFIN VARIATIONS

Berry Muffins—Increase sugar to ½ cup. Fold into muffin batter ¾ cup lightly floured blueberries, raspberries or cranberries.

Cheese Muffins—Reduce salt to ½ teaspoon and sugar to 1 tablespoon; add ¾ cup grated Canadian Cheddar cheese to muffin batter.

Sour Milk Muffins—Substitute milk for sour milk. Decrease baking powder to 1½ teaspoons. Add ½ teaspoon baking soda dissolved in 1 teaspoon lukewarm water to batter.

Wheat Germ Muffins—Substitute ½ cup Ogilvie Tonik Wheat Germ for ½ cup Five Roses Flour.

Bacon Muffins—Fold in ½ cup chopped crisp fried bacon. Substitute melted bacon fat for melted butter, if desired. Reduce salt to ½ teaspoon.

Orange Marmalade Muffins—Add 3 tablespoons orange marmalade to muffin batter.

Yum Yum Muffins—Stir in ¼ teaspoon cloves, 1 teaspoon cinnamon and ¼ teaspoon nutmeg with dry ingredients. Fold in 1 cup floured raisins.

BRAN MUFFINS

1 cup Five Roses All-purpose Flour	½ cup milk
2 teaspoons baking powder	⅓ cup molasses
½ teaspoon baking soda	1 egg, unbeaten
½ teaspoon salt	¼ cup shortening
1 cup whole bran	½ cup seedless raisins (optional)

Stir Five Roses Flour, baking powder, baking soda and salt together. Combine whole bran, milk and molasses and let stand until most of the moisture is taken up. Add egg and shortening; beat well. Add the raisins to the dry ingredients, then blend into bran mixture, stirring only until combined. Fill greased muffin pans ⅔ full. Bake in a hot oven (400°F.) about 20 minutes.

Yield: 10-12 medium-size muffins.

VITA-B MUFFINS

1 cup Ogilvie Vita-B Wheat Germ Cereal	½ teaspoon salt
	3 teaspoons baking powder
1¼ cups buttermilk	1 cup Five Roses All-purpose Flour
½ teaspoon baking soda	⅓ cup brown sugar
1 egg	¼ cup finely chopped dates
¼ cup vegetable oil	¼ cup finely chopped walnuts

Soak the Vita-B in 1 cup buttermilk for 1½ hours. Add remaining buttermilk, baking soda, egg and vegetable oil; mix well. Stir salt, baking powder, Five Roses Flour and brown sugar together; add the dates and nuts. Pour the Vita-B mixture into the dry ingredients and stir only until mixture is moistened. Spoon into well-greased muffin pans and bake at 400°F. 30 to 35 minutes.

Yield: 10-12 muffins, medium size.

SALLY'S MUFFINS

1¾ cups Five Roses All-purpose Flour	4 teaspoons baking powder
	¼ cup butter
1 teaspoon salt	3 eggs, separated
1 tablespoon sugar	1 cup milk

Stir all dry ingredients together. Cut in butter, with pastry blender or two knives, until mixture is crumbly. Beat egg yolks thoroughly; add milk and stir into dry ingredients until moistened. Fold in stiffly beaten egg whites. Fill greased muffin pans ⅔ full and bake in a hot oven (400°F.) 25 to 30 minutes.

Yield: 12-15 medium-size muffins.

ORANGE RAISIN MUFFINS

1¾ cups Five Roses All-purpose Flour	Grated rind of 1 orange
3 teaspoons baking powder	¼ cup orange juice
¾ teaspoon salt	½ cup milk
¼ cup sugar	⅓ cup vegetable oil
1 egg, well-beaten	¾ cup seedless raisins

Stir Five Roses Flour, baking powder, salt and sugar together. Combine beaten egg, orange rind, orange juice, milk and vegetable oil. Add all at once to dry ingredients, stirring just until moistened; fold in raisins. Fill greased muffin pans ⅔ full and bake in a hot oven (400°F.) for 20 to 25 minutes.

Yield: 10-12 medium-size muffins.

TEA BISCUITS

It's hard to beat tender flaky biscuits for that melt-in-your-mouth goodness. Ideal for breakfast, dinner, luncheon and for snacks. Often used as a topping for steak and kidney pie.

The Secret of Good Tea Biscuits is in the dough. It should be soft but not sticky. A little kneading improves not only the quality of biscuits but assures tall plump and tender biscuits. A hot oven (450°F.) is recommended.

Knead with a gentle touch as too much handling will produce a tough biscuit.

Perfect Tea Biscuits should be golden brown with a fairly smooth, level top. They should be slightly moist, tender, light and flaky.

Serve immediately after baking. Reheated biscuits are never as good but they may be wrapped in foil and heated in a hot oven (400°F.) 10 to 15 minutes.

TEA BISCUITS

2 cups Five Roses All-purpose Flour	¼ cup shortening
4 teaspoons baking powder	1 cup milk
1 teaspoon salt	

Mix together Five Roses Flour, baking powder and salt. Cut in shortening with 2 knives or a pastry blender, until mixture is the consistency of coarse cornmeal. Make a well in centre of these ingredients; add liquid slowly. When all the liquid has been added, stir dough rather vigorously until it comes freely from the side of the bowl. Turn dough onto lightly floured board and knead lightly for a FEW MINUTES. Roll or pat out to desired thickness — about ½ inch. Cut dough with 2-inch floured biscuit cutter; place on ungreased baking sheet. Bake in a hot oven (450°F.) 12-15 minutes.

Yield: 15-18 biscuits.

VARIATIONS OF TEA BISCUITS

Cheese—Decrease shortening to 3 tablespoons and salt to ¾ teaspoon. Cut in ½ cup grated Cheddar cheese with shortening.

Buttermilk—Decrease baking powder to 2 teaspoons; add ½ teaspoon baking soda. Substitute 1 cup buttermilk (or sour milk) for milk.

Sweet Cream—Substitute milk with ½ cup skim milk and ½ cup whipping cream.

Fruit or Nuts—Add ¼ cup granulated sugar and decrease milk to ¾ cup. Add ¾ cup raisins, currants or nuts with milk.

Whole Wheat—Use 1 cup Five Roses Whole Wheat Flour and 1 cup Five Roses All-purpose Flour.

EASY BREAKFAST ROLLS

3 cups Five Roses All-purpose Flour	½ cup granulated sugar
¼ teaspoon salt	1 teaspoon cinnamon
3½ teaspoons baking powder	¼ cup melted butter
½ cup granulated sugar	½ cup brown sugar
½ cup milk	¼ cup chopped nuts
2 eggs, beaten	¼ cup melted butter
½ cup melted butter	

Stir together Five Roses Flour, salt, baking powder and ½ cup granulated sugar. Combine milk, eggs and ½ cup melted butter; add to dry ingredients and mix well. Place on lightly floured board and knead lightly 10 times. Roll or pat into a rectangular shape, ¼-inch thick. Mix ½ cup granulated sugar, cinnamon and ¼ cup melted butter; spread over dough. Roll dough as for jelly roll, seal edges and cut into ½-inch slices. Combine remaining three ingredients and sprinkle lightly over bottoms of greased muffin pans. Arrange slices, cut side down over this mixture. Bake in a moderate oven (375°F.) 25-30 minutes. Turn pans upside down on cooling rack and lift off rolls. Serve hot.

Note: Rolls may be stored in pans in refrigerator overnight and baked in the morning.

Yield: 16 rolls.

POPPY SEED TWISTS

3½ cups Five Roses All-purpose Flour	½ teaspoon salt
	½ cup butter
8 teaspoons baking powder	1¼ cups milk

Glaze

1 egg yolk, slightly beaten	Poppy Seeds
1 tablespoon milk	

Stir Five Roses Flour, baking powder and salt together. Cut in butter with pastry blender or two knives, until mixture is crumbly. Add milk gradually, tossing with fork, until mixture holds together and comes away from sides of bowl. Knead on lightly floured board for a few minutes. Break dough into 32 equal-size pieces; roll each piece into a round pencil-like strip, 6-inches long. Tie each strip into a knot and place on a greased baking sheet. Mix slightly beaten egg yolk and milk together, then brush tops with this egg-milk mixture and sprinkle with poppy seeds. Bake in a hot oven (425°F.) 15 minutes or until lightly browned.

Yield: 32 twists.

SCONES

Richer than tea biscuits, they are ideal for luncheons and snacks.

ENGLISH CREAM SCONES

2 cups Five Roses All-purpose Flour
3 teaspoons baking powder
½ teaspoon salt
2 tablespoons sugar

¼ cup butter or shortening
2 eggs
⅓ cup milk or thin cream

Topping
2 tablespoons granulated sugar

Stir Five Roses Flour, baking powder, salt and sugar together. Cut in butter or shortening with 2 knives or pastry blender until mixture is the consistency of coarse cornmeal. Beat eggs until light, reserving a little of the egg whites to brush over tops of scones; stir in milk. Make a well in centre of dry ingredients; add liquid slowly to make a soft dough. When all liquid has been added, stir dough rather vigorously until it comes freely from side of bowl. Pat to ¾-inch thickness; cut in squares or triangles. Brush over with egg white and sprinkle with sugar. Bake on a greased cookie sheet in a hot oven (450°F.) 12-15 minutes.

Yield: 10-12 (3 x 2 inch) rectangles or 16 (2 inch) triangles.

VARIATIONS OF ENGLISH CREAM SCONES

Raisin Scones—Stir in ½ cup raisins or currants with dry ingredients. Increase sugar to 4 tablespoons.

Whole Wheat Scones—Substitute Five Roses Whole Wheat Flour for Five Roses All-purpose Flour.

Cheese Scones—Increase salt to 1 teaspoon, if using shortening. Decrease sugar to 1 teaspoon. Cut in ½ cup grated Cheddar cheese with butter or shortening.

DOUGHNUTS

A treat for the whole family — any time of the day!

The Secret of Good Doughnuts is in the dough and how you fry them.

The Dough should be as soft as can be handled. A soft dough is easier to roll when well chilled. A generous amount of flour may be used on the board for rolling — but don't work it into the dough. The flour that clings to the dough helps with browning.

Fry in deep hot fat that has been heated to 375°F. Use an electric deep fryer or a deep-fry thermometer, if possible. If fat is too hot, only the outside of the doughnuts will cook; if too cool, they will become fat-soaked. See Deep Fat Frying — (Page 168).

Don't cook too many at one time or fat will cool down too rapidly.

Turn Doughnuts only once during frying. When ready, they will rise to the top and the underside will be brown. It takes about 1 to 2 minutes on each side.

DOUGHNUTS

2¾ cups Five Roses All-purpose
    Flour
¾ teaspoon salt
3 teaspoons baking powder
1 teaspoon ground nutmeg
3 tablespoons shortening

⅔ cup sugar
2 eggs
1 teaspoon vanilla
½ cup milk
1 qt. vegetable oil

Stir first four ingredients together. Cream shortening with half of the sugar. Beat the eggs until light and add remaining sugar gradually, beating between additions; combine shortening and egg mixture and add vanilla. Add dry ingredients alternately with milk to make a dough that is soft but not sticky. Cover bowl and chill 1 hour. Press or roll dough on floured board to ¼ inch thickness, cut with floured doughnut cutter. Heat vegetable oil in deep fryer to 375°F. Fry doughnuts until golden brown; turn to do other side—takes about 1 to 2 minutes on each side. Yield: 2 dozen.

POTATO DOUGHNUTS

2¾ cups Five Roses All-purpose
    Flour
4 teaspoons baking powder
1 teaspoon salt
2 tablespoons shortening

1 cup sugar
1 cup mashed potatoes
1 egg
¾ cup milk
1 quart vegetable oil

Stir Five Roses Flour, baking powder and salt together. Cream shortening; beat in ½ the sugar and mix with mashed potatoes. Beat egg until light, gradually beat in remaining sugar and combine with potato mixture. Add dry ingredients alternately with milk, beginning and ending with dry ingredients. Chill 1 hour. Press or roll dough on floured board to ¼" thickness; cut with floured doughnut cutter. Heat vegetable oil to 375°F., and fry doughnuts until golden brown; turn to do other side — about 1 to 2 minutes on each side. Leave plain or coat with granulated or icing sugar. Yield: 2 dozen.

Note: If chilled left-over mashed potatoes are used, it is not necessary to chill dough before rolling. 3 medium-size potatoes makes 1 cup mashed.

PANCAKES AND WAFFLES

Pancakes or Waffles are a special breakfast byword. Delicious for lunch, supper and even dessert!

The Secret of Tender Pancakes or Waffles is to stir the batter only until dry ingredients are just blended. The batter will be lumpy. Use a heavy iron or aluminum frying pan or griddle for pancakes.

Pancake Griddle or Waffle Iron is hot enough when drops of water sprinkled on surface will dance. Follow manufacturer's instructions for waffle iron or electric pancake griddle. Too cool a griddle produces flat, tough pancakes. Too hot a griddle causes outside of pancakes to brown before centre is cooked. For recipes in this section, it is not necessary to grease the griddle.

Cook Pancakes until top side is full of bubbles; turn to do other side. Turn pancakes only once during cooking.

Cook Waffles in waffle iron according to manufacturer's instructions.

PANCAKES

1⅓ cups Five Roses All-purpose Flour	1 egg
3 teaspoons baking powder	1¼ cups milk
½ teaspoon salt	3 tablespoons melted butter or vegetable oil
3 tablespoons sugar	¼ teaspoon vanilla

Stir Five Roses Flour, baking powder, salt and sugar together. Beat egg thoroughly; add milk. Make a well in centre of dry ingredients; slowly add the egg-milk mixture. Add melted butter and vanilla. Stir quickly until ingredients are just mixed and batter is still lumpy in appearance. Drop by ¼ cupfuls on hot pancake griddle. Cook the pancakes until they are filled with bubbles and the under-surface is golden brown. Turn and brown the other side. Serve as hot as possible with syrup, honey, jam or jelly, bacon or sausages. Do not turn the pancakes more than once during cooking.

Yield: 10-12 pancakes.

VARIATIONS OF PANCAKES

Sour Milk Pancakes—Make pancake batter, using sour milk or buttermilk. Reduce baking powder to 1½ teaspoons; add 1 teaspoon baking soda dissolved in 1 teaspoon warm water.

Blueberry Pancakes—Make pancake batter, increasing sugar to ⅓ cup. Reduce milk to 1 cup. Add 1 cup floured blueberries. Cook slower than plain pancakes.

Apple Pancakes—Make pancake batter. Reduce milk to 1 cup. Add ¼ teaspoon vanilla, 1 cup grated raw apple and ½ teaspoon baking soda dissolved in 1 teaspoon warm water.

Ginger 'n' Spice Pancakes—Make pancake batter. To dry ingredients add: ¼ teaspoon ginger, ¼ teaspoon cinnamon and ⅛ teaspoon allspice.

Banana Pancakes—Make pancake batter. Reduce sugar to 2 teaspoons and milk to 1 cup. Add a few grains black pepper to dry ingredients. Fold in ¾ cup mashed ripe banana at end.

VITA-B PANCAKES

1 cup Five Roses All-purpose Flour	1 egg
⅓ cup Ogilvie Vita-B Cereal	1¼ cups milk
3 teaspoons baking powder	3 tablespoons melted butter
½ teaspoon salt	¼ teaspoon vanilla
3 tablespoons sugar	

Stir Five Roses Flour, Vita-B Cereal, salt, baking powder and sugar together. Beat egg thoroughly; add milk. Make a well in centre of dry ingredients; slowly add the egg-milk mixture. Add melted butter and vanilla. Stir quickly until all ingredients are just mixed and batter is lumpy in appearance. Drop by ¼ cupfuls on hot griddle; cook until surface is filled with bubbles and undersurface is golden brown. Turn and brown other side.

Yield: 10-12 pancakes.

FRENCH PANCAKES

3 eggs, separated
1 tablespoon granulated sugar
1 cup milk

¾ cup Five Roses All-purpose Flour
1 tablespoon melted butter
Currant, Apple or Raspberry Jelly

Beat egg yolks until thick and lemon coloured; add sugar and ½ cup milk. Stir in Five Roses Flour with remaining milk and melted butter. Beat egg whites until stiff but not dry; fold into batter. Drop by ⅓ cupfuls on hot pancake griddle. Cook pancakes until they are filled with bubbles and the undersurface is golden brown. Turn and brown other side. Spread each pancake with jelly and roll while hot; sprinkle with granulated or powdered sugar, if desired. Place on platter, arranging them with the lapped side down to prevent spreading; serve at once. Delicious as a dessert!

Yield: 8-10 pancakes.

WAFFLES

1¼ cups Five Roses All-purpose
    Flour
2 teaspoons baking powder
½ teaspoon salt
1 tablespoon sugar

1¼ cups milk
4 tablespoons vegetable oil
2 egg yolks, well-beaten
2 egg whites

Stir Five Roses Flour, baking powder, salt and sugar together. Combine milk and vegetable oil with beaten egg yolks; add to dry ingredients and stir only until blended. Beat egg whites until stiff but not dry; fold into batter. Cook on hot waffle iron. (For crisp waffles, use 2 tablespoons more fat and cook longer.)

Yield: 4 to 6 servings.

VARIATIONS OF WAFFLES

Bacon Waffles—Sprinkle small bits of bacon, cooked or uncooked over waffle batter after filling waffle iron.

Cheese Waffles—Use 3 tablespoons of vegetable oil instead of 4. Add ½ cup grated cheese to waffle batter.

Chocolate Waffles—Increase sugar to ¼ cup; add ¼ cup cocoa with dry ingredients. Add ¼ teaspoon vanilla to batter. This is good as a dessert, served with ice cream.

Corn Waffles—Reduce milk from 1¼ cups to 1 cup. Add one 14 oz. can cream style corn to batter. Cook until thoroughly dry.

Apple Waffles—Add 1 cup sliced and peeled apples to batter.

Blueberry Waffles—Add 1 cup fresh or frozen blueberries to batter.

Banana Waffles—Slice 1 or 2 bananas and add to batter.

POPOVERS AND YORKSHIRE PUDDING

The perfect blend of good flour, fresh milk and eggs makes these the most delicious of all quick breads. Although Yorkshire Pudding is served with Roast Beef, it is classified as a Quick Bread.

The Secret of Good Popovers and Yorkshire Pudding is proper mixing of ingredients and correct baking temperatures. Always pre-heat baking pans first and use a high oven temperature for the first 15 minutes of baking.

Perfect Popovers and Yorkshire Pudding rise high, have irregular shapes, are hollow and have a thick crusty wall. The interior should be moist but not raw. Crusts should be a golden brown.

POPOVERS

1 cup Five Roses All-purpose Flour	**1 teaspoon melted butter or**
¼ teaspoon salt	**margarine**
1 cup milk	**2 eggs**

Stir together Five Roses Flour and salt; gradually add milk, stirring constantly. Add melted butter or margarine. Beat eggs well until light in colour and foamy; add to mixture. Beat 2 minutes with electric or rotary beater. Fill hot, greased muffin pans ⅔ full. Bake in a very hot oven (450°F.) 15 minutes; reduce to moderate (350°F.) and continue baking 10 to 15 minutes or until evenly browned. Serve hot.

Yield: 8 medium-size popovers.

YORKSHIRE PUDDING

1 cup Five Roses All-purpose Flour	**2 eggs**
¼ teaspoon salt	**1 cup milk**

Stir Five Roses Flour and salt together. Beat eggs until thick and combine with milk. Make a well in centre of flour and gradually stir in milk-egg mixture. Beat with a rotary beater or electric beater at low speed until batter is smooth (about 2 minutes). Pour about 2 tablespoons of the roast drippings into a shallow 9" square pan or muffin pan; heat in oven until almost smoking hot, then pour in batter to ½ inch depth. Bake in hot oven (450°F.) until puffed and brown (15 to 20 minutes), gradually lowering the temperature to 350°F. for remainder of baking (about 15 minutes).

Yield: One 9" square or 12 individual Yorkshires.

We appreciate the fact that from time to time certain problems may arise with regard to home cooking and baking. For this reason we are pleased to remind you that our Five Roses Kitchens will always be most pleased to help you. Address all inquiries to:

PAULINE HARVEY, *Director*
FIVE ROSES KITCHENS
BOX 6089
MONTREAL, P.Q.

CAKES

Almost everybody loves cake, for there is a cake for almost every taste. Basically, however, there are only three kinds of cakes:

Butter cakes (conventional and quick-mix cakes)—containing butter or shortening.

Sponge cakes (angel and sponge cakes)—made without butter or shortening.

Chiffon cakes—combination of angel and butter cakes.

These three differ in ingredients, mixing method and baked characteristics but many cake-making rules apply to all of them.

A Guide to Successful Cake Baking

1. Select best quality ingredients. Use the ingredients suggested in the recipe and have them at room temperature. Use a good quality shortening and fine granulated sugar. Recipes in this chapter call for single-acting baking powder (phosphate and tartrate type). To substitute with double-acting, see page 10.

2. Use fresh eggs. Eggs beat easier if at room temperature but keep refrigerated until ready to use. The recipes in this chapter are based on medium to large size eggs.

3. Measure ingredients carefully using standard measuring cups and spoons (see page 7). The success of a cake depends largely on an accurate balance between various ingredients.

4. Mix or beat only as much as needed. Never double a cake recipe as you will not get proper beating or blending of ingredients.

5. Use type and size of pan called for in the recipe. Although cakes may be baked as layers, loaves, sheets, tubes or cupcakes, many recipes cannot be used interchangeably.

6. Grease sides of pan and line bottom with waxed paper, or grease sides and bottom and dredge with flour. This is done by adding a little flour to the greased pan and shaking the pan to spread the flour evenly. **Do not grease** pans for sponge, angel or chiffon cakes.

7. Fill pans only half full and spread batter evenly.

8. Bake at correct temperature for the required time in a pre-heated oven. Place pans as near the centre of the oven as possible, using centre rack position. Don't let pans touch each other or sides of oven. If necessary, use two racks but don't place pans directly over each other.

9. Cake is done when top springs back when lightly pressed with the fingertips or when a cake tester, inserted in the centre, comes out clean.

10. Let cake stand in pan 5 to 10 minutes before removing. Cool on a rack. Angel, sponge and chiffon cakes should be cooled completely in the inverted pan. A soft drink bottle will easily support the tube pan by inserting the neck of the bottle into the hollow tube.

11. To frost, see page 54.

For changes in high-altitude baking, see page 12.

CUPCAKES

Prepare muffin pans as for cake pans or line with paper-cupcake liners. Fill only ⅔ full and bake as directed in recipe.

Mixing by Hand

If you should mix cakes by hand, 225 strokes is the average for combining dry and liquid ingredients. Rich cakes should be stirred a little more. Always stir in the same direction.

Causes of Cake Failure

Cake falling
Too much leavening
Too much shortening or sugar
Too low an oven temperature
Insufficient baking
Too much batter in pan
Moving cake during baking

Undersize cake
Not enough leavening
Too large a pan
Too hot an oven

Thick, heavy crust
Over baking
Too hot an oven
Not enough shortening or sugar
Too much flour

Moist, sticky crust
Too much sugar
Insufficient baking

Peaks or cracks on top
Too hot an oven
Over mixing
Too much flour

Soggy layer or streak at bottom
Insufficient mixing
Too much sugar or baking powder

Coarse texture
Insufficient mixing
Insufficient blending of ingredients
Too much leavening
Too much sugar
Too low an oven temperature

Heavy, compact texture
Over mixing
Lack of leavening
Too much shortening, sugar or liquid
Too low an oven temperature
Insufficient baking

Dry cake
Not enough shortening, liquid or
    sugar
Too much flour or leavening
Over beaten egg whites
Over baking

Tunnels and large holes
Over mixing
Uneven distribution of leavening
    agent

Uneven shape
Uneven heat of oven
Uneven oven, cake not level, pan
    warped

ONE BOWL WHITE CAKE

2 cups Five Roses All-purpose Flour	¾ cup milk
½ teaspoon salt	1 teaspoon vanilla
3 teaspoons baking powder	½ cup shortening
1 cup sugar	2 eggs

Stir Five Roses Flour, salt, baking powder and sugar into large bowl of electric mixer. Add vanilla to milk and add to dry ingredients with shortening. Blend at No. 1 speed for 30 seconds; then mix on No. 4 speed of mixer (low speed) for 2 minutes, scraping sides of bowl frequently. Add eggs and beat 1 minute longer on No. 4 speed. Pour into greased and lined or floured 8″ square cake pan or two 8″ layer pans. Bake in a moderate oven (350°F.) 40 to 50 minutes for 8-inch square; 25 to 35 minutes for layers. Frost as desired.

Cupcakes: Bake at 350°F., 20 minutes. Makes 1½ dozen, medium size.

ONE BOWL FUDGE CAKE

1¾ cups Five Roses All-purpose Flour	⅓ cup shortening
½ teaspoon salt	2 eggs
2 teaspoons baking powder	¾ cup milk
1 teaspoon baking soda	2 squares unsweetened chocolate, melted
1 cup sugar	1 teaspoon vanilla

Stir first 5 ingredients together in large bowl of electric mixer. Add shortening (at room temperature), eggs and ½ cup of milk. Mix on No. 4 speed of mixer (low speed) for 2 minutes. Scrape sides of bowl often during mixing. Add cooled melted chocolate, vanilla and remaining milk; beat 2 more minutes on No. 4 speed. Pour into a greased and floured or lined, 9″ square cake pan. Bake in a moderate oven (350°F.) 35 to 45 minutes or until done. Frost as desired.

Cupcakes: Bake at 350°F. 15 to 20 minutes. Makes 1½ dozen, medium size.

ANGEL FOOD CAKE

¾ cup Five Roses All-purpose Flour	½ teaspoon salt
¼ cup cornstarch	1¼ teaspoons cream of tartar
1½ cups sugar	½ teaspoon vanilla (optional)
12 egg whites	

Sift Five Roses Flour, cornstarch and half of sugar (¾ cup) together, 3 times. Place egg whites in a large mixing bowl and sprinkle the salt and cream of tartar over the surface. Beat egg whites until stiff but not dry; gradually beat in remaining sugar and vanilla and continue beating until mixture forms stiff peaks but is not dry. Fold flour mixture in gently, 2 tablespoons at a time. Carefully place batter into an ungreased 10″ tube pan. Bake in moderate oven (375°F.) 25 to 30 minutes or until cake is lightly browned and springs back when lightly touched with finger tips. Invert pan so that cake does not rest on upper crust. A soft drink bottle will easily support the tube pan by inserting the neck of the bottle into the hollow tube. Leave inverted until thoroughly cooled; loosen sides and around tube with a flat knife or spatula and remove from pan. Frost, if desired.

Note: Dry ingredients MUST BE SIFTED together in making Angel Food Cake.

WHITE CAKE

2 cups Five Roses All-purpose Flour	1¼ cups sugar
3 teaspoons baking powder	2 eggs
½ teaspoon salt	1 teaspoon vanilla
½ cup shortening	1 cup milk

Stir Five Roses Flour, baking powder and salt together. Cream shortening; add sugar gradually, beating between additions. Add eggs, one at a time, beating well after each addition. Stir in vanilla. Add dry ingredients alternately with milk, beginning and ending with dry ingredients; blend well. Pour into greased and lined or floured, two 8" round layer cake pans or one 8 or 9" square cake pan. Bake in a moderate oven (350°F.) 30 to 35 minutes for layer cakes; 50 to 60 minutes for square cake. Frost as desired.

Cupcakes: Bake at 350°F. 20 to 25 minutes. Makes 2 dozen, medium size.

JELLY ROLL

1 cup Five Roses All-purpose Flour	1 tablespoon lemon juice
2 teaspoons baking powder	1 tablespoon water
¼ teaspoon salt	2 tablespoons grated lemon rind
3 eggs, separated	Fruit jelly, softened
¾ cup sugar	

Stir Five Roses Flour, baking powder and salt together. Beat egg yolks until thick and pale yellow; gradually beat in sugar. Stir in lemon juice, water and lemon rind. Fold in dry ingredients, gradually. Beat egg whites until stiff but not dry; fold into batter. Spread batter evenly in a greased and lined shallow pan, 15" x 10½" x ¾". Bake in a moderate oven (325°F.) 12-15 minutes or until lightly browned and cake springs back when lightly touched with finger. Remove from oven and turn out onto a cloth. Brush cold water on paper so that paper will come off easily; remove paper carefully. Quickly trim off side crusts, spread thinly with softened jelly and roll lengthwise. Wrap in cloth or wax paper, working very quickly so that cake will not crack. Keep wrapped until serving time. Sprinkle top with icing sugar, cut in slices.

Note: If smaller but thicker roll is desired, roll from short side.

ORANGE CHIFFON CAKE

1¾ cups Five Roses All-purpose Flour	½ cup vegetable oil
1½ cups sugar	6 egg yolks
3 teaspoons baking powder	¼ cup orange juice
1 teaspoon salt	½ cup cold water
Grated rind of 1 orange	½ teaspoon cream of tartar
	6 egg whites

Stir Five Roses Flour, sugar, baking powder, salt and orange rind together. Make a well in centre of dry ingredients and then add in this order: vegetable oil, egg yolks, orange juice and water. Beat until smooth. Add cream of tartar to egg whites in a large bowl; beat until egg whites form very stiff peaks. Gradually pour batter over beaten egg whites, gently folding in until just blended. DO NOT STIR. Pour batter into ungreased 10" tube pan. Bake in a moderate oven (325°F.) 55 minutes. Increase heat to 350°F. and bake 10 minutes longer. Invert pan, letting cake hang until cool. Remove from pan and frost with Orange Frosting (page 56).

DELUXE THREE-EGG WHITE CAKE

2 cups Five Roses All-purpose Flour	1¼ cups sugar
3 teaspoons baking powder	3 eggs, separated
½ teaspoon salt	1 teaspoon vanilla
½ cup shortening	1 cup milk

Stir Five Roses Flour, baking powder and salt together. Cream shortening; gradually add sugar, beating between additions. Add egg yolks and beat until fluffy. Add dry ingredients, alternately with milk, blending well after each addition. Stir in vanilla. Beat egg whites until stiff but not dry; fold into batter. Pour into two greased and floured or lined 8″ layer cake pans. Bake in a moderate oven (350°F.) 25 to 30 minutes or until done. Frost as desired.

CHOCOLATE CAKE

1¾ cups Five Roses All-purpose Flour	1¼ cups sugar
¼ teaspoon baking soda	2 eggs
1½ teaspoons baking powder	2 squares unsweetened chocolate, melted
½ teaspoon salt	1 teaspoon vanilla
½ cup shortening	1 cup milk

Stir Five Roses Flour, baking soda, baking powder and salt together. Cream shortening; add sugar gradually, beating between additions. Add eggs, one at a time, beating well after each. Stir in melted chocolate and vanilla, blending well. Add dry ingredients alternately with milk, blending well after each addition. Pour into greased and floured or lined 8″ or 9″ square cake pan or two 8″ layer pans. Bake in a moderate oven (350°F.) 50 to 60 minutes for square cake; 30 to 35 minutes for layer cakes. Frost as desired.

Cupcakes: Bake at 350°F. 20 to 25 minutes. Makes 2 dozen, medium size.

DUTCH APPLE CAKE

1¾ cups Five Roses All-purpose Flour	1 cup sugar
3 teaspoons baking powder	1 egg
¾ teaspoon salt	1½ teaspoons vanilla
½ cup shortening	¾ cup milk

Topping

2 medium size apples	1 teaspoon cinnamon
¼ cup sugar	

Stir Five Roses Flour, baking powder and salt together. Cream shortening; gradually add sugar, creaming well between additions. Add egg and vanilla and beat until light and fluffy. Stir in dry ingredients alternately with milk. Pour into a well greased 7″ x 11″ shallow pan. Peel and core apples; cut in eights. Place in rows on batter with sharp edges pressed in slightly. Sprinkle sugar and cinnamon on top. Bake in a moderate oven (350°F.) for 50 to 60 minutes. Serve hot with Lemon Sauce (page 104).

Yield: 8 servings.

Note: Peaches or apricots (dried or canned) may be substituted for the apples. Omit cinnamon in topping.

DUTCH BLACK CAKE

½ cup butter or shortening
4½ tablespoons cocoa
1 cup sugar
¾ cup Five Roses All-purpose Flour
2 teaspoons baking powder

¼ teaspoon salt
½ cup milk
2 eggs, unbeaten
1 teaspoon vanilla

Cook the butter or shortening and cocoa in top of double boiler until fat is melted. Stir until well mixed and smooth; let cool. Stir sugar, Five Roses Flour, baking powder and salt together. Combine milk, eggs, vanilla and chocolate mixture; stir just enough to mix. Pour the milk mixture all-at-once over the dry ingredients; stir quickly until thoroughly blended. Bake in a greased and lined 8″ square pan in a moderate oven (350°F.) 25 to 30 minutes. Cool 5 minutes before removing from pan. Top with whipped cream or frost with favourite frosting.

PRIZE GINGERBREAD

2½ cups Five Roses All-purpose
   Flour
2 teaspoons baking powder
1 teaspoon ginger
½ cup shortening
1 cup brown sugar
1 cup molasses

½ teaspoon salt
½ teaspoon nutmeg
½ teaspoon cinnamon
1 cup boiling water
1 teaspoon baking soda
2 eggs, well-beaten

Stir Five Roses Flour, baking powder and ginger together. Cream shortening and brown sugar together. Blend in molasses, salt, nutmeg and cinnamon. Pour boiling water over baking soda and add to molasses-mixture. Stir in dry ingredients, blending well. Add well-beaten eggs and mix well. Pour batter into a greased and floured 9″ x 13″ x 2″ cake pan or two 8″ square pans. Bake in a moderate oven (325°F.) 50 to 60 minutes for large pan or 35 to 45 minutes for square pans. Serve warm or cold with Whipped Cream.

APPLESAUCE CAKE

1¼ cups Five Roses All-purpose
   Flour
½ teaspoon salt
1 teaspoon baking powder
1 teaspoon baking soda
1 teaspoon nutmeg
1 teaspoon cinnamon

½ teaspoon allspice
½ cup shortening
¾ cup brown sugar
1 egg
1 cup applesauce
1 cup raisins

Leave 1 tablespoon Five Roses Flour to coat raisins. Mix all dry ingredients together. Cream the shortening; gradually add brown sugar and cream well until light and fluffy. Add egg and beat well. Add the dry ingredients alternately with the applesauce, a little at a time, beating after each addition only until smooth. Fold in the floured raisins. Bake in a greased and lined or floured 8″ square pan in a moderate oven (350°F.) for 40 to 50 minutes. Cool 10 minutes before removing from pan. Frost with Rich Butter Frosting (page 55) or Japanese Frosting (page 55).

MOM'S BEST SPICECAKE

¾ cup butter
1½ cups sugar
3 egg yolks, beaten
1 teaspoon vanilla
1 cup milk
½ teaspoon salt
2 teaspoons baking powder
½ teaspoon allspice

¼ teaspoon cloves
1 teaspoon cinnamon
2¼ cups Five Roses All-purpose
    Flour
⅔ cup chopped nuts
1 cup sultana raisins
3 egg whites

Cream butter; add sugar gradually, beating until fluffy. Add beaten yolks, vanilla and milk; beat until smooth. Stir salt, baking powder, spices and Five Roses Flour together; fold in nuts and raisins. Combine flour mixture with batter. Beat egg whites until stiff but not dry; fold gently into batter. Bake in a greased 10″ tube pan in a moderate oven (375°F.) 50 to 60 minutes. Dust with icing sugar or frost as desired.

CHERRY CAKE

1½ cups Five Roses All-purpose
    Flour
2 teaspoons baking powder
½ teaspoon salt
⅓ cup butter

¾ cup sugar
2 eggs
½ cup milk
1 cup sliced maraschino cherries

Stir Five Roses Flour, baking powder and salt together. Cream butter, gradually add sugar and cream well until light and fluffy. Add eggs, one at a time, beating well after each addition. Add dry ingredients alternately with milk, beginning and ending with dry ingredients, beating after each addition only until smooth. Fold in maraschino cherries that have been dredged with flour. Bake in a greased 9″ x 5″ x 3″ loaf pan lined with waxed paper in a moderate oven (350°F.) 50 to 55 minutes. Serve plain.

HONEY PLUM CAKE

1¾ cups Five Roses All-purpose
    Flour
½ teaspoon baking soda
½ teaspoon salt
1 teaspoon baking powder
¼ teaspoon ginger
½ teaspoon cinnamon
½ teaspoon nutmeg

¼ teaspoon cloves
½ cup shortening
½ cup brown sugar
½ cup honey
2 eggs
¾ cup milk
1 cup seedless raisins

Stir together first 8 ingredients, reserving a little of the measured flour to dust raisins. Cream shortening; gradually add brown sugar, beating between additions. Stir in honey and eggs. Add dry ingredients alternately with milk beginning and ending with dry ingredients. Fold in floured raisins. Pour into a greased and floured 8″ tube pan. Bake in a moderate oven (350°F.) 50 to 60 minutes. Frost as desired.

SPONGE CAKE

1 cup Five Roses All-purpose Flour
Few grains salt
6 eggs, separated
1 cup sugar

1 tablespoon lemon juice
1 teaspoon lemon rind
1 tablespoon cold water

Stir Five Roses Flour and salt together. Beat egg yolks until thick and pale in colour; gradually beat in sugar. Stir in lemon juice, rind and water. Fold in dry ingredients. Beat egg whites until stiff but not dry; fold into batter. Bake in an ungreased 10″ tube pan in a moderate oven (325°F.) for 1 hour or until top of cake springs back when lightly touched with finger. Invert pan on cooling rack and let hang for 1 hour or until cool. Loosen cake with spatula and shake from pan. Frost as desired.

ENGLISH POUND CAKE

1¾ cups Five Roses All-purpose
 Flour
¼ teaspoon cream of tartar
¼ teaspoon salt
¼ teaspoon mace

1 cup butter
1 cup sugar
5 eggs
½ teaspoon vanilla

Stir Five Roses Flour, cream of tartar, salt and mace together. Cream butter thoroughly; gradually add sugar, a small amount at a time, creaming well. Beat in eggs, one at a time, beating well after each. Stir in vanilla. Add dry ingredients gradually, mixing only until thoroughly blended. Pour batter into a greased and floured 8½″ x 4½″ x 2½″ loaf pan. Bake in a moderate oven (325°F.) 60 to 70 minutes or until done. Sprinkle top with icing sugar or serve plain.

RICH WEDDING CAKE

3 lbs. seeded raisins
1 lb. currants
2 lbs. dates, chopped
1 lb. figs, chopped
1 lb. candied cherries, cut in halves
1 lb. chopped mixed peel
¼ cup chopped preserved ginger
2 small apples, finely chopped
½ lb. blanched and sliced almonds
½ lb. chopped walnuts
2 teaspoons baking soda
2 teaspoons cinnamon

1 teaspoon cloves
3½ cups Five Roses All-purpose
 Flour
1 lb. (2 cups) butter
2 cups brown sugar
10 eggs
1 cup black currant jelly
2 tablespoons whipping cream
¼ cup brandy, wine or grape juice
5 drops orange extract
Juice of 1 lemon
1 teaspoon vanilla

Grease 3 wedding cake tier pans—12″, 9″ and 6″ in diameter or one 10″ and two 8″ tube pans; line with greased heavy brown paper. Combine fruits and nuts; dust with a little of the measured flour. Stir baking soda, cinnamon, cloves and Five Roses Flour together. Cream butter; add brown sugar gradually beating between additions. Add eggs, one at a time, beating well after each. Stir in currant jelly, blending well. Add cream, juice, lemon juice and flavouring; mix well. Blend in dry ingredients; fold in floured fruits and nuts. Fill prepared pans ⅔ full. Bake in a slow oven (275°F.) 4 to 6 hours, depending on size or until done. Place a shallow pan of hot water on bottom rack of oven during baking; remove during last hour. Cool before removing paper; re-wrap well and store in air-tight container in a cool place. To frost and decorate see page 59.

Yield: 13 pounds.

Note: If using grape juice, you may add a few drops of brandy or rum extract for added flavour.

LEMON QUEENS

½ cup Five Roses All-purpose Flour	1 teaspoon grated lemon rind
⅛ teaspoon salt	2 teaspoons lemon juice
¼ teaspoon baking soda	2 egg yolks, well-beaten
¼ cup butter	2 egg whites
½ cup sugar	

Stir Five Roses Flour, salt and baking soda together. Cream butter; gradually beat in sugar, creaming well after each addition. Stir in lemon rind, lemon juice and well-beaten egg yolks. Add dry ingredients and mix well. Beat egg whites until stiff but not dry and fold into batter. Pour into greased muffin pans. Bake in a moderate oven (350°F.) 20 to 25 minutes. Frost as desired.

Yield: 1 dozen medium-size cupcakes.

ALMOND CUP CAKES

1½ cups Five Roses All-purpose Flour	½ cup milk
2 teaspoons baking powder	2 eggs
½ teaspoon salt	⅓ cup melted butter
¾ cup sugar	½ teaspoon vanilla
	½ cup finely chopped almonds

Stir Five Roses Flour, baking powder, salt and sugar together. Beat together the milk, eggs and melted butter; add to dry ingredients and beat 1 minute at no. 4 (low speed) of electric mixer. Add vanilla and chopped almonds; beat 1 more minute. Pour into greased muffin pans and bake at 350°F., 20 to 25 minutes. When cool, frost as desired and top with coarsely chopped almonds, toasted or plain.

Yield: 1½ dozen medium-size cupcakes.

Quick and Easy Ways to Vary Cake Recipes

Basic cake recipes may be varied in a number of ways to make new and exciting cakes to serve. Use these suggestions as a special treat for the family or serve them at receptions and parties.

LEMON CREAM CAKE

Prepare White Cake batter and flavour with 2 teaspoons grated lemon rind. Bake in layers. When cool, fill layers with Lemon Filling (page 53) and frost with Boiled or Seven-Minute Frosting (page 57).

COCONUT LAYER CAKE

Bake favourite cake recipe in 2 layers. Spread Seven-Minute Frosting (page 57) between layers and on top and sides of cake. Sprinkle each layer and outside with shredded coconut while frosting is soft.

BURNT LEATHER CAKE

Prepare White Cake batter and flavour with ½ teaspoon caramel flavouring or Caramel Syrup (page 106). Bake in 2 or 3 layers. When cool, fill layers with Caramel Filling (page 51) and frost with Caramel Frosting (page 56) or Brown Sugar Fudge Frosting (page 56).

MAPLE CREAM CAKE

Prepare White Cake batter. Flavour with ½ teaspoon maple flavouring. Bake in layers. When cool, fill layers with Maple Cream Filling (page 51) and frost with Maple Seven-Minute Frosting (page 57).

MARBLE CAKE

Prepare White Cake batter. To half of batter, add 2 squares of melted, unsweetened chocolate. Place light and dark mixtures in alternate spoonfuls in two greased and lined 8" round layer pans. Bake as directed for cake. When cool, frost with Chocolate Frosting (page 55).

ORANGE CAKE

Prepare White Cake batter. Flavour with 1 tablespoon grated orange rind. Bake in layers. When cool, fill layers with Orange Filling (page 53) and frost with Orange Frosting (page 55).

WHIPPED CREAM PINEAPPLE CAKE

Bake White Cake in layers. Cool and then chill. Pile Whipped Cream Fruit Filling (page 52) between layers of cake and on top.

PINEAPPLE OR PEACH UPSIDE DOWN CAKE

Prepare White Cake batter. Melt ⅓ cup butter in 9" square cake pan; add 1 cup brown sugar and stir. Place drained pineapple rings (or peach halves) close together on sugar. Place a maraschino cherry in each ring or cavity. Cover with cake batter. Bake in a moderate oven (350°F.) 45 to 55 minutes or until cake is done. Allow to cool in pan 15 minutes; loosen sides of cake, invert gently on cake plate. Serve warm or cold with Whipped Cream.

DOLLY VARDEN CAKE

Prepare White Cake batter. Dredge ½ cup raisins and ½ cup chopped citron peel with 1 tablespoon Five Roses All-purpose Flour; fold into cake batter. Pour into two greased and floured 8" layer cake pans. Bake at 350°F. for 30 to 40 minutes. When cool, put together and frost with Japanese Frosting (page 55).

MOCHA CAKES

Bake Sponge Cake in a shallow pan (10" x 15" x ¾") as for jelly roll (page 42). When cold, cut in desired shapes. Split cakes through centre and put together with softened jelly. Spread Mocha Frosting (page 55) over sides and roll in coconut. Spread either Mocha Frosting or a butter frosting over top and pipe a border around top of cakes. Decorate tops as desired. Makes about 3 dozen small cakes.

PEANUT SQUARES

Make same as for Mocha Cakes. When cold, cut in desired shapes. Split cakes through centre and put together with Cream Filling (page 51) or Butter Frosting (page 55). Frost with Butter Frosting and roll in chopped peanuts.

LITTLE LEMON CAKES

Make same as for Mocha Cakes. When cold, cut in desired shapes. Split cakes through centre and put together with Lemon Filling (page 53). Frost with Japanese Frosting (page 55). Decorate, if desired, with chopped nuts, coloured candies or coloured sugar.

QUICK CHERRY CAKES

Prepare favourite cake batter. Dust ¾ cup chopped glacé cherries with Five Roses Flour; fold into batter. Fill muffin pans lined with paper-cupcake liners, ⅔ full. Bake in a moderate oven (375°F.) 20 to 25 minutes. Makes about 2 dozen medium-size cup cakes, depending on recipe. Frost with Butter Frosting (page 55) tinted pink.

PETITS FOURS

Bake a White or Chocolate cake in a greased and lined 7" x 11" x 1½" cake pan. When cool, cut into 1½" squares or triangles. Place cakes, spaced well apart, on a cake rack and put wax paper under the rack. Pour PETITS FOURS FROSTING (page 56) over cakes, moving steadily back and forth until cakes are covered. Repeat to give cakes a second coating. Scrape frosting from wax paper and reheat over medium heat until lukewarm and of pouring consistency. Add more water if necessary. Use for remaining cakes. Let cakes dry, then remove carefully from rack. Trim bottom edges with a sharp knife. Decorate as desired with coloured candies, sliced gumdrops, candied fruit, nutmeats or coconut. Makes 3 dozen.

CHOCOLATE SURPRISE CAKES

Prepare Chocolate Cake batter and bake as for cup cakes. When cold, scoop out a little of the centre of each cake; fill with Date Filling (page 52). Cut lids from removed portions; place on top and cover with Mocha Frosting (page 55).

CHILD'S PARTY CAKE

Bake favourite cake in layers. Fill layers with any desired filling or frosting. Frost with Boiled Frosting (page 57) or Japanese Frosting (page 55). Cut a slice from top of candied cherries so that cavity in centre shows. Place the cherries cut-side up on the cake, using the number of cherries corresponding with child's age. Set a tiny candle in each cherry or put one candle in centre of cake and place correct number of peppermint candy sticks around cake. Later, each guest may be given a candy to eat.

CAKE FILLINGS

An almost endless variety of appetizing and interesting cakes may be produced by the use of different fillings.

CREAM FILLING

8 tablespoons Five Roses All-purpose Flour	2 cups milk
6 tablespoons sugar	2 egg yolks
⅛ teaspoon salt	1 tablespoon butter
	1 teaspoon vanilla

Stir Five Roses Flour, sugar and salt together. Scald milk in top of double boiler. Add hot milk to dry ingredients, a little at a time, stirring between additions; mix well. Return to double boiler and cook until thickened, stirring constantly; cover and cook 20 minutes longer. Beat egg yolks slightly, add a little of the hot mixture to them, mix well, and return to double boiler; stir for 2 minutes. Remove from heat; add butter and vanilla. Let cool before using.

Yield: Enough for large layer cake.

Variations of Cream Filling

PINEAPPLE CREAM FILLING
Make Cream Filling, increasing sugar to ½ cup and substituting 1 cup of juice from canned pineapple for 1 cup of milk specified in recipe. When filling is removed from heat, fold in ½ cup drained crushed pineapple and 2 teaspoons lemon juice.

CARAMEL FILLING
Make Cream Filling. Omit vanilla and add ½ cup Caramel Syrup (page 106).

CHOCOLATE FILLING
Make Cream Filling, adding 2 tablespoons more sugar. Add 1 square melted unsweetened chocolate with butter and vanilla.

MAPLE CREAM FILLING
Make Cream Filling. Omit sugar and vanilla. Use 1 cup maple syrup in place of 1 cup of the milk specified in recipe.

COFFEE CREAM FILLING
Make Cream Filling. Substitute 1 cup prepared coffee and 1 cup light cream in place of milk.

BUTTERSCOTCH FILLING

1½ tablespoons cornstarch
½ cup brown sugar
¼ teaspoon salt
1 cup milk

2 egg yolks
2 tablespoons butter
¼ teaspoon butterscotch flavouring

Mix cornstarch, sugar and salt thoroughly in top of double boiler. Add milk then place over boiling water. Cook, stirring constantly, until thick and smooth; continue cooking for 10 minutes longer, stirring frequently. Beat egg yolks thoroughly. Stir in a little of the hot mixture into the beaten yolks, then pour back all at once, into double boiler, stirring quickly. Cook for 3 minutes longer, stirring constantly. Remove from heat, add butter and flavouring and stir until mixed. Allow to cool before putting between layers of cake.

Yield: Enough for large layer cake.

FRENCH VANILLA CREAM FILLING

⅓ cup sugar
1 tablespoon Five Roses All-purpose
   Flour
1 tablespoon cornstarch
⅛ teaspoon salt

1¼ cups milk
1 egg, beaten
1 teaspoon vanilla
½ cup heavy cream, whipped

Combine sugar, flour, cornstarch and salt. Gradually stir in milk. Cook and stir until mixture thickens and boils; cook and stir 2 to 3 minutes longer. Stir a little of hot mixture into beaten egg; return to hot mixture. Bring to boil, stirring constantly; add vanilla. Cover entire surface with clear plastic wrap or waxed paper; cool. Beat until smooth; fold in whipped cream.

Yield: Enough for 2 dozen medium size éclairs.

Note: Use half recipe to fill a layer cake.

WHIPPED CREAM FRUIT FILLING

1 cup whipping cream
1 egg white, stiffly beaten
⅓ cup fruit sugar

½ cup crushed pineapple, drained
½ teaspoon vanilla

Whip the cream and combine with remaining ingredients. Spread between layers of cake, reserving some for the top. Serve immediately.

Yield: Enough for large layer cake.

Note: If desired, increase crushed pineapple to ¾ cup.

DATE FILLING

½ lb. chopped dates
½ cup cold water
2 tablespoons brown sugar

Grated rind of ½ an orange
2 tablespoons orange juice
1 teaspoon lemon juice

Combine dates, cold water, brown sugar and orange rind in a saucepan; cook over medium heat until thick and smooth. Remove from heat, add orange and lemon juices; mix well. Cool before spreading.

Yield: 1⅔ cups filling. Enough for two 8″ or 9″ layer cakes or one recipe of date squares.

ORANGE FILLING

2 tablespoons cornstarch
⅓ cup sugar
Few grains salt
¾ cup boiling water
1 egg

1½ teaspoons lemon juice
¼ cup orange juice
Grated rind of 1 orange
2 tablespoons butter

Blend starch, sugar and salt thoroughly in top of double boiler. Add ¼ cup boiling water and beat until smooth. Add remaining water and cook until thick over boiling water. Add a little of the hot mixture to the beaten egg and return to mixture. Cook 2 minutes longer. Stir in remaining ingredients. Cool, then spread between layers of cake.

Yield: Enough for large layer cake.

LEMON FILLING

1 cup water
Grated rind of 1 lemon
4 tablespoons cornstarch
½ cup sugar

1 egg
2 tablespoons butter
2 tablespoons lemon juice

Sprinkle lemon rind in water and bring to a boil in top of double boiler, over direct heat. Mix starch and sugar together; add boiling water, a little at a time, and return to double boiler. Cook over boiling water until thickened, stirring constantly. Cover and continue cooking 20 minutes longer, without stirring. Beat egg slightly, add a little of the hot mixture. Mix well and return to double boiler. Stir for 2 minutes. Remove from heat; add butter and lemon juice. Cool before using.

Yield: Enough for large layer cake.

NOTES

FROSTINGS

A good frosting adds to the flavour of a cake and helps to keep it fresh and moist, preserving it 3 to 4 times longer than if it were not encased in this air-tight covering.

How to Frost a Cake

1. Cool cake completely and brush off loose crumbs.

2. Place bottom layer, topside down, on a plate. If desired, arrange strips of waxed paper under the edges of the cake to keep plate clean. Remove after frosting.

3. Cover top of bottom layer, spreading the frosting evenly to the edge. For best results, use a metal spatula.

4. Place top layer, bottom side down, over bottom layer. If decorating the cake, you will need a flat top, so cut off dome and place cake top side down.

5. Frost sides first to give a "base coat", then apply more frosting using free easy upward strokes, leaving a ridge of frosting around top of cake.

6. Spread frosting on top, making swirls with spatula or spoon. If decorating, have top and sides flat.

To frost Angel or Sponge cakes

Place top side down on cake plate. Frost as for layer cake or use a thin frosting or glaze and spread over top, allowing it to dribble down sides.

To frost cupcakes

Dip top of each cupcake in frosting; turn to make a swirl on top.

CONFECTIONER'S FROSTING

Sift 2 cups icing sugar. Very slowly add boiling water, a tablespoon at a time, until right spreading consistency. Spread on slightly cooled bread or rolls.

RICH BUTTER FROSTING

¼ cup butter	**2½ to 2¾ cups sifted icing sugar**
1 egg	**1 teaspoon vanilla**

Cream butter well; stir in egg. Add sugar, a little at a time, beating until light and fluffy. Stir in vanilla.

Yield: Enough for a large layer cake.

VARIATIONS

Chocolate Frosting: Melt 2 squares unsweetened chocolate. Cool slightly and beat into above icing.

Orange Frosting: Omit vanilla. Add 2 tablespoons orange juice and 1 tablespoon grated orange rind to above icing. Add more icing sugar, if necessary.

Mocha Frosting: Increase icing sugar to 3 or 3¼ cups. Stir in 2 tablespoons cocoa. Beat in strong cold coffee, a little at a time, until soft enough to spread.

Coffee Frosting: Cream 1 teaspoon dry instant coffee with butter. Reduce vanilla to ½ teaspoon.

BUTTER FROSTING

¼ cup butter	**3 to 4 tablespoons milk**
2½ cups sifted icing sugar	

Cream butter. Gradually add sifted icing sugar and milk alternately, to make of spreading consistency. Add more icing sugar or milk if necessary. Flavour and colour as desired.

Yield: Enough for a large layer cake.

Variations: Follow variations for Rich Butter Frosting.

JAPANESE FROSTING

½ cup butter	**Flavouring**
2 cups sifted icing sugar	**Food colouring (optional)**
2 egg whites	

Cream butter; gradually stir in ½ cup icing sugar, beating until smooth. Beat egg whites until stiff but not dry; gradually beat in 1 cup icing sugar. Combine both mixtures and continue adding icing sugar until of good spreading consistency. Add desired flavouring and food colouring. Frosting should be stiff enough to hold its shape. Good for decorating cakes.

Yield: Enough for large layer cake.

ORNAMENTAL FROSTING

3 egg whites	**½ teaspoon cream of tartar**
2½ cups sifted icing sugar	

Put egg whites and ½ cup of icing sugar into a large bowl. Beat vigorously 10 minutes; add another ½ cup icing sugar and beat again. Add cream of tartar. Continue adding icing sugar and beating until mixture will hold its shape when forced through a bag or tube. Use for decorating special occasion cakes. By using decorating tubes, effective motifs such as roses or stars may be made.

Yield: 3 cups.

CARAMEL FROSTING

½ cup butter
½ cup brown sugar
¼ cup milk

1¾ to 2 cups sifted icing sugar
1 teaspoon vanilla

Melt butter in small saucepan. Add brown sugar and cook until sugar melts; stir in milk. Cool; beat in enough icing sugar to make a good spreading consistency. Add vanilla.

Yield: Enough for 8″ or 9″ square cake.

BROWN SUGAR FUDGE FROSTING

2 cups brown sugar
⅔ cup milk
2 tablespoons corn syrup

4 tablespoons butter
Few grains salt
½ teaspoon vanilla

Combine all ingredients together (except vanilla) in large saucepan. Bring to boiling point over medium heat, stirring constantly until sugar is dissolved. Boil without stirring until mixture reaches the soft ball stage (238°F.). Cool to lukewarm. Add vanilla and beat vigorously until creamy and stiff enough to spread.

Yield: Enough for large layer cake.

ORANGE FROSTING

Grated rind of 1 orange
3 tablespoons orange juice
1 tablespoon lemon juice

1 tablespoon butter
3 tablespoons light cream
3 to 4 cups sifted icing sugar

Mix first 5 ingredients together. Gradually add icing sugar until of good spreading consistency.

Yield: Enough for large layer cake.

PETITS FOURS FROSTING

3 cups icing sugar
5 to 6 tablespoons cold water

1 teaspoon soft butter

Mix icing sugar and 5 tablespoons water together in a saucepan. Heat over medium heat until mixture feels lukewarm and is of good pouring consistency. Stir in butter. Add more water, if necessary. Pour over cakes twice to give a good coating.

To colour: When frosting is ready to pour, tint delicately with food colouring.

WHIPPED CREAM FROSTING

1 teaspoon unflavoured gelatin
2 tablespoons cold water
2 tablespoons boiling water

½ pint whipping cream
¼ cup icing sugar
Few grains salt

Sprinkle gelatin over cold water in small bowl to soften. Pour boiling water over gelatin; stir until dissolved. Refrigerate until consistency of unbeaten egg white, then beat until smooth. Whip cream; stir in sugar and salt. Fold in gelatin mixture.

Yield: Enough for a 4 layer cake.

BOILED FROSTING

2 cups granulated sugar	2 egg whites
⅓ cup corn syrup	1 teaspoon vanilla
⅓ cup water	

Combine sugar, corn syrup and water in top of double boiler. Cook over boiling water until syrup will spin a long thread when dropped from a spoon or until candy thermometer reads 238°. Remove from heat. Meanwhile, have ready stiffly beaten egg whites. Add the beaten egg whites and vanilla and beat until mixture is almost cold, becomes creamy and will hold its shape when spread on cake. Grated lemon or orange rind or almond flavouring may be used instead of vanilla. Chopped nuts or shredded coconut may be folded in at end. Use immediately.

Yield: Enough for large layer cake.

Honey Boiled Frosting: Make as for Boiled Frosting but substitute honey for corn syrup. Omit vanilla.

Coffee Boiled Frosting: Make as for Boiled Frosting but substitute cold strong coffee for water. Omit vanilla.

SEVEN-MINUTE FROSTING

1 cup granulated sugar	1 egg white, unbeaten
⅛ teaspoon cream of tartar	⅓ cup boiling water
Few grains salt	½ teaspoon vanilla

Mix all ingredients together (except vanilla) in top of double boiler; stir to dissolve sugar. Set pan over boiling water and beat with rotary or electric beater until stiff enough to stand in peaks. Remove from heat; add vanilla and continue beating until stiff enough to spread. Use immediately.

Yield: Enough for large layer cake.

Note: It is preferable to use an enamel or pyrex double boiler. The beating will take longer if a rotary hand beater is used instead of an electric beater.

MAPLE SEVEN MINUTE FROSTING

¾ cup hot maple syrup	2 teaspoons granulated sugar
⅛ teaspoon cream of tartar	1 egg white, unbeaten

Combine hot maple syrup, cream of tartar and sugar in top of double boiler. Place over boiling water and add unbeaten egg white. Beat with rotary or electric beater until thick and smooth. Remove from heat and use immediately.

Yield: Enough for large layer cake.

APRICOT GLAZE

1 cup dried apricots	2½ cups granulated sugar
2½ cups water	

Place apricots and water in 1½ quart saucepan. Bring to boil and boil uncovered for 10 minutes. Force apricots through a sieve. Should yield about 2 cups purée— if not, add enough water to purée to make 2 cups. Return purée to saucepan and add sugar. Bring to boil and boil gently, stirring constantly, until purée is as thick as marmalade. Cool before using. Use for glazing fruit cakes.

Yield: 2 cups glaze.

CHRISTMAS CAKES
AND
PLUM PUDDING

The aging of fruit cake, plum pudding and mincemeat might be compared to the aging of wine. Time seems to put mellow deliciousness into them that no art can imitate. All rich fruit cakes should be prepared long enough ahead for them to ripen to moist, spicy lusciousness. The richer the cake is in fruits, the longer the time required for ripening.

PREPARING INGREDIENTS

The actual labour of making Christmas Cakes will seem considerably lighter if fruits and nuts are prepared the day before. Fruits should never be stale or dry.

Currants, seedless raisins, sultana raisins—wash and drain well. Leave whole.

Seeded raisins—wash, drain and cut in halves with wet scissors.

Candied pineapple, citron and fruit peels—chop finely or slice thinly.

Candied cherries—usually cut in halves.

Dates—cut in quarters with floured knife or wet scissors.

Nuts—chop in quarters. Always blanch almonds.

Dredge fruit lightly with flour so that pieces will not stick together.

PREPARING PANS

Use deep pans. Grease pans lightly and line with crossed strips of heavy waxed paper or greased brown paper, cut to fit, and large enough to reach top of pan. Glass or ovenware casseroles are attractive to use. Grease lightly but do not line with paper. After baking and cooling, cover and set cakes aside to ripen. Fill prepared pans about ⅔ full.

BAKING CHRISTMAS CAKES

Bake fruit cakes in a slow oven for recommended time. Always place a shallow pan of hot water on bottom of oven during baking. This prevents the cakes from drying out. Remove pan of water during last hour of baking.

STORING CHRISTMAS CAKES

Cool fruit cakes thoroughly in the pan. Remove the lining papers left attached to the cake or leave on for storage. Re-wrap well in aluminum foil or heavy waxed paper. Seal securely. Store in air-tight container, in a cool place. If desired, sprinkle cakes lightly with brandy, once a week until used. This helps keep the cake moist and improves the flavour.

DECORATING CHRISTMAS CAKES

Invert cakes in order to procure a flat surface for the paste. When cake has a rounded top and will not set flat on plate, cut off a thin slice to make it set evenly.

Brush tops of cake with egg white. Spread Almond Paste (page 62) evenly on top—about ¼-inch thick. Let stand until firm.

Spread Ornamental Frosting (page 55) evenly over Almond Paste and sides of cake; decorate with remaining frosting. If you have had no experience with work of this kind, practice on an inverted cake tin. Frosting can be scraped off and used again.

Decorate top of cake with garlands of "holly", cutting leaves from slices of citron, stems from angelica and using tiny red candies for berries. "Mistletoe" may be formed on a pale green frosting, using tiny white candies for berries, citron for leaves and angelica for stems.

A light, wholesome cake for the children's Christmas can be frosted with Boiled or Butter Frosting and decorated with tiny Christmas trees cut from thin slices of citron peel. If the peel is pale in colour, smear the back of each "tree" with a little green frosting or dip peel in green food colouring and allow to dry before putting on cake.

STEAMING CHRISTMAS PUDDING

See Steamed Pudding section, page 100.

Small Plum Puddings make attractive gifts. Cool thoroughly, wrap in saran and then in gay wrapping paper.

REHEATING STEAMED PUDDINGS

Place pudding in container or bowl. Cover and steam 2 to 3 hours, depending on size.

LIGHT FRUIT CAKE

3 cups sultana raisins
4 cups chopped mixed peel
1½ cups glacé cherries, cut in
    halves
2 cups sliced, blanched almonds
Grated rind and juice of lemon

4½ cups Five Roses All-purpose
    Flour
½ teaspoon salt
1 teaspoon baking powder
2 cups butter
2 cups granulated sugar
9 eggs

Line three 9" x 5" x 3" loaf pans or three 8" tube pans with heavy waxed or brown paper. Combine fruits, nuts and lemon rind; dust with a little of the measured Five Roses Flour. Stir Five Roses Flour, salt and baking powder together. Cream butter until creamy and light; add sugar gradually, beating between additions. Add eggs, one at a time, beating well after each. (If mixture curdles add a little of the dry ingredients, then continue to add eggs.) Blend in dry ingredients. Fold in lemon juice, fruits and nuts. Fill prepared pans ⅔ full. Bake in a slow oven (275°F.) 3 - 3½ hours depending on size or until done. Place a shallow pan of hot water on bottom rack of oven during baking; remove during last hour. Cool before removing paper; re-wrap well and store in an airtight container in a cool place.

Yield: 6¾ lbs.

DARK FRUIT CAKE

3 cups seedless raisins
3 cups sultana raisins
½ cup chopped glacé cherries
½ cup chopped candied pineapple
½ cup chopped citron peel
¼ cup chopped lemon peel
¼ cup chopped orange peel
1 cup chopped walnuts
1½ cups Five Roses All-purpose
    Flour

½ teaspoon salt
¼ teaspoon baking soda
1 teaspoon cinnamon
1 teaspoon allspice
¼ teaspoon nutmeg
¼ teaspoon mace
1 cup shortening
1 cup brown sugar
6 eggs
½ cup molasses

Line two 9" x 5" x 3" loaf pans or two 8" tube pans with heavy waxed or brown paper. Prepare fruits and nuts; dust with ¼ cup of the Five Roses Flour. Stir remaining Five Roses Flour, salt, baking soda and spices together. Cream shortening and brown sugar together until fluffy. Add eggs, one at a time, beating well after each. Add molasses; mix well. Blend in dry ingredients; fold in fruit and nut mixture. Fill prepared pans ⅔ full. Bake in a slow oven (300°F.) 2 hours or until done. Place a shallow pan of hot water on bottom rack of oven during baking; remove during last hour. Cool before removing paper; re-wrap well and store in an airtight container in a cool place.

Yield: 4¼ lbs.

TUTTI FRUTTI CHRISTMAS CAKE

1 lb. glacé cherries, cut in halves
2 cups chopped citron peel
1½ lbs. sultana raisins
½ lb. seedless raisins
6 oz. almonds, blanched and sliced
4½ cups Five Roses All-purpose
    Flour
2 teaspoons baking powder
1 teaspoon salt
1 teaspoon nutmeg

1 tablespoon cornstarch
1½ cups butter
1 cup sugar
7 eggs
1 cup crabapple jelly
1 cup pineapple jam
½ cup brandy, rum or fruit juice
1 teaspoon vanilla
1 teaspoon almond extract

Grease two 9" x 5" x 3" loaf pans and one 8½" x 4½" x 2½" loaf pan (or two 8" tube pans) and line with heavy waxed or brown paper. Combine fruit and almonds; dust with a little of the measured flour. Stir Five Roses Flour, baking powder, salt, nutmeg and cornstarch together. Cream butter; add sugar gradually, beating between additions. Add eggs, one at a time, beating well after each. Blend in a little of the dry ingredients, then beat in the jelly and jam. Stir in juice and flavourings. Add remaining dry ingredients, mix well. Fold in floured fruit and almonds. Fill prepared pans ⅔ full. Bake in a slow oven (275°F.) 3½ to 4 hours depending on size or until done. Place a shallow pan of hot water on bottom rack of oven during baking; remove during last hour. Cool before removing paper; re-wrap well and store in an airtight container in a cool place.

Yield: Two 9" x 5" x 3" and one 8½" x 4½" x 2½" cakes.

Note: Cake appears dry when cooled. However, it softens as it ripens, and after 4 to 6 weeks storage it will be moist and delicious.

A Wonderful Christmas Favourite **LIGHT FRUIT CAKE**
page 59

BRAZIL NUT CHRISTMAS LOAF

¾ cup Five Roses All-purpose Flour
½ teaspoon baking powder
½ teaspoon salt
3 cups (12 oz.) whole brazil nuts
1 lb. whole, pitted dates

1 cup maraschino cherries, well
    drained
3 eggs
¾ cup sugar
1 teaspoon vanilla

Stir Five Roses Flour, baking powder and salt together. Add the brazil nuts, dates and maraschino cherries; mix well until fruits and nuts are well coated. Beat eggs and sugar together with a fork until slightly foamy; stir in vanilla. Combine the egg mixture and floured nuts and fruit; mix well. Turn into a greased and lined 9″ x 5″ x 3″ loaf pan. Bake in a slow oven (325°F.) 1½ to 2 hours. Cool in pan. When cooled, wrap in heavy waxed paper or foil and store in refrigerator.

To decorate: If desired, spread top of cake with a thin layer of hot jam. Cover with Almond Paste, then frost as desired. Decorate with candied red or green cherries.

ALMOND PASTE

2 cups blanched almonds
1 egg white

1¼ cups icing sugar
2 teaspoons lemon juice

Chop almonds very finely, preferably with a blender. Add egg white gradually, then 1 cup icing sugar and lemon juice. Knead with more icing sugar until a soft dough is formed. Roll out to desired shape, about ¼ inch thick.

Yield: 1¼ lbs.

PLUM PUDDING

1 cup soft bread crumbs
1 cup seedless raisins
1 cup currants
1 cup chopped dates
½ cup chopped citron peel
½ cup chopped walnuts
1 cup Five Roses All-purpose Flour
1 teaspoon baking powder
¼ teaspoon baking soda
¼ teaspoon salt

½ teaspoon cinnamon
¼ teaspoon nutmeg
¼ teaspoon cloves
¼ teaspoon all-spice
½ cup butter
½ cup brown sugar
2 eggs
⅓ cup molasses
1 cup milk

Prepare bread crumbs, fruits and nuts; dust with a small amount of Five Roses Flour. Stir Five Roses Flour, baking powder, baking soda, salt and spices together. Cream butter and sugar together well. Add eggs, one at a time, beating well after each. Blend in molasses. Add milk alternately with dry ingredients, beginning and ending with the dry ingredients. Fold in fruits, nuts and bread crumbs. Fill a greased 1½ qt. pudding bowl or individual moulds ⅔ full; cover tightly. Steam 3 hours or until done for large mould; 1 to 2 hours for small moulds. Serve hot with sauce.

Note: If made ahead of time, reheat for serving by steaming 2-3 hours.

CHRISTMAS WREATH

Steam pudding in a greased ring mould. Turn out onto serving dish and decorate with cherries and candied citron to look like a Christmas Wreath.

COOKIES

Cookies may be crisp or soft, thick or thin, dark or light, plain or full of fruits and nuts, frosted, filled or decorated. The cookies in this chapter are divided into 8 principal groups, based on the way that they are made.

The Secret of Good Cookies is in the dough. No matter what type of cookie, the softest dough that can be handled and baked into the desired form will give the most tender product. Chilling the dough for rolled cookies prevents stickiness and therefore, the dough will not take up so much flour during the rolling process.

Place Baking Sheet in centre of oven. If using 2 racks, never place one baking sheet directly over the other. For proper heat circulation, have at least 2 inches of rack showing around the edges of each baking sheet.

Cool cookies on a rack before storing.

Store crisp cookies in a loosely covered container; soft cookies in an air-tight container. If crisp cookies should become soft after storing, the crispness may be restored by placing the cookies on an ungreased baking sheet and letting them stand in a slow oven (300°F.) for 3 to 5 minutes.

DROP COOKIES

STANDARD DROP COOKIES

1 cup Five Roses All-purpose Flour	1 egg
½ teaspoon baking powder	1 tablespoon milk
⅛ teaspoon baking soda	½ teaspoon vanilla
½ teaspoon salt	½ cup chopped nuts
⅓ cup butter	½ cup glacé cherries, halved
⅓ cup brown sugar	

Stir Five Roses Flour, baking powder, baking soda and salt together. Cream butter; add brown sugar gradually, beating well after each addition. Add egg, milk and vanilla; mix well. Blend in dry ingredients. Fold in nuts and cherries. Drop by teaspoonfuls onto greased cookie sheet, allowing space for spreading. Bake in a moderate oven (375°F.) 8 to 10 minutes or until browned.

Yield: 2½ dozen. Recipe may be doubled.

HERMITS

Add to Standard Drop Cookie dough—½ teaspoon cinnamon, ⅛ teaspoon cloves, ⅛ teaspoon nutmeg, 1 cup raisins, ½ cup coconut and increase nuts to 1 cup.

CHERRY ALMOND DROP COOKIES

Add to Standard Drop Cookie dough—¾ cup chopped almonds (in place of ½ cup chopped nuts), ½ teaspoon almond extract and increase glacé cherries to 1 cup.

CHRISTMAS DROP COOKIES

Add to Standard Drop Cookie dough—½ cup chopped lemon peel, 1 cup sultana raisins and ½ cup chopped almonds.

OATMEAL DROP COOKIES

Make Standard Drop Cookies, using only ¾ cup Five Roses Flour and increasing baking soda to ¼ teaspoon. Add ½ cup Ogilvie Quick Oats and ¼ teaspoon cinnamon to dry ingredients. Omit chopped nuts and cherries, if desired.

COCONUT DROP COOKIES

Add to Standard Cookie dough—1 cup shredded coconut. Omit nuts and cherries, if desired.

CHOCOLATE NUT DROPS

1¾ cups Five Roses All-purpose Flour	2 eggs, well-beaten
¼ teaspoon baking soda	2 tablespoons milk
½ teaspoon salt	2 squares unsweetened chocolate, melted
1 teaspoon baking powder	½ teaspoon vanilla
½ cup shortening	1 cup chopped nuts
1¼ cups brown sugar	

Stir Five Roses Flour, baking soda, salt and baking powder together. Cream shortening; add brown sugar gradually, beating well after each addition. Add well-beaten eggs, milk, melted chocolate and vanilla; mix well. Blend in dry ingredients; fold in nuts. Drop by teaspoonfuls onto a greased cookie sheet and bake in a moderate oven (375°F.) 10 to 12 minutes.

Yield: 5 dozen.

CHOCOLATE CHIP COOKIES

1 cup Five Roses All-purpose Flour	1 egg
½ teaspoon salt	½ teaspoon vanilla
½ teaspoon baking soda	½ cup chocolate chips
½ cup butter or margarine	½ cup chopped walnuts
⅔ cup brown sugar	

Stir Five Roses Flour, salt and baking soda together. Mix 2 tablespoons of the dry ingredients with the chocolate chips and nuts. Cream butter; add brown sugar gradually, beating until creamy. Beat in egg and vanilla. Add dry ingredients, mixing well. Fold in the chocolate chips and nuts. Drop by teaspoonfuls onto greased cookie sheet. Bake in a moderate oven (375°F.) 8 to 10 minutes or until done. Cool slightly before removing from pan.

Yield: 3½ dozen.

ROLLED COOKIES

SUGAR COOKIES

1½ cups Five Roses All-purpose Flour
1½ teaspoons baking powder
¼ teaspoon salt
½ cup butter

½ cup sugar
1 egg yolk, slightly beaten
3 tablespoons milk
½ teaspoon vanilla

Stir Five Roses Flour, baking powder and salt together. Cream butter; add sugar gradually, beating between additions. Add egg yolk; mix well. Add dry ingredients alternately with milk; add vanilla. Chill dough thoroughly. Roll ¼" thick on lightly floured board; cut with fancy cookie cutters. Bake on an ungreased cookie sheet in a moderate oven (375°F.) 8 to 10 minutes.

Yield: 3 dozen medium-size cookies.

Note: If desired, ice the cookies with butter icing and decorate.

GINGERSNAPS

½ cup shortening
⅔ cup molasses
2 cups Five Roses All-purpose Flour
1 teaspoon salt

½ teaspoon baking soda
2 teaspoons ginger
1 teaspoon cinnamon

Cream shortening. Heat molasses to boiling; cool slightly and pour over shortening, mixing well. Stir dry ingredients together; mix in to first mixture. Chill 1 hour or more. Roll out dough ¼" thick on a lightly floured board. Cut with cookie cutter. Bake at 375°F. 5 to 7 minutes or until delicately brown.

Yield: 5 dozen 2" round cookies.

Note: The crispness of the cookies will depend largely on how thin the dough is rolled and how evenly the baking is done.

Gingerbread Men: Follow above recipe. Cut out with cutter. Bake. Decorate with icing, candies or bits of citron.

BUTTERSCOTCH COOKIES

3 cups Five Roses All-purpose Flour
½ teaspoon baking powder
½ teaspoon salt
1 teaspoon baking soda

¾ cup butter
1½ cups brown sugar
2 eggs
1 teaspoon vanilla

Stir Five Roses Flour, baking powder, salt and baking soda together. Cream butter; gradually add brown sugar, beating between additions. Add eggs and beat well. Stir in dry ingredients, a little at a time, mixing well after each addition; add vanilla. Chill dough 1 hour. Roll dough ⅛" thick on lightly floured board and cut with cookie cutter. If desired, shape into balls; place on greased cookie sheet and flatten with floured fork. Decorate cookies, if desired. Bake at 375°F. 10 to 12 minutes.

Yield: 5 to 6 dozen.

CHOCO-PECAN BUTTERSCOTCH

Add ½ cup pecans and ⅓ cup chocolate chips to Butterscotch Cookie dough.

GRANDMOTHER'S OATMEAL COOKIES

2 cups Five Roses All-purpose Flour	1 cup brown sugar
1 teaspoon baking soda	½ cup butter
1 teaspoon salt	½ cup shortening
2 cups Ogilvie Quick Oats	½ cup sour milk

Stir first 5 ingredients together. Melt fats and mix with dry ingredients. Stir in milk, mixing well. Chill dough ½ hour. Roll out ¼″ thick on lightly floured board. Cut with round cookie cutter, about 2″ in diameter. Place on greased baking sheet and bake in a moderate oven (350°F.) 10 to 15 minutes or until lightly browned.

Yield: 5 to 6 dozen.

FOUNDATION FILLED COOKIES

3 cups Five Roses All-purpose Flour	1 cup sugar
3 teaspoons baking powder	2 eggs, beaten
½ teaspoon salt	1 teaspoon vanilla
½ cup shortening	¼ cup milk

Stir Five Roses Flour, baking powder and salt together. Cream shortening; add sugar gradually, beating between additions. Add beaten eggs and vanilla; mix well. Add dry ingredients alternately with milk, beating between additions until well blended. Work dough with hand until smooth; chill 15 minutes. Roll ⅛″ thick; cut with floured 1½″ cookie cutter. Place a teaspoon of filling in centre of cookie, cover with another and press edges together. Bake on a greased baking sheet in a moderate oven (375°F.) 8 to 10 minutes.

Fillings

Jam Cookies: Use 1 cup jam or jelly to fill centres.

Mincemeat Cookies: Use 1 cup mincemeat to fill centres.

Date Cookies: Use 1 cup Date Filling (page 52) to fill centres.

Yield: 3 dozen.

PRIZE SHORTBREAD

2 cups Five Roses All-purpose Flour	½ teaspoon salt
1 cup butter	⅛ teaspoon nutmeg
½ cup icing sugar	1 egg yolk

Soften butter slightly, but do not allow to become oily. Stir in sugar, salt, nutmeg and egg yolk with a wooden spoon. Add flour, a little at a time, until mixture is too stiff to work with spoon. Turn onto floured board and knead lightly, drawing in flour all the time until dough just **begins to crack**. Roll out dough ¼″ thick and cut into desired shapes with cookie cutter; place on an ungreased cookie sheet. Bake at 350°F. 10 minutes or until delicately brown.

Yield: 3½ dozen.

To Decorate — Top with strips of red and green maraschino cherries before baking.

Top to Bottom:
CHERRY ALMOND MERINGUES
page 71

SUGAR COOKIES
page 65

CHOCOLATE NUT DROPS
page 64

CHOCOLATE CHIP COOKIES
page 64

PEANUT BUTTER COOKIES
page 69

PINWHEELS
page 68

REFRIGERATOR COOKIES

ICE BOX COOKIES

⅔ cup butter	2 cups Five Roses All-purpose Flour
1 cup brown sugar	¼ teaspoon salt
1 egg	½ teaspoon baking soda
1 teaspoon vanilla	

Cream butter; gradually add brown sugar and cream well. Add egg, vanilla and beat well. Mix Five Roses Flour, salt and baking soda together; stir into batter. Use dough as it is or in any of the variations listed. Shape finished dough into long rolls, about 2″ in diameter. Wrap with waxed paper and chill until hard (about 1-2 hours). Slice thinly; place on ungreased cookie sheet. Bake at 350°F for 8-10 minutes.

Yield: 5 dozen.

Variations
(Use ⅓ of dough for each variation)

ORANGE
Add 1½ tablespoons grated orange rind.

CHOCOLATE NUT
Add 1 square melted unsweetened chocolate for chocolate dough. Add 4 tablespoons chopped nuts.

LEMON-COCONUT
Add ½ teaspoon lemon extract and 2 tablespoons shredded coconut.

TURTLES
Between 2 slices of chocolate dough, place whole pecan (for head) and 4 pieces chopped pecan (for legs).

SANDIES
Bake a plain cookie. Dredge with (colored) powdered fruit sugar while still warm.

BLACK AND WHITE
Use chocolate dough. Top with miniature marshmallows for last 3 minutes of baking.

JEWEL
Add 2 tablespoons chopped red and/or green maraschino cherries, drained well and 2 tablespoons chopped nuts.

PINWHEELS
Roll out rectangles of chocolate and vanilla dough, ⅛″ thick. Place one on top of other and roll together.

ALMOND
Add ½ teaspoon almond extract. Before baking, top each cookie with blanched almond half.

LEMON PECAN DAINTIES

1¾ cups Five Roses All-purpose Flour	1 cup sugar
1 teaspoon baking powder	1 egg
½ teaspoon salt	1 tablespoon grated lemon rind
⅔ cup butter	1 tablespoon lemon juice
	1 cup chopped pecans

Stir Five Roses Flour, baking powder and salt together. Cream butter and sugar together; beat in egg, lemon rind and juice. Add dry ingredients gradually; stir in chopped pecans. Shape into 2 rolls, 1½″ in diameter; wrap in waxed paper and chill thoroughly. Slice thinly and place on greased cookie sheet. Bake in a moderate oven (375°F.) 12 to 15 minutes.
Yield: 5 dozen.

SHAPED COOKIES

PEANUT BUTTER COOKIES

½ cup butter	½ teaspoon salt
½ cup brown sugar	½ teaspoon baking soda
½ cup granulated sugar	1 cup Five Roses All-purpose Flour
1 egg	½ teaspoon vanilla
½ cup peanut butter	

Cream butter; add sugars gradually, beating until creamy. Mix in egg, peanut butter, salt and baking soda. Blend in Five Roses Flour, slowly. Add vanilla and mix well. Roll into small balls (or drop by teaspoonfuls) and place on a greased cookie sheet. Press the balls flat with a floured fork. Bake in a moderate oven (350°F.) 10-12 minutes.
Yield: 4½-5 dozen.

BUTTER BALLS

2½ cups Five Roses All-purpose Flour	2 egg yolks
	2 egg whites
¼ teaspoon salt	1 cup chopped nuts
1 cup butter	Jelly
½ cup sugar	

Stir Five Roses Flour and salt together. Cream butter; add sugar gradually beating between additions. Add egg yolks, mix well. Blend in dry ingredients gradually. Shape dough into 1″ balls. Roll in slightly beaten egg whites and then in chopped nuts. Place on a greased baking sheet; make an indentation in centre of cookies. Bake in a moderate oven (325°F.) 20 to 25 minutes. Cool; fill centres with jelly.
Yield: 4 dozen.
Note: If desired, omit rolling in egg whites and nuts; leave plain.

ORANGE NUT CRISPS

½ cup granulated sugar	Grated rind of 1 orange
⅓ cup butter	Grated rind of 1 lemon
1 cup Five Roses All-purpose Flour	1 cup chopped nuts
1 egg	

Cream sugar and butter together, mixing well. Beat in egg. Add Five Roses Flour gradually, stirring well. Stir in orange rind, lemon rind and chopped nuts. Shape into balls; place on greased cookie sheet. Press balls flat with a floured fork. Bake in a moderate oven (350°F.) 12-15 minutes.
Yield: 3 dozen.

PRESSED COOKIES

PRESSED COOKIES

2 cups Five Roses All-purpose Flour
½ teaspoon baking powder
⅛ teaspoon baking soda
½ teaspoon salt
½ cup butter

½ cup sugar
1 egg
2 tablespoons orange juice
1 teaspoon orange rind

Stir Five Roses Flour, baking powder, baking soda and salt together. Cream butter; gradually add sugar, creaming well after each addition. Add egg and beat well. Stir in dry ingredients; add orange juice and orange rind, mixing well. Place dough in cookie press and press dough onto ungreased cookie sheet. Bake in a moderate oven (350°F.) 10-12 minutes or until lightly browned around edges.

Yield: 3 dozen.

CHOCOLATE SPRITZ COOKIES

1 cup butter
⅔ cup sugar
1 egg
1 egg yolk
½ teaspoon vanilla

2 squares semi-sweet chocolate,
    melted
2¼ cups Five Roses All-purpose
    Flour
¼ cup cocoa
¼ teaspoon salt

Cream butter; gradually add sugar, beating until light and fluffy. Add egg and egg yolk, mixing well. Stir in vanilla and melted chocolate. Combine Five Roses Flour, cocoa and salt; gradually add to creamed mixture, mixing thoroughly. Place dough in cookie press and press dough onto ungreased cookie sheet. Bake at (400°F.) 10 to 12 minutes.

Yield: 5 dozen.

UNBAKED COOKIES

HONEY NUTLETS

½ lb. dates
½ lb. nuts

1½ tablespoons honey
1½ teaspoons lemon juice

Chop dates and nuts finely or put through food chopper. Mix dates and ½ of the nuts, then moisten with a mixture of honey and lemon juice. Roll mixture into 1" balls, then roll in the remainder of the nuts.

Yield: 2½ dozen.

Note: If desired, roll in icing sugar or granulated sugar.

OAT DELIGHTS

2 cups sugar
6 tablespoons cocoa
½ cup butter
½ cup milk

½ teaspoon vanilla
1 cup shredded coconut
3 cups Ogilvie Instant Oats

Combine sugar, cocoa, butter and milk in saucepan; bring to a boil. Add vanilla. Remove from heat and stir in coconut and Ogilvie Oats. Drop by teaspoonfuls onto wax paper; chill.

Yield: 4½ dozen.

MERINGUES AND MACAROONS

CHOCOLATE COCONUT MACAROONS

2 squares unsweetened chocolate, melted
4 cups, packed, shredded coconut

1 can (14 oz.) sweetened condensed milk
1 teaspoon vanilla

Mix melted unsweetened chocolate with sweetened condensed milk; add shredded coconut and mix thoroughly. Stir in vanilla. Drop by teaspoonfuls onto well greased baking sheet, 1″ apart. Bake in a moderate oven (350°F.), 8 to 10 minutes. Cool slightly before removing from pan.

Yield: Approximately 3½ dozen, depending on size.

PLAIN COCONUT MACAROONS — Omit the chocolate and use 1 lb. shredded coconut. Mix and bake as above.

Yield: Approximately 4 to 4½ dozen, depending on size.

HARD MERINGUES

3 egg whites
Few grains salt
½ teaspoon cream of tartar

¾ cup granulated sugar
½ teaspoon vanilla

Combine egg whites, salt and cream of tartar and beat at medium speed of electric mixer until mixture turns foamy-white and doubles in volume. Increase speed and start adding sugar very slowly—takes about 10 minutes. Beat 5 to 10 minutes longer to dissolve every grain of sugar. Rub a little of the meringue between fingers. If it feels smooth, the sugar is dissolved. Fold in vanilla. Drop meringue by teaspoonfuls onto ungreased paper lined cookie sheet. Bake in a slow oven (250°F.) for 1 hour. Turn oven off and leave to dry in oven, 1 hour longer.

Yield: 3 dozen.

VARIATIONS:

Coconut Meringues: Substitute vanilla with a few drops almond extract. Fold in 1½ cups shredded coconut and ⅓ cup glacé red cherries.

Cherry Almond Meringues: Omit vanilla and fold in ½ cup glacé red cherries, ½ cup glacé green cherries, ½ cup chopped almonds and ¼ teaspoon almond extract.

Chocolate Chip Meringues: Increase vanilla to ¾ teaspoon. Fold in ¾ cup chocolate chips.

RAGGED ROBINS

2 egg whites
½ cup sugar
½ cup maraschino cherries

1½ cups cornflakes
½ cup chopped nuts
1 teaspoon vanilla

Beat egg whites until stiff but not dry; gradually add sugar, beating between additions. Drain the maraschino cherries well on absorbent paper. Add to egg whites along with cornflakes, nuts and vanilla and blend well. Drop by teaspoonfuls onto greased baking sheet. Bake in a moderate oven (350°F.) 12 to 15 minutes.

Yield: 2 dozen.

SQUARES AND BARS

CHINESE CHEWS

⅔ cup Five Roses All-purpose Flour
1 teaspoon baking powder
¼ teaspoon salt
¾ cup sugar

1 cup chopped dates
1 cup chopped walnuts
2 eggs, well-beaten
½ teaspoon vanilla
Fruit sugar

Stir Five Roses Flour, baking powder and salt together. Add sugar, dates and nuts, then stir in the eggs and vanilla. Spread about ½" thick on a well greased 9" square pan. Bake in a moderate oven (325°F.) for 25-30 minutes. Cut in small squares (while warm) and roll into balls; dredge with fruit sugar.

Yield: 4 dozen.

WALNUT SLICES

Pastry

1½ cups Five Roses All-purpose
  Flour

¼ cup brown sugar
½ cup butter

Meringue Topping

2 egg whites
1 cup brown sugar
2 tablespoons Five Roses
  All-purpose Flour

½ teaspoon baking powder
½ cup shredded coconut
1 cup chopped nuts

Mix ingredients for pastry together until crumbly. Press into a shallow greased pan, 7" x 11". Bake in a moderate oven (375°F.) for 10 minutes or until mixture begins to brown; let cool to lukewarm. Beat egg whites until stiff but not dry. Gradually beat in sugar, beating well after each addition. Blend in baking powder and Five Roses Flour. Fold in coconut and nuts. Spread mixture evenly on top of cooled pastry. Bake in a moderate oven (325°F.) until meringue mixture is delicately browned (about 15 to 20 minutes). Cut while warm into finger-size slices and allow to cool in pan.

CHOCOLATE BROWNIES

½ cup butter or margarine
2 squares unsweetened chocolate, melted
1 cup sugar

2 eggs, well-beaten
½ cup Five Roses All-purpose Flour
½ cup chopped walnuts

Cream butter; add melted chocolate and mix well. Blend in sugar well. Add well-beaten eggs; mix well. Blend in Five Roses Flour. Stir in the chopped nuts. Pour into a greased 8″ or 9″ square pan, spreading evenly. Bake in a moderate oven (350°F.) 25-30 minutes. Cool; cut into squares.

Note: If desired, ice brownies with a butter icing.

BUTTERSCOTCH BROWNIES

¾ cup Five Roses All-purpose Flour
1 teaspoon baking powder
¼ cup butter
1 cup brown sugar

1 egg, slightly beaten
¼ teaspoon salt
1 teaspoon vanilla
½ cup chopped nuts

Stir Five Roses Flour and baking powder together. Melt butter and brown sugar over low heat. Stir in slightly beaten egg; blend in dry ingredients, mixing well. Add vanilla and nuts. Bake in a greased and floured 8″ square pan in a slow oven (300°F.) 25 to 35 minutes. Cut while warm.

DATE SQUARES

1½ cups Five Roses All-purpose Flour
½ teaspoon baking soda

1½ cups Ogilvie Quick Oats
1½ cups brown sugar
1 cup butter

Date Filling

1 lb. pitted dates, chopped
½ cup hot water
¼ cup sugar
Pinch of salt

¼ cup orange juice
Rind of ½ orange
2 teaspoons lemon juice
1 teaspoon vanilla

Prepare filling. Combine dates, hot water, sugar, salt, orange juice, orange rind and lemon juice together in a saucepan. Cook over medium heat until dates are soft and water is absorbed; add vanilla and let cool.

Stir Five Roses flour and baking soda together; add to Oats and brown sugar and mix well. Work in butter, with fork, until mixture is crumbly. Spread ½ the mixture in bottom of a greased 8″ square pan and pat down. Cover with cold date filling. Pat remaining mixture on top. Bake in a moderate oven, 350°F., 30 minutes.

Yield: 22 squares of 2″ x 2″.

Note: For thinner date squares, use a larger pan, 9″ x 13″.

PASTRIES AND PIES

Every woman wants to make that perfect "melt-in-your-mouth" pastry that the family will brag about. Follow these simple but important rules and a light, tender pastry will result.

Important Rules

1. Have all ingredients as cold as possible.
2. Measure accurately. See page 7.
3. Handle mixture lightly and carefully.
4. Use just enough water to bind mixture.
5. Bake at correct temperature.

Good Pastry has a blistery, pebbled surface that promises flakiness. It is tender, easily cut with a fork, but not crumbly. The colour is golden brown, with a slightly richer brown at the edges. It is always rolled fairly thin so that the entire crust (bottom as well as rim) will be crisp and fragile.

KINDS OF PASTRY

Pastry may be divided into two general classes:
1. Pastry—used for pies, tarts, etc.
2. Puff pastry—used for patty shells, fancy pastries, etc.

TO BAKE PASTRY

Baking makes pastry flaky and tender and develops a rich golden brown colour all over. Bake it at a high temperature to cook the pastry quickly so that the particles of fat surrounded by layers of dough will be melted quickly without mixing into the dough. A low temperature produces an oily and crumbly crust. If a filling is used, the temperature is reduced after first 10 minutes of baking so that filling may cook without burning the pastry.

TO BAKE PUFF PASTRY

The oven should be hot enough to make the pastry rise quickly. Layers of cold air have been incorporated into the crust and the heat of the oven is necessary to expand this cold air quickly, thus making the crust light. When pastry is fully risen, the temperature is reduced for the remainder of the baking time. If the oven is too hot the top of the pastry will become scorched before the pastry has risen to its full height; if it is not hot enough, the pastry will become heavy and sodden.

TEMPERATURE GUIDE FOR BAKING PASTRY

Double Crust Fruit Pies—Bake in a hot oven (450°F.) for 10 minutes, then lower heat to 350°F. for remaining time, until filling is cooked.

Pie Shell Filled with an Uncooked Filling—Unbaked pie shells filled with mixtures of milk and eggs (custard and pumpkin pies) should be baked in a hot oven (450°F.) for 10 minutes, then in a moderate oven (325°F.) for remaining time.

Baked Single Pie Shell or Tart Shells—Bake in a hot oven (450°F.) 10 to 12 minutes or until pastry is golden brown.

Puff Pastry—Bake in a very hot oven (450°F. to 500°F.) for 10 minutes or until pastry has risen to full height. Then lower heat to 350°F. for remaining time.

CAUSES OF PASTRY SHRINKING IN PAN

Too much handling

Pastry stretched tightly in pan

Dough stored too long in refrigerator

Too slow an oven

Unbalanced recipe

STANDARD PASTRY

1½ cups Five Roses All-purpose Flour

½ teaspoon salt

½ teaspoon baking powder

½ cup shortening

⅓ cup ice-cold water

Mix Five Roses Flour, salt and baking powder together. Cut in shortening with 2 knives or pastry blender. Add water, a little at a time, using just enough to bind mixture so that dough can be patted lightly to form a ball. HANDLE AS LITTLE AS POSSIBLE. Form ⅔ of dough into a round disc and place on lightly floured board. Save remaining dough for top crust. Roll dough from centre outward, with a light, even pressure, to form a circle ⅛" thick and an inch larger than pie plate. Fold double and lift gently into pie plate. Unfold and fit loosely in place. DO NOT STRETCH. Trim edges, allowing ¼" to ½" extra all around. Put in generous amount of filling. Heap fruit filling in centre because it will cook down during baking. Roll out top crust; fold double and cut slits or fancy design near centre to allow steam to escape. Brush edges of undercrust with water, fit top crust over filling and lightly press top edge over undercrust. Trim edges evenly and flute. Bake as directed for pie filling.

Yield: One 9" double crust pie or two 9" single shells.

Single Shell—Use only ½ of dough for each single shell. Arrange undercrust as above. Press pastry to rim of pie plate; flute. Add filling. Bake as directed for filling.

Baked Single Shell—Arrange undercrust as above. Prick pastry well all over with a fork. Bake in a hot oven (450°F.) 10 to 12 minutes or until golden brown. Cool before adding cooked filling.

Tarts—Roll pastry as for pie shell. Cut with round cookie cutter 1" larger than tart wells. Ease gently into tart pans but do not stretch pastry. Add filling and bake as directed for filling. For BAKED TART SHELLS, Prick sides and bottom with fork. Bake in a hot oven (450°F.) 12 to 15 minutes or until golden brown. Fill with favourite cooked filling.

Yield: 12 medium-size tarts or 18 small tarts.

CHEESE PASTRY

Follow recipe for pastry. Reduce shortening to 7 tablespoons. Add ⅓ cup grated Cheddar cheese to dry ingredients with shortening. Continue as for pastry. Delicious for apple pies.

DECORATIVE FINISHES

LATTICE TOP

Roll pastry ⅛″ thick and cut into ½″ strips. Weave strips, lattice fashion, directly on top of filled pie. Trim ends and press strips to the moistened edge of bottom crust. Flute edges.

FLUTED EDGE

Fold edge of pastry under and build up edge. With one finger make indentations on one side and with two fingers of the other hand, bring the points up around the finger. Use for single or double crust pie.

FORK EDGE

Fold edge of pastry under and build up edge. Press edge firmly with tines of fork. Dip fork in flour to prevent sticking. Use for single or double crust pie.

SPOON EDGE

Fold edge of pastry under and build up edge. Press down on edge with inverted spoon at 1″ intervals. Dip spoon in flour to prevent sticking. Vary by doing 2 or 3 rows. Use for double crust pie.

RICH FLAKY PASTRY

2 cups Five Roses All-purpose Flour
½ teaspoon salt
¼ teaspoon baking powder
2 tablespoons sugar

¼ cup lard
½ cup butter
About 9 tablespoons <u>ice-cold</u> water

Stir Five Roses Flour, salt, baking powder and sugar together. Cut in lard and butter with pastry blender until mixture is crumbly. Add water, a little at a time, using just enough to bind mixture so that dough can be patted lightly to form a ball. HANDLE AS LITTLE AS POSSIBLE. Roll as for Standard Pastry (page 75). Bake as directed for filling.

Baked Single Shell—Use ⅓ of dough for each single shell. Arrange undercrust in pie plate. Prick pastry well all over with a fork. Bake at 450°F. 10 to 12 minutes or until golden brown. Cool before adding cooked filling.

Tarts—See Standard Pastry (page 75).

Yield: Enough dough for—three 9″ single shells, or one 9″ double crust pie and 1 single shell or 1½ dozen medium-size tarts.

HOT WATER PASTRY

⅔ cup shortening
½ cup boiling water
1 teaspoon salt

2 cups Five Roses All-purpose Flour
1 teaspoon baking powder

Place shortening in bowl; add water and beat with rotary beater until cooled and creamy. Stir Five Roses Flour, salt and baking powder together; add all-at-once to shortening and stir until well mixed. Work dough lightly to shape into a round disc, then proceed as for Standard Pastry.

Yield: Makes two 8″ or 9″ single shells or one 9″ double crust pie.

ELECTRIC MIXER PASTRY

1 cup shortening
¼ cup butter
1 teaspoon salt

3 cups Five Roses All-purpose Flour
½ cup <u>cold</u> water

Cream shortening and butter thoroughly with electric beater. Stir salt and Five Roses Flour together; gradually add to shortening mixture creaming well. Add water and mix thoroughly. Mixture will be sticky at first. Use immediately or wrap in waxed paper and store in refrigerator until needed. Pastry will not become tough and will keep, if well wrapped, in refrigerator for 10 days. (Before using chilled pastry, allow it to stand at room temperature to soften.)

Double Crust Pie—Place ½ of dough on **heavily** floured board. Use only ⅔ of this and form it into a round disc. Save remainder for top crust. Roll dough from centre outward, using a light even pressure to form a circle ⅛″ thick and 1″ larger than inverted pie plate. Fold double and lift gently into pie plate. Unfold and fit loosely into place. DO NOT STRETCH. Trim edges, allowing ¼″ to ½″ extra all around. Add filling. Roll out top crust; fold double and cut slits or fancy design near centre to allow steam to escape. Brush edges of undercrust with water; fit top crust over filling and lightly press top edge over undercrust. Trim edges evenly and flute. Bake as directed for pie filling.

Single Shell—Use only ⅓ of dough for each single shell. Arrange undercrust as above. Press pastry to rim of pie plate; flute. Add filling. Bake as directed for filling.

Baked Single Shell—See Standard Pastry (page 75).

Tarts—See Standard Pastry (page 75).

Yield: Enough dough for two 9″ double crust pies, or three 9″ single shells, or 18 medium-size tarts or 24 small tarts.

GRAHAM CRACKER CRUST

1½ cups Graham Cracker crumbs	¼ cup melted butter
1 teaspoon Five Roses All-purpose Flour	2 teaspoons sugar

Combine all ingredients together. Press firmly into buttered 9″ pie plate to make an even layer of uniform thickness on bottom and sides. Bake in a moderate oven (325°F.) for 10 minutes. Let chill at least 45 minutes before filling. Fill with pre-cooked pie filling.

DOUBLE CRUST PIES

DELUXE APPLE PIE

6 cups thinly sliced apples	¼ teaspoon salt
6 tablespoons granulated sugar	¼ cup butter
6 tablespoons brown sugar	½ teaspoon lemon rind
⅓ cup Five Roses All-purpose Flour	6 tablespoons whipping cream
1 teaspoon cinnamon	1 pastry recipe

Prepare pastry and line a 9″ pie plate, reserving some for top crust. Core, peel and slice apples. Combine sugars, Five Roses Flour, cinnamon and salt together, then mix with apples. Spread apple mixture into unbaked pastry shell. Dot with butter; sprinkle with lemon rind. Pour whipping cream over top; then cover with top crust, sealing carefully and making slits to allow steam to escape. Bake in a hot oven (450°F.) 10 minutes. Reduce heat to 350°F. and continue baking 20 to 30 minutes or until apples are cooked.

Note: Hard green cooking apples will keep their shape better than other varieties of apples.

DEEP APPLE PIE

6 to 8 apples, medium size	2 tablespoons butter
¾ cup fruit sugar	1 pastry recipe
½ teaspoon cinnamon	

Pare, core and slice apples. Place in deep oven proof baking dish (9″ square). Sprinkle with fruit sugar and cinnamon. Dot with butter. Prepare pastry and roll to a 10″ x 10″ square. Place over apples, bringing edges just over sides of dish. Press dough just over edge and flute. Make several slits on top to allow steam to escape. Bake at 450°F. for 10 minutes; reduce temperature to 350°F. and continue baking 50 to 60 minutes, or until apples are done.

Note: Other canned or fresh fruit may be substituted for apples.

Tender, Flaky Pastry

CHERRY PIE
page 80
(Lattice top)
page 76

PUFF PASTRY
page 84
(shaped into horns)

RHUBARB PIE

2 cups rhubarb, cut in ½" pieces
1 cup sugar
2 tablespoons Five Roses All-purpose
    Flour

1 egg, unbeaten
1 pastry recipe

Combine sugar, Five Roses Flour and egg; add to rhubarb. Prepare pastry and line a 9" pie plate, reserving some for top crust. Add rhubarb mixture and cover with top crust; seal and flute edges. Make slits in top crust to allow steam to escape. If desired, make a lattice top with top crust. Bake in a hot oven (450°F.) 10 minutes; reduce temperature to 350°F. and continue baking 40 to 50 minutes longer or until rhubarb is cooked and pastry is a golden brown.

CHERRY PIE

4 cups fresh or canned pitted
    cherries
¼ cup Five Roses All-purpose Flour
2 tablespoons sugar

1 tablespoon butter
Cinnamon
1 pastry recipe

Prepare pastry; line an 8" or 9" pie plate, reserving some for top crust. Mix cherries with Five Roses Flour and sugar. Pile into pastry shell. Dot with butter; sprinkle with cinnamon. Cover with top crust. Make slits in top crust to allow steam to escape. Seal edges. Bake in a hot oven (450°F.) 10 minutes; reduce temperature to 350°F. and bake 30 to 35 minutes longer, until done.

FRESH BERRY PIE

3 to 3½ cups berries*
¾ to 1 cup sugar
¼ cup Five Roses All-purpose Flour
⅛ teaspoon salt
½ teaspoon cinnamon

½ teaspoon nutmeg
½ teaspoon grated lemon rind
1 teaspoon lemon juice
1 tablespoon butter
1 pastry recipe

Prepare pastry; line an 8" or 9" pie plate, reserving some for top crust. Pile berries into pastry shell, piling higher in centre. Combine sugar (amount will depend on sweetness of berries), Five Roses Flour, salt, cinnamon, nutmeg and lemon rind; sprinkle over berries. Sprinkle lemon juice on top; dot with butter. Cover with top crust, making slits to allow steam to escape. Seal edges and flute. Bake at 400°F. 40 to 50 minutes or until pastry is golden brown.

*Use strawberries, raspberries, blueberries, blackberries or loganberries. For strawberries or raspberries, omit lemon rind, juice and spices.

Frozen Berry Pie

Substitute partially thawed frozen berries for fresh berries. Drain before using. Reduce sugar to ½ cup or less.

MINCEMEAT PIE

1 pastry recipe

2 cups mincemeat

Prepare pastry and line a 9" pie plate. Add mincemeat. Prepare top crust and make slits to allow steam to escape. Place top crust over mincemeat; seal and flute. Bake in a hot oven (450°F.) 10 minutes; reduce temperature to 350°F. and continue baking 30 to 35 minutes longer or until crust is browned.

SINGLE CRUST PIES

PRIZE PUMPKIN PIE

2 tablespoons Five Roses All-purpose
Flour
½ teaspoon salt
½ teaspoon ginger
½ teaspoon mace
½ teaspoon nutmeg
½ teaspoon cinnamon

⅓ cup brown sugar
¼ cup maple syrup
1 cup scalded milk
2 eggs, well-beaten
1½ cups canned pumpkin
1—10" unbaked pie shell
Whipped cream (optional)

Mix all ingredients together except whipped cream. Pour mixture into unbaked pie shell. Bake in a hot oven (450°F.) 10 minutes; reduce heat to 325°F. and bake 30 to 40 minutes longer or until filling is firm. (Knife inserted in centre should come out clean.) Cool before serving. If desired, serve with whipped cream.

Note: Filling may be cooked in top of double boiler. Mix all ingredients together except eggs. Cook 15 minutes. Beat eggs, add a little of the filling to the eggs, then add eggs to filling, stirring constantly. Cook until thick, about 5 minutes, stirring occasionally. Pour into **baked** pie shell.

CUSTARD PIE

⅓ cup sugar
2 eggs
2 egg yolks
Few grains salt

½ teaspoon vanilla
2½ cups hot milk
1—9" or 10" unbaked pie shell

Beat sugar, eggs, egg yolks and salt until perfectly smooth. Add hot milk gradually, stirring constantly. Add vanilla. Pour into an unbaked pie shell. Bake at 450°F. for 10 minutes; reduce heat to 325°F. and continue baking for 20 to 25 minutes or until filling is set.

CREAM PIE

8 tablespoons Five Roses All-purpose
Flour
6 tablespoons sugar
⅛ teaspoon salt
2 cups milk

2 egg yolks
1 tablespoon butter
1 teaspoon vanilla
1—8" or 9" baked pie shell

Stir Five Roses Flour, sugar and salt together. Scald milk in top of double boiler. Add hot milk to dry ingredients, a little at a time, stirring between additions; mix well. Return to double boiler and cook over boiling water until thickened, stirring constantly; cover and cook 20 minutes longer. Beat egg yolks slightly; stir a little of the hot mixture into the beaten yolks, then pour back all at once, into double boiler, stirring quickly. Cook for 2 minutes longer, stirring constantly. Remove from heat; stir in butter and vanilla. Pour into baked pie shell. When cool, top with meringue, using leftover egg whites. (See page 82).

BANANA CREAM PIE

Make Cream Pie as directed. Chop or slice bananas and fold into filling before pouring it into pie shell, or pour filling into pie shell and decorate top with sliced bananas. Top with meringue.

DATE CREAM PIE

Make Cream Pie as directed. Fold chopped dates into filling before pouring it into pie shell. Top with meringue.

LEMON MERINGUE PIE

2 cups boiling water
Grated rind of 1 lemon
¾ cup sugar
10 tablespoons Five Roses
   All-purpose Flour

2 egg yolks
¼ cup butter
4 tablespoons lemon juice
¼ teaspoon lemon extract
1—9" baked pie shell

Scald lemon rind with water in top of double boiler over direct heat. Mix sugar and Five Roses Flour together; add boiling water, a little at a time and return to double boiler. Cook over boiling water until thickened, stirring constantly. Cover and continue cooking 20 minutes longer without stirring. Beat egg yolks slightly. Add a little hot mixture to them, mix well and return to double boiler; stir for 2 minutes. Remove from heat; stir in butter, lemon juice and lemon extract. Cool to lukewarm before pouring into baked and cooled pie shell.

Meringue: Make meringue with 2 egg whites and ¼ cup sugar (see below). Bake as directed.

BUTTERSCOTCH MERINGUE PIE

6 tablespoons Five Roses All-purpose
   Flour
¾ cup brown sugar
½ teaspoon salt
2 cups scalded milk

3 eggs, separated
3 tablespoons butter
½ teaspoon vanilla
1—8" baked pie shell

Mix Five Roses Flour, brown sugar and salt thoroughly in top of double boiler. Add 1 cup of the scalded milk and stir over direct heat until smooth; add remaining milk, then place over boiling water. Cook, stirring constantly until thick and smooth (about 5 minutes); continue cooking for 10 minutes longer, stirring frequently. Beat egg yolks thoroughly; stir in a little of the hot mixture into the beaten yolks, then pour back all at once into double boiler, stirring quickly. Cook for 3 minutes longer, stirring constantly. Remove from heat, add butter and vanilla and stir until mixed. Pour into baked and cooled pastry shell.

Meringue: Make meringue using leftover egg whites and 6 tablespoons sugar. (See below.) Bake as directed.

MERINGUE FOR PIES

Beat egg whites until stiff but not dry. For each egg white, gradually add 2 tablespoons sugar, beating between additions. Beat until mixture holds its shape. Pile gently onto cooled pie filling. Spread to edge of crust. Swirl or peak for an attractive top. Bake in a moderate oven (350°F.) 7 to 10 minutes or until lightly browned.

SUGAR PIE

1½ cups brown sugar
½ cup Five Roses All-purpose Flour
¼ cup milk or cream

½ teaspoon vanilla
1—9" unbaked pie shell

Mix all ingredients together; pour into unbaked pie shell. Bake in a hot oven (425°F.) for 10 minutes; reduce heat to 350°F. and continue baking 25 to 30 minutes longer or until filling is set. Cool before serving.

TARTS

PRIZE BUTTER TARTS

1 pastry recipe	2 tablespoons milk
1 egg beaten	½ cup raisins, currants or
⅓ cup butter	chopped pecans
1 cup brown sugar	1 teaspoon vanilla

Prepare pastry; roll ⅛" thick and cut into 4" rounds. Press into medium-size tart pans. Mix all ingredients together; fill tart shells ⅔ full. Bake in a hot oven (450°F.) 8 minutes; reduce temperature to 350°F. and bake 15 to 20 minutes longer or until pastry is delicately brown.

Yield: 12 to 15 tarts.

MAID OF HONOUR TARTS

1 pastry recipe	1 egg, well-beaten
2 tablespoons butter	1 cup chopped walnuts
1 cup fruit sugar	¼ teaspoon vanilla

Prepare pastry; roll ⅛" thick and cut in 4" rounds. Press into medium-size tart pans. Cream butter; gradually add sugar, beating between additions. Stir in well-beaten egg, chopped nuts and vanilla. Place a spoonful of mixture in each tart shell; bake at 400°F. 12 to 15 minutes or until set. Let cool before serving.

Yield: 1½ dozen.

Note: If desired, a little jam or jelly may be placed in each tart shell before adding filling.

ALMOND MERINGUE TARTLETS

1 pastry recipe	⅓ cup icing sugar
Jam or jelly	¼ teaspoon almond flavouring
¼ cup ground almonds	1 egg

Prepare pastry; roll ⅛" thick and cut into 4" rounds. Press into medium-size tart pans. Place a ½ teaspoon jam or jelly in each tart shell and bake in a hot oven (450°F.) until shells are half-baked—about 5 minutes. Remove from oven. Combine ground almonds and icing sugar. Add almond flavouring to egg and beat well. Work beaten egg into sugar mixture. Place a tablespoon of filling into each tart shell. Bake in a moderate oven (350°F.) 7 to 10 minutes or until delicately browned.

Yield: 1½ dozen.

Note: Shredded coconut may be substituted for ground almonds.

PEACH TARTLETS

Into each baked and cooled tart shell, place a peach half hollow side up. Fill cavity with jam or jelly and top with whipped cream.

JAM TARTS

Into each small, unbaked tart shell, place 1 teaspoon jam. If tarts are more than half full, they will bubble over. Bake at 400°F. 20 to 25 minutes.

MINCEMEAT TARTS

1 pastry recipe   **2 cups mincemeat**

Prepare pastry; roll ⅛" thick. Cut twelve 4" rounds and press into medium-size tart pans. Fill ⅔ full with mincemeat. Cut remaining pastry to fit tops of tart wells; make slits in centre to allow steam to escape. Place on top of filling; seal edges. Bake in a hot oven (450°F.) 10 minutes; reduce temperature to 350°F. and continue baking 30-35 minutes longer or until crust is browned.

Yield: 12 tarts.

CRANBERRY TARTS

1 cup chopped dates   **1½ cups Cranberry Sauce (page 123)**
⅓ cup chopped walnuts   **1 pastry recipe**

Prepare pastry; roll ⅛" thick and cut into 4" rounds. Press into medium-size tart pans. Cut remaining pastry into thin strips. Combine dates and nuts with the cranberry sauce. Fill tart shells ½ full; arrange twisted strips of pastry across the tarts, lattice fashion. Bake in a hot oven (425°F.) 20-25 minutes or until nicely browned. Serve plain or with whipped cream.

Yield: 10 to 12 tarts.

PUFF PASTRY

Puff pastry is the foundation for Patty Shells and Napoleons. It may also be used for cream rolls, horns, etc. To make these, use the special forms which are available and follow the manufacturer's directions on how to use them. Patty Shells are very popular as containers for creamed foods.

PUFF PASTRY

1½ cups butter   **3 cups Five Roses All-purpose Flour**
About 1 cup ice-cold water

Wash butter with very cold water, squeezing lightly until it is waxy and smooth; reserve 3 tablespoons. Add about 2 tablespoons flour to remaining butter and shape into a rectangle, ½" thick. Wrap butter in waxed paper and chill. Work the 3 tablespoons of butter into Five Roses Flour; mix to a dough with just enough ice-cold water to bind mixture. Turn out on lightly floured board; knead 5 minutes, cover and let stand for 5 minutes. Pat with rolling pin and roll to form a rectangle about 11" x 16" and ¼" thick, keeping corners square. Place chilled butter in centre; fold one end of dough over butter to centre line, fold other end over to centre and slightly overlap. Press with fingers to seal ends and centre seam. Turn so that centre seam faces you and roll with a gentle even pressure to form a rectangle slightly larger than before, in order to distribute butter evenly. Fold again in 3; cover and chill for 30 minutes. Repeat this 3 more times, chilling each time. Chill before shaping. If desired, wrap well and keep in refrigerator overnight.

To Shape Patty Shells: Roll dough ¼" thick—keeping corners square and dough even. Cut with 2½" or 3" round doughnut cutter. Set aside dough from holes for tops and chill. Press remaining scraps of dough together and roll ⅛" thick; cut same number of rounds but do not make holes. Brush these rounds with water;

place the rounds with holes on top. Chill. Place chilled shells and tops on baking sheet covered with 3 thicknesses of brown paper. Bake on second rack from bottom of a hot oven (450°F. to 500°F.) for 10 minutes or until shells have risen; reduce heat to 350°F. and continue baking 10 more minutes or until shells have finished cooking. Place a pan underneath if shells are browning too quickly. Turn baking sheet around during baking to brown evenly. For a smoother top, brush tops with slightly beaten egg before baking.

Yield: 2 dozen patty shells.

NAPOLEONS

Prepare Puff Pastry. To shape: Roll out dough to a 13" x 11" rectangle. Trim edges and cut in twenty-four 3" x 1½" rectangles. Chill. Place on ungreased cookie sheet. Bake in a hot oven (450°F.) 10-12 minutes, until delicately browned. Reduce temperature to 350°F. and bake 15 minutes longer, until golden brown and crisp. Reduce oven to 200°F. and let pastries dry out for 15 minutes. Just before serving, split each rectangle lengthwise into 2 layers. Spread French Vanilla Cream Filling (page 52) between layers. Frost with Confectioner's Frosting (page 54) using light cream instead of water. Melt 2 squares of semi-sweet chocolate and dribble over top to create design.

Yield: 24 Napoleons.

NOTES

CHOU PASTRY, CREAM PUFFS AND ECLAIRS

Chou Pastry is the foundation for Cream Puffs and Eclairs. Tiny Cream Puffs may be used as containers for dainty confections for afternoon tea or as hors d'oeuvres; larger shells may be used as containers for salads, hot creamed foods and for light, dainty desserts.

CHOU PASTRY

1 cup boiling water	1 cup Five Roses All-purpose Flour
½ cup butter	3 or 4 eggs

Place boiling water in a small saucepan; add butter and place over medium heat. When butter is melted and while mixture is boiling, add Five Roses Flour, all at once. Stir rapidly until mixture makes a ball that comes away from the sides of the pan. DO NOT OVERCOOK. Remove from heat; add unbeaten eggs, one at a time. Beat each one in thoroughly before adding the next. Add the fourth egg, only if mixture is not smooth enough. **The secret of tenderness in cream puffs is long and patient beating**. A good rule is to beat the batter until you can cut through with a clean knife without anything sticking to the blade.

VARYING THE PASTRY

When Chou Pastry is to be used for making shells for desserts, a little grated lemon or orange rind and a few grains of sugar may be added to the paste. When used for creamed foods, add a little grated cheese and paprika to the paste.

CREAM PUFFS

Drop dough by spoonfuls on greased cookie sheet, a few inches apart, and twirl slightly to give a peaked effect.

    small puffs—1 teaspoon of paste
    large puffs—1 tablespoon of paste

Bake in a hot oven (425°F.) 30 minutes; reduce temperature to 325°F. and continue baking until puffs are dry, about 10 to 15 minutes for small ones and 20 to 25 minutes for large ones. Slit each puff with a sharp knife in one of the natural divisions made by the expanding dough; let cool on rack before filling. Fill puffs with sweetened and flavoured whipped cream, sprinkle tops with icing sugar. If desired, add chopped or sliced fruits to whipped cream.

Yield: 2 dozen large puffs; 3 dozen small puffs.

PARTY PUFFS

Make Small Cream Puffs. Fill each with jam; top with Orange Frosting (page 56).

ICE CREAM PUFFS

Make large or small Cream Puffs. Cut tops off and fill with ice cream; replace tops. Serve with Chocolate Fudge Sauce (page 104) or crushed and sweetened strawberries, raspberries or peaches.

ECLAIRS

To shape Eclair Shells, use a pastry bag with a plain tube or large funnel of strong paper. Shape paste ¾″ wide and 3½″ long. Bake on a greased cookie sheet in a hot oven (450°F.) 20 minutes; then reduce temperature to 325°F. and continue baking until shells are dry—about 15 to 20 minutes. Slit each shell with a sharp knife in one of the natural divisions made by the expanding dough; let cool on rack before filling.

Yield: 2 to 3 dozen, depending on size.

CHOCOLATE ECLAIRS

Fill each shell with French Vanilla Cream Filling (page 52). Frost with Chocolate Frosting (page 55).

COFFEE ECLAIRS

Fill each shell with Coffee Cream Filling (page 51). Frost with Coffee Frosting (page 55).

CHOU PASTRY SHELLS FOR SALADS

Shape paste as for Cream Puffs or Eclairs. Remove tops completely. Fill with one of the following salad mixture suggestions.

1. Cheese and nut salad.
2. Cheese, date and raisin salad.
3. Cottage or cream cheese and olive salad.
4. Lobster salad.
5. Shrimp salad.
6. Chicken and celery salad.

CHOU PASTRY SHELLS FOR CREAMED FOODS

Shape paste as for Cream Puffs or Eclairs. Fill with your favourite creamed savoury mixture. Creamed chicken or turkey, eggs, oysters, lobster, shrimp or mushrooms are all suitable fillings.

DESSERTS

Plain or fancy, desserts are the crowning touch to any meal. Serve light desserts with heavy meals and rich desserts with light meals.

FRUIT DESSERTS

FRUIT COMPOTE

2 cups drained, cooked prunes
1 fresh grapefruit, sectioned
2 fresh oranges, sectioned

1 (14 oz.) can pears
Brown sugar
Lemon slices

Arrange layers of fruit (except lemon) in 1½ quart casserole. Sprinkle each layer sparingly with brown sugar. Bake in a moderate oven (350°F.) 30 minutes. Arrange lemon slices over fruit and bake 10 minutes longer. Remove lemon slices and serve hot or cold.

Yield: 6 to 8 servings.

STEWED RHUBARB

2 cups rhubarb, cut in 1-inch pieces
¾ cup sugar

1 teaspoon grated orange rind
¼ cup water

Place cut rhubarb in saucepan and sprinkle with sugar and grated orange rind. Add just enough water to prevent burning (about ¼ cup). Cover and simmer gently until rhubarb is soft—about 20 to 25 minutes. Taste and add more sugar if necessary.

Yield: 4 servings.

PINEAPPLE AMBROSIA

⅔ cup whipping cream
2 teaspoons lemon juice
2 tablespoons sugar

8 large marshmallows, cut in ¼'s
1 cup drained pineapple chunks

Pour cream into a chilled bowl; add lemon juice and beat until stiff. Fold in sugar and marshmallows; chill. Chill pineapple chunks; fold into whipped cream mixture when ready to serve. Serve immediately.

Yield: 4 to 6 servings.

Note: Any fresh or frozen fruit may be used instead of pineapple chunks. If frozen berries are used, keep in refrigerator until almost thawed. When used, they should be slightly icy in centre.

BAKED APPLES

6 large red apples	2 cups water
1 cup sugar	

Wash and core apples. Peel ⅓ way down from stem end. Arrange in shallow baking dish with pared sides up. For colour, add skins and cores to water and boil for 10 minutes; discard skins and cores. Add sugar to water; boil 5 minutes. Pour over apples, filling cavities. Bake apples in a moderate oven (350°F.) ½ to 1 hour or until apples are tender. (Time varies with size of apples.) Spoon syrup from pan over apples frequently during baking. When tender, remove to individual serving dishes; pour syrup over top. Serve cold or warm, as is or with cream, whipped cream or ice cream.

Note: May also fill each cavity with a mixture of brown sugar and cinnamon.

FRENCH PEARS

1 (14 oz.) can pear halves	2 oranges, peeled and sliced
2 cups orange juice	1 recipe Custard Sauce (page 103)
2 teaspoons grated orange rind	

Drain pears and cover with orange juice; chill thoroughly. Drain pears again and arrange in individual dessert dishes. Surround with Custard Sauce and garnish with orange rind and thin orange slices.

Yield: 5 to 6 servings.

RHUBARB STRAWBERRY MERINGUE

3 cups rhubarb, cut in ½″ pieces	2 tablespoons water
2 tablespoons Five Roses All-purpose Flour	2 cups strawberries, fresh or frozen
1⅓ cups sugar	2 eggs, separated

Combine cut rhubarb, Five Roses Flour and 1 cup sugar in a saucepan. Add water and simmer for 10 minutes, stirring frequently; add strawberries and remove from heat. Beat egg yolks and slowly stir into fruit mixture. Turn into an 8″ square baking dish and bake in a moderate oven (350°F.) for 10 minutes. Beat egg whites until stiff but not dry; gradually add remaining sugar and beat until smooth and thick. Arrange on top of fruit and bake at 300°F. for 20 minutes. Serve immediately.

Yield: 6 to 8 servings.

PEACH MELBA

1 pkg. frozen raspberries or strawberries	1 tablespoon cold water
½ cup currant jelly	Peach halves
1½ teaspoons cornstarch	Vanilla Ice Cream

Mash raspberries or strawberries in a saucepan. Add currant jelly; bring to a boil. Mix cornstarch with cold water and add to mixture. Cook over medium heat, stirring frequently, until clear (about 5 minutes); cool. Place peach halves on servings of ice cream; cover with the cooled melba sauce.

Yield: 6 to 8 servings.

CUSTARDS AND PUDDINGS

BAKED CUSTARD

4 eggs	**¼ teaspoon vanilla**
½ cup sugar	**2 cups scalded milk**
¼ teaspoon salt	**½ teaspoon nutmeg**

Beat eggs slightly with a fork. Stir in sugar, salt and vanilla. Add a little of the hot milk to the egg mixture and stir; add remaining milk and mix well. Strain. Pour into 1 quart mould or 8 individual moulds; sprinkle top with nutmeg. Set mould or moulds in a pan containing about 1-inch of hot water. Bake at 350°F. 50 to 60 minutes or until firm. To test: run a sharp knife through centre, if knife comes out clean, then custard is done. Serve as is, or unmould into serving dishes.

Yield: 8 servings.

FLOATING ISLAND

2 eggs, separated	**Few grains salt**
1 whole egg	**2 cups milk**
7 tablespoons sugar	**1 teaspoon vanilla**

Combine egg yolks and egg; beat slightly. Add 3 tablespoons sugar and salt; mix well. Scald milk in top of double boiler; add a little of the hot milk to the egg mixture. Stir well and return to double boiler. Cook, stirring constantly, over lightly boiling water until mixture thickens and coats spoon — about 4 minutes. Pour custard into a shallow baking dish. Beat egg whites until stiff but not dry; gradually add remaining sugar and beat until stiff peaks form. Drop large spoonfuls of meringue into sauce. Bake in a hot oven (500°F.) 2 to 3 minutes or until meringues are lightly browned.

Yield: 6 servings.

BLANC MANGE

⅓ cup sugar	**2 cups scalded milk, cooled**
¼ cup cornstarch	**½ teaspoon vanilla**
¼ teaspoon salt	

Sift together sugar, cornstarch and salt; mix thoroughly in top of double boiler. Gradually add milk, stirring constantly. Cook over lightly boiling water until mixture thickens, stirring constantly. Remove from heat and stir in vanilla. Pour into serving dishes. Serve warm or cold, plain or with a sauce.

Yield: 6 servings.

Suggested Sauces: Whipped cream, Fresh Strawberry Sauce (page 107), Chocolate Fudge Sauce (page 104).

VARIATIONS

Chocolate Blanc Mange: Add 1 square unsweetened chocolate, melted, with the vanilla.

Fruit Blanc Mange: Fold in 1 cup canned or fresh fruits with the vanilla.

BUTTERSCOTCH PUDDING

1 tablespoon butter	¼ teaspoon salt
½ cup brown sugar	¼ cup cold milk
2 cups scalded milk	1 teaspoon vanilla
3 tablespoons cornstarch	

Melt butter, add brown sugar and cook until sugar melts, stirring constantly. Add slowly to hot, scalded milk and stir until well blended. Mix cornstarch and salt with cold milk; add to scalded milk mixture. Cook 15 minutes in top of double boiler over boiling water, stirring constantly until mixture thickens, then stirring occasionally. Cool slightly, add vanilla. Pour into individual serving dishes. Serve warm or cold, plain, with chopped nuts or with milk.

Yield: 4 to 6 servings.

TRIFLE

3 cups cubed cake, white or sponge	2 cups Custard Sauce (page 103)
½ cup raspberry or strawberry jam	

Cut fresh or leftover cake in small cubes to measure 3 cups. Place in individual serving dishes or large serving bowl. Spoon jam over cake, then pour Custard Sauce over top. Top with a spoonful of jam.

Yield: 4 to 6 servings.

LEMON SPONGE PUDDING

3 tablespoons Five Roses All-purpose Flour	1 tablespoon butter
1 cup sugar	1 cup milk
2½ tablespoons lemon juice	2 egg yolks
2 teaspoons grated lemon rind	2 egg whites, stiffly beaten

Mix Five Roses Flour and sugar together. Add lemon juice, lemon rind, butter, milk and egg yolks; blend well. Fold in stiffly beaten egg whites. Pour into a buttered 1½ quart casserole; place casserole in a pan of hot water. Bake in a moderate oven (350°F.) 45-50 minutes.

Yield: 4 to 6 servings.

OLD-FASHIONED BAKED RICE PUDDING

½ cup long grain rice	⅓ cup sugar
2 cups milk	½ teaspoon nutmeg
1 cup water	½ teaspoon salt
½ tablespoon butter	⅓ cup raisins

Stir all ingredients (except raisins) together in a buttered 1½ quart casserole. Bake in a slow oven (300°F.) 1 hour without disturbing rice. Reduce temperature to 250°F. and continue baking 1½ hours. Add raisins ½ hour before removing from oven.

Yield: 6 servings.

BAKED DESSERTS

CHOCOLATE SOUFFLÉ

¼ cup butter
⅓ cup Five Roses All-purpose Flour
Few grains salt
1½ cups milk
2 squares unsweetened chocolate,
    melted

4 eggs, separated
¾ cup sugar
1 teaspoon vanilla

Melt butter in medium-size saucepan. Stir in Five Roses Flour and blend well. Add salt, milk and melted chocolate; stir constantly over direct heat until sauce boils and thickens. Beat egg yolks with half the sugar. Add a small amount of the hot mixture to the beaten egg yolks and return to rest of mixture in saucepan. Cook 2 minutes longer, stirring constantly. Remove from heat; cool slightly and stir in vanilla. Beat egg whites until stiff but not dry; gradually beat in remaining sugar and beat until thick and glossy. Fold into cooled chocolate mixture. Turn into an ungreased 2 quart soufflé dish or casserole dish. Bake in a slow oven (300°F.) for 1 hour. Serve immediately with Foamy Sauce (page 104) or Vanilla Sauce (page 103).

Yield: 6 to 8 servings.

STRAWBERRY SHORTCAKE
(Basic Shortcake Dough)

2¼ cups Five Roses All-purpose
    Flour
4 teaspoons baking powder
½ teaspoon salt
2 tablespoons sugar

¼ cup butter
¾ cup milk
¼ cup water
Strawberries
Whipped Cream

Stir dry ingredients together. Cut in butter with 2 knives or pastry blender until mixture is crumbly. Combine milk and water in a saucepan and heat until just warm. Make a well in dry ingredients and pour only ⅞ cup of milk and water mixture into well; toss mixture lightly with fork until liquid is absorbed. Knead lightly (about 10 times) on lightly floured board. Divide dough in two parts and place in two greased 8-inch layer pans; pat down dough with hand. Bake in a hot oven (450°F.) 10 to 12 minutes or until lightly browned. Serve warm. Place sweetened strawberries between layers and on top. Garnish with whipped cream.

Yield: 6 servings.

Note: Other fruits such as peaches, stewed rhubarb and other berries may be substituted for the strawberries. This Shortcake Dough is the basis for many desserts.

SWEET DUMPLINGS

Make Shortcake Dough (above) and mix with a fork to a soft dough. Follow one of the following variations. Makes 6 to 8 servings.

1. Butterscotch

Make Butterscotch Syrup (page 105) in heavy saucepan and dilute with ¾ cup of water. Bring to boil over medium heat. Drop spoonfuls of dough lightly on top of boiling sauce. Cover and let boil 12 to 15 minutes. Serve with the hot sauce.

2. Orange Marmalade

Mix 2 cups sugar, 1 cup water, ½ cup orange juice and 2 tablespoons grated orange rind together in a heavy saucepan; boil 5 minutes. Add 1 tablespoon grated orange rind to dough. Knead and roll to ¼-inch thickness. Cut into 4-inch squares. Spoon 1 teaspoon marmalade in centre. Fold dough over to form triangle; seal edges. Drop lightly on top of boiling syrup. Cover and let boil 12 to 15 minutes. Serve immediately, using syrup for a sauce.

3. Grandpères

Combine 1½ cups maple syrup and 2 cups water in heavy saucepan; bring to a boil. Drop spoonfuls of dough into boiling syrup. Sprinkle with chopped nuts. Cover and let boil 12 to 15 minutes. Serve with the hot syrup.

DO NOT PLACE THE DUMPLINGS TOO CLOSE TOGETHER. LEAVE PLENTY OF ROOM TO RISE.

APPLE TURNOVERS

1 recipe shortcake dough (page 92)	¼ cup butter
6 apples, medium size	1 egg yolk, slightly beaten
½ teaspoon cinnamon	1 teaspoon water
½ cup brown sugar	

Prepare shortcake dough; roll ¼-inch thick. Cut in 6-inch squares. Peel and core medium size apples—do not core all the way through the apple. Place an apple on each square of dough. Mix cinnamon, brown sugar and butter; fill cavities of apples with this mixture. Fold edges of dough on top; pinch together to seal. Brush dough with egg yolk that has been diluted slightly with 1 teaspoon water. Place in a buttered pan and bake in a hot oven (450°F.) 10 minutes; reduce temperature to 375°F. and continue baking 25 to 30 minutes longer or until apples are baked. Serve warm with Butterscotch Sauce or Syrup (page 105).

Yield: 6 servings.

RHUBARB TURNOVERS

Prepare dough as above. Combine 2 cups uncooked, chopped rhubarb, ¾ cup sugar, ½ teaspoon cinnamon and ¼ cup butter. Divide mixture equally and place on each square of dough. Seal and proceed as for Apple Turnovers.

Enough for 6 to 8 turnovers.

CHERRY OATMEAL CRISP

2 cups (2 - 14 oz. cans) Bing cherries, pitted and drained	¾ cup Ogilvie Quick Oats
4 teaspoons lemon juice	½ teaspoon cinnamon
¾ cup brown sugar	¼ teaspoon nutmeg
¾ cup Five Roses All-purpose Flour	¼ teaspoon salt
	½ cup soft butter

Place cherries in a greased baking dish, 8-inch square or 1½ quart casserole. Sprinkle lemon juice over the cherries. Blend remaining ingredients together until crumbly; sprinkle over cherries. Bake in a moderate oven (375°F.) 30 to 40 minutes. Serve plain or with whipped cream.

Yield: 6 to 8 servings.

FRUIT COBBLER

Use any white cake recipe or mix. Grease a shallow 8-inch square pan. Spread a generous layer of sweetened, chopped fruit (or your favourite canned fruit pie filling) in bottom of pan. Top with cake batter. Bake in a moderate oven (375°F.) 40 to 45 minutes or until cake is done. Serve warm with any hot pudding sauce.

Makes 6 to 8 servings.

FRUIT CRUMBLE

Fruit of any kind	**¾ cup Five Roses All-purpose Flour**
½ cup butter	**¼ teaspoon cinnamon**
½ cup brown sugar	**¼ teaspoon cloves**

Cover bottom of an 8-inch square cake pan with a 1-inch layer of any fruit prepared in the usual way. Cream butter; add brown sugar gradually, creaming well. Add Five Roses Flour and spices and mix to a crumbly consistency. Crumble topping over fruit and bake in a moderate oven (350°F.) 40 to 45 minutes or until fruit is cooked. Serve plain or with whipped cream.

Yield: 6 to 8 servings.

Note: If canned fruit is used, drain thoroughly.

GELATIN DESSERTS

The unflavoured gelatin mentioned in these recipes refers to the ¼ oz. (7 gram) size envelope.

CHERRY MOUSSE

½ cup finely chopped maraschino	**Few grains salt**
cherries	**4 eggs, separated**
¼ cup orange juice	**½ cup milk**
¼ cup maraschino cherry juice	**¼ cup sugar**
1 envelope unflavoured gelatin	**1 cup whipping cream**
¼ cup sugar	**4 drops cherry flavouring**

Combine chopped cherries with orange juice and beat well or blend in electric blender. Set aside. Pour cherry juice into a small bowl; sprinkle with gelatin and let stand 5 minutes. Mix softened gelatin, ¼ cup sugar and salt. Beat in egg yolks with wire whisk until light. Gradually stir in milk. Cook over boiling water, stirring constantly until slightly thickened and gelatin dissolves—about 10 minutes. Add cherry mixture. Chill until of egg white consistency. Beat egg whites until foamy; gradually add ¼ cup sugar, beating until stiff. Whip the cream and fold with beaten egg whites into gelatin mixture. Turn into a 1-quart soufflé dish or mould. Chill until firm. Decorate with maraschino cherries or whipping cream, if desired.

Yield: 6 to 8 servings.

Note: If desired, substitute Kirsch for orange juice.

SPANISH CREAM

2 envelopes unflavoured gelatin	3 eggs, separated
3 cups cold milk	¼ teaspoon salt
¾ cup sugar	1½ teaspoons vanilla

Soften gelatin in 1 cup of cold milk—about 10 minutes. Pour remaining milk into top of double boiler; add ¼ cup sugar, egg yolks and salt. Cook over lightly boiling water, stirring constantly, until sauce thickens and coats a spoon. Add softened gelatin and stir until melted; stir in vanilla. Chill until mixture has the consistency of an egg white. Remove from refrigerator and beat until smooth. Beat egg whites until stiff but not dry; gradually beat in remaining ½ cup sugar and continue beating until stiff peaks form. Fold into gelatin mixture. Pour into serving dish and chill until set. Serve plain or with a sauce.

Yield: 6 to 8 servings.

Suggested sauces: Custard Sauce (page 103), Melba Sauce (page 106), Caramel Sauce (page 106).

BAVARIAN CREAM

1 envelope unflavoured gelatin	Few grains salt
2 tablespoons cold water	2 cups scalded milk
2 egg yolks	2 teaspoons vanilla
1 whole egg	1 cup whipping cream
½ cup sugar	

Soften gelatin in cold water. Combine egg yolks, egg, sugar and salt in top of double boiler; stir with a wooden spoon until smooth and creamy. Gradually add hot milk, stirring vigorously. Cook over lightly boiling water, stirring constantly, until thick and smooth. Add vanilla and softened gelatin, stirring until gelatin is thoroughly dissolved. Remove from heat and strain into a bowl. Cool, stirring occasionally to prevent a crust from forming. When partially set, whip cream and fold into mixture. Pour into a slightly oiled mould or serving dish. Chill at least 4 hours before serving. Serve plain or with a sauce.

Yield: 6 to 8 servings.

Note: ¼ cup cooking brandy may be added to the whipped cream.

Suggested sauces: Lemon Sauce (page 104), Almond Sauce (page 103), Melba Sauce (page 106).

COFFEE BAVARIAN

Make Bavarian Cream but omit vanilla. Dissolve 1½ teaspoons dry instant coffee in the cold water before adding the gelatin.

PEACH BAVARIAN

Make Bavarian Cream but omit vanilla. Use 2 envelopes gelatin, softened in 4 tablespoons cold water. Fold in 2 cups mashed peaches with whipped cream.

ALMOND BAVARIAN

Make Bavarian Cream but omit vanilla and replace with 1 teaspoon almond flavouring. Scald the milk with 1 cup ground almonds. To serve, sprinkle with toasted slivered almonds.

PINEAPPLE BAVARIAN

1 envelope unflavoured gelatin	1 cup whipping cream
5 tablespoons cold water	3 tablespoons lemon juice
1 (19 oz.) can crushed pineapple,	½ cup sugar
drained	½ cup chopped almonds (optional)

Soften gelatin in cold water for 5 minutes. Reserve juice from the pineapple and heat to boiling. Stir in gelatin until dissolved and set aside to cool. Whip cream until fluffy; add lemon juice and sugar and beat until stiff. Fold in gelatin mixture, crushed pineapple and almonds, gently but thoroughly. Pour into chilled sherbet or parfait glasses. Chill. Decorate with red or green maraschino cherries if desired.

Yield: 6 servings.

ICE CREAM AND SHERBETS

OLD-FASHIONED VANILLA ICE CREAM

3 teaspoons cornstarch	2 eggs
¼ teaspoon salt	2 cups whipping cream
¾ cup sugar	2 teaspoons vanilla
3 cups milk	1 cup light cream

Combine cornstarch, salt, sugar and 2 cups of milk in top of double boiler. Cook over boiling water for 20 minutes, stirring occasionally. Beat eggs until light; gradually stir in a small amount of the hot milk mixture and add to mixture in double boiler. Cook 2 minutes longer, stirring constantly. Cool, then strain. Stir in remaining milk, whipping cream and vanilla. Pour into freezer tray and freeze thoroughly. Remove from freezer; break into small pieces and place in large bowl of electric mixer. Add light cream and beat with electric mixer until smooth and creamy—about 10 minutes. Return to freezer tray and freeze.

Yield: 8 cups (12 to 14 servings).

APRICOT ICE CREAM

1 can (28 oz.) apricots	2 egg whites, stiffly beaten
1 cup apricot juice	1 cup whipping cream
¼ cup sugar	

Drain apricots and reserve juice; put through food chopper, electric blender or rub through a sieve to make a purée. Chill. Boil juice and sugar together until syrup threads—about 10 minutes. Pour hot syrup gradually over stiffly beaten egg whites and beat until thick and smooth. Whip cream and fold in chilled apricot purée; fold in egg white mixture, gently but thoroughly. Turn into freezer tray and freeze until firm.

Yield: 6 cups (8 to 10 servings).

PEPPERMINT ICE CREAM

1¾ cups crushed after-dinner soft
    mints (12 oz. pkg.)
1 cup milk
Pinch of salt

2 cups whipping cream
2 drops peppermint flavouring
Few drops green food colouring
    (optional)

Use a rolling pin or potato masher to crush the mints. Add milk and salt to crushed mints and pour into freezer tray; freeze until of mushy consistency. Place the partially frozen mixture into a chilled bowl and beat until smooth. Whip the cream and fold into mixture. Add flavouring and food colouring, if desired. Return to freezer trays and freeze until firm.

Yield: 4 cups (8 to 10 servings).

ORANGE CREAM SHERBET

1¼ cups sugar
1½ cups orange juice
1 tablespoon orange rind

Pinch of salt
1 cup thin cream
2 cups milk

Combine sugar, orange juice, rind and salt; stir until sugar is dissolved. Add orange mixture gradually to cream, blending well; stir in milk. Turn into freezer tray and freeze until firm.

Yield: 4 cups (6 to 8 servings).

LEMON MILK SHERBET

Grated rind of 2 lemons
1 cup lemon juice
2 cups sugar

1 cup thin cream
4 cups milk

Combine lemon rind, juice and sugar; stir until sugar is dissolved. Gradually add lemon mixture to cream, blending well; stir in milk. Turn into freezer tray and freeze until firm.

Yield: 6 cups (8 to 10 servings).

DESSERTS FOR SPECIAL OCCASIONS

COLD LEMON SOUFFLÉ

1 envelope unflavoured gelatin
¼ cup cold water
4 eggs, separated
3 teaspoons lemon rind
½ cup lemon juice

1¼ cups sugar
½ teaspoon salt
1 teaspoon vanilla
1¼ cups whipping cream

Soften gelatin in cold water; set aside. Combine egg yolks with 2 teaspoons lemon rind, lemon juice, ½ cup sugar and salt together in top of double boiler. Cook over boiling water, stirring constantly, until slightly thickened. Remove from heat; add softened gelatin and vanilla and mix well. Cool to lukewarm. Beat egg whites until stiff but not dry; gradually beat in remaining ¾ cup sugar. Whip the cream and fold into the beaten egg whites. Fold cooled egg mixture into the whipped cream mixture. Slightly oil a 1 quart mould or serving dish and sprinkle with 1 teaspoon lemon rind. Pour the soufflé into the mould and chill for at least 3 hours. Serve plain or with Lemon Sauce (page 104).

Yield: 6 to 8 servings.

BAKED ALASKA

⅔ cup Five Roses All-purpose Flour	2 teaspoons cold water
Few grains salt	1 pint ice cream
4 eggs, separated	5 egg whites
⅔ cup sugar	10 tablespoons sugar
2 teaspoons lemon juice	Pinch salt
½ teaspoon lemon rind	Slivered, blanched almonds

Mix first 7 ingredients as for Sponge Cake (see page 46). Bake in an ungreased 8-inch tube pan in a moderate oven (325°F.) 45 minutes or until top of cake springs back when lightly touched with finger. Invert pan on cooling rack and let hang for 1 hour or until cool. Loosen with spatula and shake from pan. Place on wooden board or heavy cardboard covered with foil. Leave cake inverted so that it rests on widest part. Cut a slice from top, ½-inch thick. Carefully lift off and set aside. Hollow out cake, leaving just the shell—about ¼-inch on sides and ½-inch on bottom. Fill cavity with scoops of ice cream. Replace top. Make meringue by beating egg whites and salt until stiff but not dry. Gradually beat in sugar until meringue holds its shape. Spread meringue over the top and sides of cake, covering it completely. Sprinkle with slivered almonds, if desired. Bake in a very hot oven (500°F.) for 3 to 5 minutes or until meringue is delicately browned. Serve immediately.

Yield: 8 to 10 servings.

CHEESE CAKE

Crust

1 cup Graham cracker crumbs	1 teaspoon cinnamon
2 tablespoons sugar	¼ cup melted butter

Combine all ingredients together and mix well. Line bottom of an 8″ spring form pan or bottom and sides of 9″ pie plate; refrigerate.

Filling

½ lb. cream cheese	¾ cup sugar
¼ cup lemon juice	½ cup commercial sour cream
2 eggs	

Have cheese at room temperature and cream well with lemon juice. Beat eggs slightly with a fork. Add sugar and mix well; fold in sour cream. Combine egg and cheese mixtures; strain. Pour into chilled crust and bake in a moderate oven (350°F.) for 30 minutes. Remove from oven; gently spread with topping. Return to oven and bake 10 minutes longer. Chill thoroughly before serving.

Topping

½ cup commercial sour cream	1 teaspoon lemon juice
2 tablespoons brown sugar	1 teaspoon lemon rind

Combine all ingredients and blend thoroughly.

Yield: 8 to 10 servings.

ORANGE CHARLOTTE RUSSE

¼ teaspoon salt
1 cup sugar
2 tablespoons cornstarch
1½ cups milk
2 eggs, separated
2 envelopes unflavoured gelatin

1½ cups orange juice
1 tablespoon lemon juice
2 tablespoons grated orange rind
2 cups (1 pint) whipping cream
Lady Fingers

Stir salt, ⅔ cup sugar and cornstarch together in top part of double boiler; slowly add milk and blend well. Beat egg yolks slightly with a fork and mix with milk mixture. Sprinkle gelatin in ¼ cup orange juice; set aside to soften. Cook milk mixture over lightly boiling water until thickened. Add softened gelatin and stir until dissolved; strain into a bowl. Blend in remaining orange juice, lemon juice and rind. Chill until consistency of egg white. Beat egg whites until stiff but not dry; gradually beat in remaining ⅓ cup sugar and continue beating until peaks form; whip cream. Fold both into orange mixture. Line sides of 8″ spring form pan with Lady Fingers. Fill pan with orange mixture and set in refrigerator to chill for several hours. Remove from pan to serve.

Yield: 10 to 12 servings.

STEAMED PUDDINGS

Steamed puddings make a typical winter dessert. Some are hearty and have a rich and distinctive flavour and some are light and delicate.

Moulds—Use a special pudding mould, large or individual size, fitted with tight covers or use small tins, pyrex bowls or custard cups. To cover, use a piece of aluminum foil or a piece of muslin (folded 2 or 3 times). Fit tightly on bowl and tie with a string or elastic band to secure.

To Fill Moulds—Grease moulds. Fill not more than ⅔ full to allow for expansion. Cover.

To Steam in Steamer or Deep Kettle—Place a rack under moulds in steamer or kettle so that steam can get all around the pudding. Add BOILING water until it comes halfway up around the moulds. Cover steamer or kettle tightly. Adjust heat to keep water boiling throughout steaming. Add more water as it boils away but make sure you add boiling water.

To Steam in Pressure Cookers—Set moulds on rack. Surround with water according to manufacturer's directions and steam.

To Steam in Double Boiler—Grease top part of double boiler. Fill not more than ⅔ full. Set over boiling water and steam. Keep water boiling, adding more as it boils away.

To Unmould—Remove pudding from mould as soon as it is taken from steamer. Set mould in cold water for a few seconds. Uncover and run a flat knife or spatula around sides of mould to loosen pudding. Unmould. If pudding is too moist, set in oven for a few minutes.

To Serve—Serve warm with a sauce.

To Store—Cool pudding completely before storing. Wrap and store in airtight container in a cool place.

To Reheat—Return pudding to greased mould; cover and steam 1 to 3 hours, until hot. Time will depend on size of pudding.

For Christmas Plum Pudding see page 62.

STEAMED SUET PUDDING

½ cup Five Roses All-purpose Flour	2 tablespoons grape juice
1½ teaspoons baking soda	1 cup (¼ lb.) ground suet
½ teaspoon cinnamon	1 cup fine dry bread crumbs
½ teaspoon allspice	1½ cups sultana raisins
⅛ teaspoon cloves	2 tablespoons chopped orange peel
1 teaspoon salt	2 tablespoons chopped lemon peel
2 eggs	½ cup slivered, blanched almonds
½ cup molasses	2 teaspoons brandy flavouring
1¼ cups buttermilk	

Stir dry ingredients together. Combine eggs, molasses, buttermilk and grape juice. Add to dry ingredients and blend well. Stir in ground suet and bread crumbs. Combine fruits and almonds; fold into batter. Add flavouring. Turn into a well-greased 1½ quart mould. Cover mould and steam in a covered steamer for 3 to 3½ hours or until done. Serve warm with hot pudding sauce or Hard Sauce (page 106).

Yield: 8 to 10 servings.

Note: 2 tablespoons brandy may be substituted for grape juice and brandy flavouring.

CARROT PUDDING

1¼ cups grated raw carrot	½ teaspoon cinnamon
1½ cups grated apple	¼ cup butter
1 cup Five Roses All-purpose Flour	1 cup brown sugar
2 teaspoons baking powder	¾ cup seeded raisins
1 teaspoon salt	¼ cup grape juice
½ teaspoon cloves	1 teaspoon baking soda
½ teaspoon nutmeg	

Grate carrot and apple; measure and set aside. Reserve a tablespoon of the measured Five Roses Flour to dust raisins. Stir remaining flour, baking powder, salt, cloves, nutmeg and cinnamon together. Cream butter; gradually add brown sugar, beating well after each addition. Add dry ingredients alternately with grape juice, blending well after each addition. Add grated carrot and half of the grated apple and floured raisins. Dissolve baking soda in remaining grated apple and add at end; mix lightly. Pour into a greased 1½ quart mould; cover tightly and steam 4½ to 5 hours. Serve warm with hot pudding sauce or Hard Sauce (page 106).

Yield: 6 to 8 servings.

CHOCOLATE STEAMED PUDDING

¾ cup Five Roses All-purpose Flour
2½ teaspoons baking powder
½ teaspoon salt
½ teaspoon cinnamon
½ teaspoon cloves
1½ squares unsweetened chocolate
2 teaspoons butter

3 eggs, separated
¾ cup sugar
½ cup milk
1 teaspoon vanilla
¼ cup slivered, blanched almonds
  (optional)

Stir first 5 ingredients together. Melt chocolate and butter; cool. Beat egg yolks until light and foamy; add sugar and continue beating until fluffy. Blend in melted chocolate and butter. Add dry ingredients alternately with milk, mixing well after each addition. Stir in vanilla. Beat egg whites until stiff but not dry; fold into batter. Fold in almonds, if used. Turn into well greased 1½ to 2 quart mould; cover tightly. Steam in a covered steamer for 1½ hours or until done. Serve warm with hot pudding sauce.

Yield: 6 to 8 servings.

FIVE ROSES PUDDING

2 cups Five Roses All-purpose Flour
4 teaspoons baking powder
½ teaspoon salt
4 tablespoons butter or shortening
4 tablespoons sugar

1¼ cups milk
Fruit
2 tablespoons butter
¼ cup brown sugar

Stir Five Roses Flour, baking powder and salt together. Cut in shortening with 2 knives or pastry blender. Stir in sugar. Add milk gradually, mixing with a fork to make a stiff batter. Fold in desired fruit or leave plain. Mix 2 tablespoons butter and brown sugar together; coat the inside of a 1½ quart mould. Pour in pudding batter. Cover mould and steam 2 hours. Serve warm with a hot pudding sauce.

Yield: 6 to 8 servings.

Fruit: Use 1 cup raisins, currants, figs or chopped dates.

Apple: Use 1 cup coarsely chopped peeled apple and 1 teaspoon cinnamon.

NOTES

SWEET SAUCES FOR DESSERTS

A good sauce adds a festive touch to the simplest pudding.

CUSTARD SAUCE

2 egg yolks
2 tablespoons sugar
Pinch of salt

1 cup scalded milk
¼ teaspoon vanilla

Beat yolks slightly; stir in sugar and salt, blending well. Slowly stir in the scalded milk. Pour mixture into top part of double boiler; cook over boiling water, stirring constantly, until mixture is thickened and will coat a spoon. Remove from heat; strain and cool. Add vanilla.

Yield: 1 cup.

Note: Use leftover egg yolks for sauce, increase sugar and milk according to number of egg yolks used.

Suggested uses: gelatin desserts, dessert soufflés, tapioca, trifle, cream puffs, fruit.

ALMOND SAUCE

Make Custard Sauce as directed. Substitute almond flavouring for vanilla. Add slivered blanched almonds, if desired.

VANILLA SAUCE

¼ cup sugar
1 tablespoon Five Roses All-purpose
  Flour
Few grains salt

1 cup boiling water
2 tablespoons butter
1 teaspoon vanilla
Few grains nutmeg

Combine sugar, Five Roses Flour and salt in a saucepan. Add boiling water gradually, stirring constantly. Cook and stir over low heat until clear and thickened—about 5 minutes. Remove from heat; add butter, vanilla and nutmeg. Brandy, rum or sherry may replace vanilla.

Yield: 1 cup.

Suggested uses: bread pudding, steamed pudding, cottage pudding, dessert soufflés.

FOAMY SAUCE

½ cup butter
1 cup sifted icing sugar
Few grains salt

1 teaspoon vanilla
1 egg (or 2 egg yolks), well-beaten

Cream butter; gradually add sugar and beat until well blended. Beat in salt, vanilla and eggs; set over hot water. Cook and beat with rotary beater or wire whisk until it has thickened and is smooth and light—about 7 minutes. Serve hot or cold. Yield: 1½ cups.

Suggested uses: gelatin desserts, dessert soufflés, sponge puddings, steamed puddings.

LEMON SAUCE

½ cup sugar
1 tablespoon cornstarch
Few grains salt
½ teaspoon lemon rind

1 cup boiling water
2 tablespoons butter
1½ tablespoons lemon juice

Combine sugar, cornstarch, salt and lemon rind in a saucepan. Add boiling water gradually, stirring constantly. Cook and stir mixture over low heat until clear and thickened—about 5 minutes. Remove from heat and stir in butter and lemon juice. Yield: 1 cup.

Suggested uses: steamed pudding, cottage pudding, apple crisp, gelatin desserts.

CHOCOLATE FUDGE SAUCE

1 tablespoon butter
2 squares unsweetened chocolate
⅓ cup boiling water
¾ cup sugar

2 tablespoons corn syrup
Few grains salt
1 teaspoon vanilla

Melt butter and chocolate in top of double boiler. Gradually stir in boiling water. Add sugar, corn syrup and salt. Cook over boiling water, stirring occasionally, until slightly thickened. Remove from heat; add vanilla. If desired, substitute vanilla with sherry or brandy. Serve hot or cold. Yield: 1¼ cups.

Suggested uses: ice cream, meringues, cream puffs, cottage pudding, un-iced cake, blanc mange.

COCOA SYRUP

½ cup cocoa
½ cup cold water
¼ cup boiling water

½ cup sugar
1 teaspoon vanilla

Mix cocoa and cold water to a paste in a saucepan. Add boiling water and sugar. Bring to boil over medium heat and boil 3 minutes, stirring constantly to prevent burning. Remove from heat. Cool and add vanilla. Pour into a sterilized jar; seal. Store in a cool place and use as required. Yield: 1 cup.

Suggested uses: as a sauce or for flavouring puddings, pie fillings, beverages.

RICH BUTTERSCOTCH SAUCE

½ cup brown sugar
½ cup corn syrup
½ cup light cream

Few grains salt
2 tablespoons butter
1 teaspoon vanilla

Combine brown sugar, corn syrup and cream in top of double boiler. Cook 30 minutes over boiling water, stirring occasionally. Remove from heat and stir in remaining ingredients. Serve hot or cold.

Yield: 1¼ cups.

Suggested uses: custard, cottage pudding, ice cream, steamed puddings.

BUTTERSCOTCH SYRUP

1½ tablespoons butter
2 cups brown sugar

1 cup boiling water
½ teaspoon vanilla

Mix butter and 1 cup brown sugar in a saucepan. Cook and stir over medium heat until sugar is melted, but not dark. Add boiling water and remaining brown sugar. Bring to boiling point, stirring constantly, and cook until sugar is melted—about 10 minutes. Remove from heat and add vanilla. Serve warm.

Yield: 2 cups.

Suggested uses: ice cream, cottage pudding, sweet dumplings, steamed puddings.

MAPLE SAUCE

1 cup maple syrup

2 tablespoons chopped nuts

Boil syrup 5 minutes; add nuts and serve immediately.

Yield: 1 cup.

Suggested uses: custard, blanc mange, cottage pudding, ice cream, waffles, un-iced cake.

QUICK HONEY SAUCE

⅔ cup honey
½ cup thin cream

½ teaspoon lemon or orange rind

Mix all ingredients to make a smooth sauce.

Yield: 1 cup.

Suggested uses: any simple pudding.

OLD-TIME BRANDY SAUCE

2 eggs, separated
1 cup icing sugar

3 tablespoons brandy

Beat egg yolks until thick and lemon coloured. Slowly add half of the sugar, beating constantly. Beat egg whites until stiff; add remaining sugar, a little at a time, beating constantly. Fold beaten egg whites into yolk mixture. Add brandy.

Yield: 2 cups.

Suggested uses: steamed puddings, baked fruit, chocolate bread pudding.

CARAMEL SAUCE

1 cup corn syrup	½ cup milk
1 cup brown sugar	¼ cup Five Roses All-purpose Flour
¼ teaspoon salt	3 tablespoons butter

Blend corn syrup, brown sugar, salt, milk and Five Roses flour, in a saucepan. Slowly bring to a boil, and cook five minutes, stirring occasionally. Remove from heat, add butter.

Yield: 1¼ cups.

Suggested uses: custard, cottage pudding, ice cream.

CARAMEL SYRUP

1 cup granulated sugar	½ cup boiling water

Melt ½ cup sugar in a small smooth saucepan and allow to brown slightly. Slowly add ½ cup boiling water. Stir until caramelized sugar is dissolved. Add another ½ cup of sugar and continue cooking until the consistency of syrup. Store in a tightly covered jar and use as required.

Yield: ½ cup.

Suggested uses: for flavouring pie fillings, puddings, sauces.

MELBA SAUCE

1 cup berries, fresh or canned	¼ cup sugar

Crush berries. Strain to remove seeds, if desired. Add sugar and cook over low heat, stirring constantly, until mixture is the consistency of a heavy syrup. Syrup will also thicken on cooling. Use only small amount per serving.

Yield: ½ cup.

Suggested uses: ice cream, custard, blanc mange, fruit, cottage pudding.

HARD SAUCE

½ cup butter	⅓ cup whipping cream
¾ cup brown sugar	1 teaspoon vanilla
¾ cup icing sugar	2 teaspoons brandy (optional)

Cream butter; gradually add sugars, beating thoroughly. Slowly add cream and vanilla, beating constantly. Pile into sauce dish. Make a well in centre; add brandy and let sit until brandy is all soaked up. Chill well before serving.

Yield: 1½ cups.

Suggested uses: steam pudding, bread pudding, mince pie.

VARIATIONS

Lemon Hard Sauce: Add 1 teaspoon lemon juice and 1 tablespoon grated lemon rind.

Spicy Hard Sauce: Add ½ teaspoon lemon juice, ½ teaspoon cinnamon and ¼ teaspoon cloves.

FRESH STRAWBERRY SAUCE

⅓ cup butter 1 cup icing sugar	⅔ cup fresh strawberries, slightly mashed

Cream butter; add sugar gradually, creaming well. Add strawberries, a few at a time, blending well.

Yield: 1⅓ cups.

Suggested uses: blanc mange, tapioca, cottage pudding, ice cream.

WHIPPED CREAM

1 cup whipping cream 2 tablespoons sifted icing sugar	½ teaspoon vanilla

Chill bowl and beaters. Beat cream until it begins to thicken. Fold in sugar and vanilla; continue beating until cream just holds its shape.

Yield: 2 cups whipped cream.

Suggested uses: pies, puddings, gingerbread, as a filling for cakes, eclairs and cream puffs.

COFFEE WHIPPED CREAM

Substitute 1½ teaspoons instant coffee for vanilla. Chopped nuts may be folded in at end.

PINEAPPLE CREAM SAUCE

½ cup crushed pineapple, well drained	¼ cup fruit sugar ½ cup whipping cream

Mix crushed pineapple and fruit sugar together; let stand 1 hour. Just before serving, whip the cream and fold into pineapple.

Yield: 1 cup.

Suggested uses: ice cream, cottage pudding, sponge cake, un-iced cake, meringues.

MARSHMALLOW SAUCE

¾ cup sugar 1 tablespoon corn syrup ¼ cup milk	½ lb. marshmallows 2 tablespoons water 1 teaspoon vanilla

Combine sugar, corn syrup and milk in a saucepan. Cook and stir over low heat until sugar is dissolved. Bring to boil and simmer 5 minutes. Melt marshmallows with water in top of double boiler. Pour syrup over melted marshmallows and beat well. Add vanilla. Serve warm. To reheat: Place over hot water and beat well before serving.

Yield: 2 cups.

Suggested uses: ice cream, chocolate cake, gingerbread.

BEVERAGES

Rules for Making Coffee

1. Always start with a perfectly clean coffee maker.
2. Use fresh cold water.
3. Use fresh coffee. Buy only one week's supply at a time and store in an airtight container.
4. Use the right type of grind for your coffee maker.
5. Measure coffee accurately, with coffee measure or standard measuring spoon. Suggested measurements for 1 cup of water are:
   weak   —1 tablespoon
   medium—2 tablespoons
   strong   —3 tablespoons
6. Depending on what type of coffee maker you have, these measurements may vary. Read manufacturer's instructions carefully.

ICED COFFEE

Fill glasses with ice cubes. Pour hot coffee over the ice and stir, using 2 teaspoons dry instant coffee per cup of boiling water.

Rules for Making Tea

1. Pour boiling water in a clean tea pot and let stand a few minutes; empty.
2. Measure tea into pot—allow ½ to 1 teaspoon per cup. If tea bags are used— allow 2 bags for 3 cups of tea.
3. Pour **freshly** boiling water over tea leaves.
4. Cover and let steep 3-5 minutes.
5. Stir and serve; strain, if desired, to remove loose tea leaves.
6. Keep boiling water on hand. Tea becomes stronger on standing and needs to be diluted if serving seconds.

ICED TEA

Prepare a strong brew. Follow rules above, using 2 tea bags per cup of boiling water. Let steep. Pour over glasses filled with ice cubes. Sweeten if desired. Serve with lemon slices.

HOT CHOCOLATE

2 squares unsweetened chocolate	Pinch of salt
1 cup water	3 cups of milk
6 tablespoons sugar	

Cook chocolate and water over medium heat until chocolate is melted. Add sugar and salt; boil 5 minutes stirring constantly. Add milk gradually, stirring constantly until hot. Beat until frothy; serve immediately. For variety, serve with marshmallows, whipped cream or long cinnamon sticks.

Yield: 6 servings.

HOT COCOA

4 tablespoons cocoa	1 cup water
4 tablespoons sugar	3 cups milk
Pinch of salt	

Mix cocoa, sugar, salt and water together. Boil three minutes over medium heat, stirring constantly. Proceed as for Hot Chocolate.

Yield: 6 servings.

CHOCOLATE SYRUP

2½ squares unsweetened chocolate	2 tablespoons corn syrup
1 cup boiling water	⅛ teaspoon salt
1 cup sugar	

Melt chocolate over hot water. Add boiling water and cook over direct heat, stirring constantly, until thickened—about 2 to 3 minutes. Stir in sugar, corn syrup and salt; cook 5 minutes more, stirring constantly. Store in airtight jars.

Yield: 2 cups.

Note: Use for making hot chocolate, chocolate milk, chocolate milkshakes. Allow 1 to 2 tablespoons of syrup per cup of milk.

BANANA MILKSHAKE

1 cup cold milk	1 ripe banana

Slice banana into a bowl and beat with rotary beater until creamy. Add milk; beat thoroughly. Serve cold.

Yield: 1 large serving.

STRAWBERRY MILKSHAKE

1 cup milk	2-3 tablespoons strained
2 teaspoons sugar	strawberries

Crush strawberries and press through a coarse sieve to measure 2-3 tablespoons. Combine with milk and sugar; beat well. Serve cold.

Yield: 1 large serving.

CHOCOLATE MILKSHAKE

Add 2 tablespoons chocolate syrup to 1 cup cold milk. Mix well with rotary beater.

FROSTED MILKSHAKES

Make milkshake as directed. Add 1 scoop of ice cream and 4 oz. of soda pop to each glass. Stir well.

EGGNOG

1 egg, beaten	¼ cup milk
1 tablespoon sugar	¼ teaspoon vanilla
Pinch of salt	Pinch of nutmeg

Combine beaten egg with sugar and salt. Add milk and vanilla; mix well. Serve cold in a tall glass and sprinkle with nutmeg.

Yield: 1 serving.

LEMONADE

1½ cups lemon juice	Crushed ice
3 cups Sugar Syrup	Water

Mix lemon juice and Sugar Syrup together. Pour ¼ cup in each glass. Fill glasses with crushed ice and water. Garnish with mint leaves or cherries.

Yield: 12 servings.

1 serving: Mix 2 teaspoons lemon juice and ¼ cup Sugar Syrup in a tall glass. Fill with crushed ice and water.

SUGAR SYRUP

2 cups water	2 cups sugar

Boil water and sugar together for 5 minutes, stirring only **until sugar is dissolved**. Chill and store in covered jars until ready to use.

Yield: Approx. 3 cups.

HOLIDAY PUNCH

2 cups cranberry juice cocktail	Maraschino cherries
4 cups lemonade	Lemon slices
1 cup orange juice	3 (6 oz.) bottles ginger ale

Mix all ingredients (except ginger ale) together in a large bowl; chill. Add chilled ginger ale just before serving. Add ice-cubes, if desired.

Yield: 18 punch-cup servings.

SPICED APPLE CIDER

4 cups apple cider	2 cinnamon sticks
10 whole cloves	Few grains salt
10 whole allspice	¼ cup brown sugar

Pour cider into saucepan; add spices and brown sugar. Place over low heat and stir until sugar is dissolved. Cover and heat to boiling point. Heat should be so low that it takes a ½ hour to come to a boil. Remove from heat and strain. Serve hot in punch cups. If desired, use fresh cinnamon sticks as stirrers.

Yield: 8 to 10 servings.

SANDWICHES

Sandwiches are right at home for luncheons, suppers, snacks, picnics, lunch boxes or even elegant receptions. Vary their shapes and forms and use a variety of breads. Occasionally, try a Quick Bread such as Date Bread.

Rules for Making Fancy Sandwiches

1. Prepare filling first, refrigerate until ready to use.
2. Prepare garnishes; store in crisper or refrigerator jars.
3. Cream butter until soft and pliable. Melted butter will soak into the bread.
4. Use very fresh bread for rolled or pinwheel sandwiches. Fresh bread will slice easier if chilled in refrigerator first.
5. Use a **sharp** knife for slicing bread.
6. Keep bread from drying out. As you slice the bread, cover slices with a damp linen towel.

To Store Filled Sandwiches

If sandwiches are to be made ahead of time, leave crusts on and wrap in waxed paper, then in a slightly dampened linen towel. Store in refrigerator until ready to serve. Trim party sandwiches just before serving.

To Freeze Filled Sandwiches

Do not freeze fillings with mayonnaise, lettuce, tomato or hard-cooked eggs. Add these just before serving. Wrap sandwiches in waxed paper and then in aluminum foil or put in an airtight plastic bag. Do not wrap sandwiches with different fillings in the same package as odors will mingle. Thaw sandwiches before unwrapping. Frozen tea sandwiches do not keep in the freezer for a long time—about 1 to 3 weeks only.

OPEN FACE SANDWICHES (PARTY SPECIALS)
1. Prepare all ingredients in advance, assemble just before serving.
2. Cut sliced bread into desired shapes with buttered cookie cutter.
3. Spread with butter, then desired filling.
4. Garnish as desired.

RIBBON SANDWICHES

1. Spread 2 slices of bread (1 white and 1 brown) with butter, cream cheese or jam. Press together. Spread top side.
2. Place another slice (either brown or white) on top so that the two outside slices are the same colour; press together to form 3 slices.
3. Wrap in foil or waxed paper; chill for 1 hour or more.
4. Just before serving, trim off crusts using a sharp knife. Cut into ½" slices. If desired, cut each slice into halves, thirds or triangles.

PINWHEEL SANDWICHES

1. Trim crusts from bread slices.
2. Roll slices with rolling pin.
3. Cover slice with butter, cream cheese or desired filling.
4. Place red or green cherries, gherkins, pitted dates, stuffed olives, vienna or cocktail franks at one end.
5. Roll up carefully and wrap in foil or waxed paper; twist ends to seal.
6. Chill for 1 hour or more.
7. Just before serving, cut into thin slices.

ROLLED SANDWICHES

Make as for Pinwheels, but place cooked asparagus spears or stuffed celery at one end. Wrap and chill. Do not cut to serve.

TOASTED ROLLED SANDWICHES

Fasten Rolled Sandwiches with a toothpick. Toast in a hot oven (450°F.) 5 to 7 minutes. Remove toothpicks and serve hot.

CLUB SANDWICHES

1. Allow 3 slices buttered toast for each sandwich.
2. Arrange lettuce, crisp bacon, sliced tomato and mayonnaise on first slice; cover with another slice of toast, butter side up.
3. Arrange lettuce, sliced chicken and mayonnaise on second slice; cover with third slice of toast; butter side down.
4. Serve warm.

SANDWICH FILLINGS

Egg Salad

Mix chopped, hard-cooked eggs with mayonnaise, salt and pepper to taste, chopped onion (1 teaspoon per egg) and chopped celery.

Variations: Add crisp bacon bits and chopped parsley, chopped cooked chicken and pimiento or tuna or salmon and chopped pickle.

Chicken and Mayonnaise

Season finely chopped cooked chicken and mix with mayonnaise or salad dressing to moisten.

Variations: Add chopped celery, chopped pimiento, chopped ham, bacon bits, pineapple bits, shredded cabbage, chopped hard-cooked egg (or a combination) to the above.

Cold Meat

Use slices of cold chicken, turkey, ham, veal, beef or lamb. Cover with lettuce and slices of tomato. Spread with mayonnaise or salad dressing. You may also use liver paste, devilled ham or canned luncheon meats.

Variations: Chop or mince the meat, mix with mayonnaise or salad dressing. Season to taste. Add bacon bits, chopped pickle, chopped celery, chopped onion, chopped shallots or chives, chopped green pepper or chopped hard-cooked egg (or a combination).

Salmon or Tuna

Mix tuna or salmon with mayonnaise. Season to taste.

Variations: Add chopped cucumbers, chopped celery, chopped green pepper, chopped apple, crushed pineapple, chopped pickle or cottage cheese (or a combination) to the above.

Crab, Lobster or Shrimp

Mix with mayonnaise. Season to taste. Vary as above.

Cream Cheese

Vary by combining the cream cheese with chopped cooked chicken, chipped beef, shrimp, bacon bits, chopped walnuts, chopped dates, chopped maraschino cherries or chopped pimiento.

Peanut Butter

Vary it with banana, jam, marmalade, honey, chopped dates and nuts, lettuce, bacon, cream cheese, onion and mayonnaise.

SANDWICH LOAF

1 sandwich loaf	Thin cream or mayonnaise
½ cup creamed butter	Fillings as suggested
1 pkg. (8 oz.) cream cheese	

Select a small sandwich loaf or use ⅔ of a large one; remove outside crusts with a very sharp knife. Cut loaf lengthwise into 4 slices, parallel with bottom of loaf. Spread bread with butter on both sides except bottom and top slices which are spread on one side. Spread bottom layer with desired filling; cover with a slice of bread that has been buttered on both sides and spread with another filling. Repeat and place top slice, buttered side down, on top. Press down gently. Mix cream cheese to a smooth paste with a little thin cream or mayonnaise; spread over entire loaf. Chill for 1 hour or until needed. Just before serving, decorate top with bits of parsley or pimiento. Slice into 1″ slices to serve.

Yield: 10 to 12 servings.

Fillings: Select your favourite sandwich filling. The most popular for Sandwich Loaves are:

Lettuce and tomatoes with mayonnaise
Chopped or ground meat with pickle
Egg salad
Cream or sliced cheese.

HOT SANDWICHES

WESTERN SANDWICH

3 tablespoons finely chopped onion	**4 eggs, slightly beaten**
2 tablespoons butter	**Salt and pepper**
½ cup chopped cooked ham	**8 slices buttered toast**

Sauté onion in butter until soft. Add ham and eggs and stir until eggs are cooked. Season with salt and pepper to taste. Spread between slices of buttered toast. Serve hot.

Yield: 4 sandwiches.

HOT ROAST BEEF SANDWICH

Cut thin slices of leftover roast beef and reheat in leftover gravy. Do not allow gravy to boil. Place on buttered slices of bread toasted on outside only. Sprinkle with salt, pepper and horse-radish (optional). Cover with more bread and serve with hot gravy. If desired, garnish with slices of onion.

HOT CHEESE SANDWICH

1 cup grated Cheddar cheese	**12 slices bread, ½″ thick**
2 eggs, well-beaten	**6 slices bacon**
½ teaspoon dry mustard	**1 teaspoon Worcestershire Sauce**
½ teaspoon salt	

Cream cheese; add eggs and seasonings, blending well. Cut bread slices into 3″ rounds; spread with cheese mixture. Cut bacon strips in half and place on each round. Bake in a hot oven (475°F.) until bacon is cooked—about 5 to 10 minutes. Serve with a green salad.

Yield: 12 sandwich rounds.

We appreciate the fact that from time to time certain problems may arise with regard to home cooking and baking. For this reason we are pleased to remind you that our Five Roses Kitchens will always be most pleased to help you. Address all inquiries to:

PAULINE HARVEY, *Director*
FIVE ROSES KITCHENS
BOX 6089
MONTREAL, P.Q.

SOUPS

Soups are for all seasons and all occasions. Add extra seasonings to suit your own tastes. Monosodium glutamate will intensify the flavour—use according to manufacturer's directions.

CREAM SOUP BASE

1 tablespoon butter	Salt and pepper to taste
1 tablespoon Five Roses All-purpose Flour	1 bay leaf
	Few grains onion powder
2 cups milk or light cream	Few grains celery seed

Melt butter; slowly stir in Five Roses Flour and cook for 3 minutes after mixture bubbles. Add milk gradually and cook over direct heat, stirring constantly, until mixture is thick and smooth. Add seasonings.

Yield: 2 cups soup base.

CREAM OF VEGETABLE SOUP

Use 2 cups soup base and add 1 cup puree of any of the following vegetables—asparagus, potato, pea, corn, carrot, dried peas, beans or lentils. Makes about 6 servings.

Note: Puree means any vegetable boiled or steamed and rubbed through a sieve. Or if desired, you may use an electric blender instead of the sieve.

SEASONING THE SOUPS

The seasoning of Cream Soups is important. Use in small amounts and to taste. We suggest the following for:

Tomato Soup—Onion, peppercorns, celery or celery seed, bay leaf, salt and pepper.

Potato Soup—Onion juice, salt, pepper, celery salt, cayenne and parsley.

Asparagus Soup—Salt, pepper, paprika and a grating of cheese.

Celery, Corn and Carrot Soups—Salt, pepper, paprika and onion juice.

SOUP STOCKS

Rich soup stock is the basis for many fine soups. Although it is often more convenient to use canned consomme or stock made with bouillon cubes or meat concentrate, nothing can surpass the flavour of home made stock.

Meats for Stock. Use shin bone (preferably middle cut), brisket or other soup meat. Use ⅔ lean meat and ⅓ bone and fat. Have bones cracked. Add to the stock any left over cooked meat and bones. Do not use burned pieces, smoked or corned meats, raw mutton or lamb.

To Store Stock. Cover and refrigerate. Use the soup pot or pour into clean, empty milk bottles. Do not remove cake of fat which forms on stock when cold as this aids in preserving it. Remove fat only when ready to use.

To Remove Fat. Run a knife around edge of pan or bottle and carefully lift off fat. A warm damp cloth may be passed around edge and over top of stock to remove the small amounts of fat remaining.

To Clear Stock. Remove fat from stock and put quantity to be cleared in a clean pan. Taste at this point and add further seasonings if needed. To 4 cups of stock, add 1 egg white, beaten slightly with a fork and diluted with 2 teaspoons cold water. Add egg shell, broken in small pieces. Bring to boiling point, stirring constantly; let boil 2 minutes. Leave for 20 minutes over low heat. Strain through fine strainer, lined with double thickness of cheese cloth.

BROWN STOCK

3 lbs. brisket, shinbone or other soup meat and bone	¼ teaspoon marjoram
	2 sprigs parsley
10 cups cold water	¼ cup diced raw carrots
½ teaspoon peppercorns	¼ cup diced raw turnips
2 whole cloves	¼ cup chopped onions
½ bay leaf	¼ cup chopped celery
⅛ teaspoon thyme	1 tablespoon salt

Remove lean meat from bones and cut in 1-inch cubes. Brown slightly in 3 tablespoons fat or marrow from the bone. Put fat, bone and browned meat cubes in large kettle. Rinse skillet with measured water to retain all rich colour and flavour. Cover with cold water and let stand 1 hour, to draw out juices from meat. Heat slowly to boiling point and simmer 3 hours or more. Skim fat off top from time to time. Add spices and vegetables, the last half hour of cooking. Strain. Cool very quickly, uncovered, to prevent souring. Store until needed.

Yield: 10 cups.

CHICKEN BROTH OR BOUILLON

4 lbs. chicken, cut in 5 or 6 pieces	½ bay leaf
6 cups cold water	¼ teaspoon peppercorns
1 carrot, sliced	Salt to taste
2 stalks celery, sliced	Pepper to taste
1 onion, sliced	

Clean and wipe chicken; put all except breast meat in a large kettle. Add water, vegetables and seasonings. Heat gradually to boiling point; add breast meat. Cover and cook slowly until breast meat is tender. Cool and remove fat. Bring to boiling point again; strain. Add more seasonings if needed. Cool quickly, then store until needed.

Yield: 5 cups.

SPLIT PEA SOUP

½ lb. dried peas
2 tablespoons barley
Cold water
½ lb. fat salt pork, cut in cubes
1 medium size onion, minced

¼ cup chopped celery
1 bay leaf
Salt and pepper to taste
⅛ teaspoon marjoram
Few grains thyme

Cover dried peas and barley with cold water. Soak several hours or over night. Drain. Add 5 cups cold water, fat salt pork, minced onion, chopped celery and bay leaf. Salt and pepper to taste. Add marjoram and thyme. Simmer over medium-low heat for 4 hours or until peas are soft.

Yield: 5 cups (6 to 8 servings).

VEGETABLE SOUP

5 tablespoons butter
½ cup chopped carrots
½ cup chopped turnips
½ cup chopped celery
½ cup thinly sliced onions

½ cup chopped potatoes
2½ cups brown stock
2½ cups water
Salt and pepper to taste
½ tablespoon finely chopped parsley

Melt 4 tablespoons butter in large kettle; add vegetables (except potatoes) and sauté 10 minutes, stirring constantly. Add potatoes, cover and sauté 2 more minutes. Add liquid; bring to boil and simmer for 1 hour, or until vegetables are soft. (Add more water if necessary.) Season to taste with salt and pepper. Add remaining butter and parsley.

Yield: 5 cups (6 to 8 servings).

PRIZE ONION SOUP

2 cups thinly sliced onion
2 tablespoons butter
2 tablespoons Five Roses All-purpose
    Flour

5 cups (1 quart) milk
Salt and pepper to taste
Few grains paprika
1 cup grated Cheddar cheese

Sauté onions in butter until golden brown; stir in Five Roses Flour until blended. Heat milk in top of double boiler, over boiling water. Add salt and pepper to taste and paprika. Stir in fried onions. Allow mixture to heat, but not boil, for 10 minutes. Sprinkle grated cheese over milk mixture and stir until cheese is melted. DO NOT BOIL. Serve immediately.

Yield: 5 cups (6 to 8 servings).

LEFTOVER TURKEY SOUP

Break the carcass in 5 or 6 pieces; add any leftover gravy and all scraps of skin, dressing, etc. Add leftover giblets, if any. Add 2 carrots, 2 onions and a few stalks of celery.

Add 1 teaspoon each of poultry seasoning and savoury, 2 teaspoons salt, ¼ teaspoon pepper and ½ teaspoon monosodium glutamate. (If a small turkey (4-5 lbs.) is used, decrease amount of seasoning.) Cover with cold water, bring to boiling point and simmer for 3 hours. Strain. Add additional seasoning, if necessary. If desired, vary soup by adding noodles or rice.

VICHYSSOISE

2 tablespoons butter
2 leeks sliced (white part only)
4 tablespoons minced onion
2 cups chicken broth
1 sprig of parsley
1 thinly sliced potato (medium-size)

⅓ cup chopped celery
Few grains nutmeg
Salt and pepper to taste
1 to 2 drops Worcestershire Sauce
½ cup whipping cream

Melt butter in a large saucepan. Add sliced leeks and minced onion. Sauté until tender but not brown. Add remaining ingredients, except whipping cream. Cook until potato is tender (about 40 minutes). Put through a very fine sieve or mix in an electric blender. Add more stock if necessary. Reheat to serve and stir in cream.

Yield: 3 cups (4 to 6 servings).

Cold Vichyssoise

Chill in serving dish or individual dishes. Sprinkle lightly with finely chopped parsley or chives.

CLAM CHOWDER

2 tablespoons diced salt pork
3 tablespoons butter or margarine
2 tablespoons chopped onion
1 cup boiling water
2 cups potato cubes

1 teaspoon salt
Few grains pepper
1 (10 oz.) can baby clams
2½ cups scalded milk

Sauté salt pork in butter until golden brown and crisp. Add onion; cook until golden. Add water, potatoes, salt and pepper, cover. Boil 15 minutes, stirring occasionally. Add clams with liquid; heat. Add milk; season to taste, then serve at once.

Yield: 6 servings.

SHRIMP BISQUE

3 tablespoons butter
2 tablespoons chopped celery
4 tablespoons chopped mushrooms
2 tablespoons chopped onions
2 tablespoons chopped carrots
1 bay leaf
¼ teaspoon marjoram

Few grains mace
½ teaspoon peppercorns
Salt and pepper to taste
1 tablespoon lemon juice
2 cups chicken broth
1 cup small shrimps (4½ oz. can)
1 cup whipping cream

Melt butter in large saucepan; add vegetables, seasonings and lemon juice. Cook slowly for 5 minutes. Add chicken broth and simmer 20 minutes; strain. Add small shrimps (or large ones, chopped) and cook 5 minutes longer. Add cream just before serving.

Yield: 4 to 6 servings.

SAVOURY SAUCES, GRAVIES AND DRESSINGS

All sauces have the same fundamental purpose—to enhance the flavour and appearance and often the nutritive value of the foods they accompany. A good sauce should never dominate the dish.

WHITE SAUCE

2 tablespoons butter	1 cup milk
2 tablespoons Five Roses All-purpose Flour	¼ teaspoon salt
	⅛ teaspoon pepper

Melt butter in a small saucepan. Slowly stir in Five Roses Flour; cook and stir over medium heat, 3 to 5 minutes after mixture bubbles. Gradually stir in milk. Add seasonings. Cook, stirring constantly, until mixture is smooth and thick and comes to a boil.

Yield: 1 cup.

Thin White Sauce—Follow above recipe but use only 1 tablespoon each of butter and Five Roses Flour.

Thick White Sauce—Follow above recipe but use 4 tablespoons each of butter and Five Roses Flour.

Variations

Make White Sauce, using the following variations:

Cream Sauce—Use cream instead of milk.

Cheese Sauce—Add 2 to 4 tablespoons grated cheese to hot sauce; stir over low heat until cheese melts.

Egg Sauce—Add 2 hard-cooked eggs, chopped in coarse pieces to cooked sauce.

Foamy Egg Sauce—Separate 1 egg. Add a little of the hot sauce to the yolk; stir and return to sauce and cook 1 minute longer. Remove from heat. Beat egg white until stiff; fold into sauce. Serve at once.

Asparagus Sauce—Add a little of the hot sauce to 1 egg yolk; stir and return to sauce and cook 1 minute longer. Add ½ cup cooked or canned asparagus.

Parsley Sauce—Add 1 tablespoon parsley.

Curry Sauce—Add ¼ to ½ teaspoon curry powder.

Horse-Radish Sauce—Add 1½ tablespoons grated horse-radish.

Velouté Sauce—Heat 1 cup milk in top of double boiler. Add to it a little celery, carrot and ½ bay leaf. Cook for 20 minutes over boiling water. Strain. Use this milk for making White Sauce.

Allemande Sauce—Make Velouté Sauce. Add a little of the cooked sauce to 1 egg yolk. Stir and return to sauce. Cook 1 minute longer.

Béchamel Sauce—Cook 1 tablespoon each of chopped carrot, onion and celery in the butter that is to be used for making the sauce. Do not allow the butter to brown. Remove vegetables; add flour and continue as for White Sauce. For **Yellow Béchamel Sauce:** add a little of the cooked sauce to 1 egg yolk. Stir and return to sauce. Cook 1 minute longer.

Mock Hollandaise Sauce—Season the White Sauce with a little pepper and cayenne. Add a little of the cooked sauce to 1 or 2 egg yolks. Stir and return to sauce. Cook 1 minute longer. Add ¼ cup butter, a little at a time, and 1 tablespoon lemon juice.

Drawn Butter Sauce—Same as Mock Hollandaise but made with water instead of milk.

Onion Sauce—Cook ¼ cup chopped onion for 5 minutes in the butter that is to be used for making the sauce, being careful not to brown the onion. Proceed as for White Sauce.

Cucumber Sauce—Use water instead of milk. Add ½ tablespoon white vinegar and ¼ cup chopped cucumber at end.

Mushroom Sauce—Make White Sauce, using consomme instead of milk. Season with salt, pepper, 1 teaspoon scraped onion, ¼ teaspoon oregano. Add ½ cup sautéed mushrooms.

HOLLANDAISE SAUCE

½ **cup butter**	**Dash of salt and white pepper**
4 egg yolks	**2½ tablespoons lemon juice**

Divide butter into 3 portions. Put 1 piece in top of double boiler with slightly beaten egg yolks. Cook over hot, but never boiling water, stirring constantly until butter melts. Add second piece of butter and stir until sauce thickens. Add third piece and remove pan immediately from heat. Beat with wooden spoon until glossy. Add seasonings and lemon juice, a teaspoon at a time. If separation occurs, stir in 2 tablespoons boiling water, a drop at a time.

Yield: 1 cup.

Suggested uses: meat, fish, egg and vegetable dishes.

TOMATO SAUCE

¼ **cup chopped onion**	**1 bay leaf**
6 tablespoons butter	½ **teaspoon celery salt**
3 tablespoons + 1 teaspoon Five	**3 whole cloves**
Roses All-purpose Flour	**2 teaspoons sugar**
¼ **teaspoon salt**	**3 cups tomato juice**
Few grains pepper	

Cook onion until golden in butter. Stir in flour, salt and pepper. Cook until golden, stirring constantly. Add remaining ingredients and cook 5 minutes. Put through a strainer and serve very hot.

Yield: 3 cups.

Suggested uses: steaks, veal, pork chops or stuffed green peppers.

SPANISH SAUCE

4 strips of bacon
1 medium-size onion, chopped
½ green pepper, chopped
2 cups canned tomatoes

⅛ teaspoon pepper
¼ teaspoon salt
1 teaspoon sugar
4 chopped olives

Cook bacon in frying pan until light brown; remove and chop in small pieces. Sauté chopped onion and green pepper in bacon fat until slightly brown. Add tomatoes, pepper, salt and sugar; cook until thickened. Add chopped bacon and olives just before serving.

Yield: 2 cups.

Suggested uses: omelets, cheese soufflé, savoury soufflé, leftover meat dishes.

BROWN SAUCE

2 teaspoons chopped onion
2 tablespoons butter
½ teaspoon salt

2½ tablespoons Five Roses Flour
1 cup liquid*

Sauté onion in butter until pale yellow. Stir in Five Roses Flour and salt; cook until mixture is brown. Slowly stir in liquid and cook until smooth and thick, stirring constantly.

Yield: 1 cup.

*For liquid, use consomme, brown stock or water in which a bouillon cube has been dissolved.

BROWN MUSHROOM SAUCE

Add sautéed mushrooms to Brown Sauce.

Suggested uses: use as a gravy for leftover meats, steaks or chops.

BREAD SAUCE

1 medium-size onion
4 whole cloves
2 cups milk
Dash of cayenne

½ teaspoon salt
⅓ cup fine dry bread crumbs
⅔ cup soft bread crumbs
2 tablespoons butter

Stud onion with cloves and place in top of double boiler. Add milk, cayenne, salt and bread crumbs. Cook over boiling water for 30 minutes until sauce is thickened. Stir in butter. Serve warm or cold.

Yield: 2 cups.

Suggested uses: wild game and poultry.

GRAVY

¼ cup meat drippings
¼ cup Five Roses All-purpose Flour
Salt and pepper to taste

2 cups liquid (stock, bouillon or water)

Remove meat from pan and keep warm. Pour off fat and drippings and return ¼ cup back into pan. Blend in Five Roses Flour. Cook and stir over low heat until mixture thickens and browns. Slowly stir in liquid; cook and stir until gravy thickens and comes to a boil. Season to taste. If necessary, strain before serving.

Yield: 2 cups.

Variations

Cream Gravy—Use milk or cream as the liquid.

Giblet Gravy—Use giblet stock as liquid and add chopped, cooked giblets to chicken or turkey gravy.

Mushroom Gravy—Sauté ½ cup sliced mushrooms in meat drippings until tender. Then add Five Roses Flour and proceed as above.

Savoury Gravy—Add ½ teaspoon Worcestershire Sauce and 2 teaspoons ketchup or chili sauce to gravy.

Wine Gravy—Use part red wine for liquid.

RAISIN SAUCE

¼ cup brown sugar	Few grains pepper
1½ teaspoons dry mustard	1½ cups water
1 tablespoon Five Roses All-purpose Flour	2 tablespoons lemon juice
⅛ teaspoon salt	¼ cup seedless raisins

Mix dry ingredients together in a saucepan. Slowly stir in water and lemon juice. Add raisins. Cook over medium heat, stirring constantly, until of syrup consistency. Serve hot or cold.

Yield: 1 cup.

Suggested uses: ham, tongue, ham croquettes.

CREOLE SAUCE

¼ cup butter	½ cup chopped green pepper
½ cup minced onion	2 cups cooked or canned tomatoes
1 garlic clove	1 teaspoon salt

Melt butter in saucepan; sauté onions, garlic and green pepper. Remove garlic and add remaining ingredients. Bring to boil and let simmer 15 minutes.

Yield: 2 cups.

Suggested uses: fish loaf, baked or broiled fish, liver.

HOT TARTAR SAUCE

2 tablespoons butter	Dash of pepper
2 tablespoons Five Roses All-purpose Flour	2 tablespoons chopped pickle
1 cup milk	¼ cup mayonnaise
¼ teaspoon salt	Paprika (optional)

Melt butter in small saucepan; gradually blend in Five Roses Flour. Add milk, a little at a time, stirring constantly. Cook over direct heat, stirring constantly until mixture is thick and smooth. Stir in salt, pepper and chopped pickle; fold in mayonnaise. Serve hot; sprinkle with paprika if desired.

Yield: 1 cup.

Suggested uses: hot fish dishes.

COLD TARTAR SAUCE: Substitute Five Roses Flour, butter and milk with ½ cup whipping cream, beaten stiff. Fold in salt, pepper and mayonnaise. Just before serving, add the chopped pickle. Serve cold.

Yield: 1 cup.

Suggested uses: cold fish dishes and fish salads.

LEMON BUTTER

¼ cup butter	Salt and pepper
2 tablespoons lemon juice	1 tablespoon chopped parsley

Mix together butter, lemon juice, salt and pepper to taste and chopped parsley. Shape into small balls; chill. If desired, melt butter and add remaining ingredients; serve hot.

Yield: ¼ cup.

Suggested uses: steaks, chops, fish dishes, vegetables.

SEAFOOD COCKTAIL SAUCE

1 tablespoon prepared horse-radish	2 drops Tabasco
¼ cup ketchup	1 tablespoon grated onion
¼ cup chili sauce	1 teaspoon Worcestershire Sauce
2 tablespoons lemon juice	2 tablespoons minced celery
½ teaspoon salt	

Mix all ingredients together thoroughly. Chill before serving.

Yield: 1 cup.

Suggested uses: oysters, shrimp, lobster.

BARBECUE SAUCE

¼ cup white vinegar	½ cup minced onion
1 cup ketchup	1 teaspoon salt
1 cup water	¼ teaspoon pepper
1 tablespoon Worcestershire Sauce	1 tablespoon butter
¼ cup brown sugar	Dash of Tabasco

Combine all ingredients in a saucepan. Simmer over low heat 15 minutes. Use sauce to baste meat or poultry while roasting, broiling or grilling.

Yield: 2¼ cups.

CRANBERRY SAUCE

2 cups sugar	1 lb. fresh or frozen cranberries
1 cup water	Rind and pulp of ½ orange

Combine sugar and water in saucepan. Bring to boil and boil for 5 minutes. Add cranberries and finely chopped orange rind and pulp. Cook, stirring occasionally, over low heat, until cranberries start popping. Remove from heat and chill.

Yield: 4 cups.

SAVOURY BREAD STUFFING

½ cup butter or margarine	¼ cup snipped parsley
⅓ cup minced onion	¾ teaspoon poultry seasoning
9 cups day-old bread crumbs (lightly packed)	¾ teaspoon salt
	⅛ teaspoon pepper
2 tablespoons chopped celery	¼ teaspoon monosodium glutamate

Sauté onion in butter until tender in a large skillet or kettle. Combine remaining ingredients and add to onion. Heat well without browning, stirring frequently.

Yield: 5 to 6 cups. Enough for neck and body cavity of a 10 to 12 lb. turkey or two roasting chickens.

Variations

Giblet Dressing—Add coarsely chopped, cooked giblets.

Mushroom Dressing—Sauté ½ lb. sliced mushrooms and ⅓ cup chopped green pepper (optional) with onions in butter.

UNCOOKED DRESSING

4 cups dried bread cubes	1 teaspoon salt
2 cups cold water	⅛ teaspoon pepper
1 small onion, finely chopped	½ teaspoon savory
2 tablespoons butter	1 teaspoon Worcestershire Sauce

Soak bread cubes in water and measure to make 2 cups when squeezed out. Sauté onion in butter until golden brown; add remaining ingredients (except bread) and blend well. Press remaining water gently from bread and crumble it into pan. Toss lightly until fluffy and stir in remaining ingredients. Press down gently and chill. Cut in squares.

Yield: 4-6 servings.

Suggested uses: cold meats.

APPLE STUFFING FOR GOOSE OR DUCK

3 cups stale bread cubes	¼ teaspoon pepper
2 tablespoons melted butter	1 small onion, finely chopped
1 teaspoon salt	2 large apples, cut in quarters

Combine ingredients and stuff bird.

Yield: 4 cups. Enough for a 6-8 lb. duck or goose.

We appreciate the fact that from time to time certain problems may arise with regard to home cooking and baking. For this reason we are pleased to remind you that our Five Roses Kitchens will always be most pleased to help you. Address all inquiries to:

PAULINE HARVEY, *Director*
FIVE ROSES KITCHENS
BOX 6089
MONTREAL, P.Q.

LUNCHEON AND SUPPER DISHES

Casseroles and one-dish meals are the perfect answer to a busy homemaker or hostess. Most can be prepared ahead of time and reheated just before serving.

SPAGHETTI WITH MEAT SAUCE

2 tablespoons olive oil
2 garlic cloves, minced
½ cup chopped onion
½ cup chopped celery
¾ cup sliced mushrooms
2 tablespoons chopped parsley
½ cup chopped green pepper
1 lb. ground beef
½ lb. ground pork
1 (28 oz.) can tomatoes

1 (5½ oz.) can tomato paste
1 tablespoon salt
⅛ teaspoon paprika
⅛ teaspoon cayenne
½ teaspoon basil
¼ teaspoon oregano
¼ teaspoon pepper
1 bay leaf
16 oz. spaghetti

Sauté vegetables in oil until onion is golden. Add beef and pork and cook until lightly browned. Add remaining ingredients and simmer 2 hours. Cook spaghetti according to directions on package. Pour sauce over spaghetti and if desired, sprinkle with grated Parmesan cheese.

Yield: 8 servings.

Note: If more liquid is needed, add water.

MACARONI AND CHEESE CASSEROLE

3 cups ready-cut macaroni
4 tablespoons butter
4 tablespoons Five Roses All-purpose Flour
2 cups milk

1 cup grated process or strong Cheddar cheese
Salt and pepper to taste
¼ teaspoon dry mustard

Topping

½ cup fine dry bread crumbs
2 tablespoons butter

2 tablespoons grated process or strong Cheddar cheese
Few grains paprika

Cook macaroni according to directions on package. Melt butter; add Five Roses Flour and stir until bubbling. Gradually add milk and stir constantly until smooth and thickened. Add grated cheese and stir until melted; blend in seasonings. Place a layer of macaroni in a greased 1½ quart casserole, cover with a layer of sauce. Repeat procedure until dish is full, ending with sauce. Prepare topping: mix bread crumbs with butter and spread over top; sprinkle with grated cheese and paprika. Bake at 375°F. 25 to 30 minutes or until mixture is heated through and crumbs are brown.

Yield: 6 to 8 servings.

CHILI CON CARNE

½ cup chopped onion	2 (14 oz.) cans kidney beans
2 tablespoons vegetable oil	3 teaspoons chili powder
1 lb. ground beef	1 teaspoon salt
1 (14 oz.) can tomatoes	1 teaspoon oregano

Sauté onion in vegetable oil; add ground beef and stir until beef is well done. Stir in remaining ingredients; cover. Bring to boil; reduce heat and cook slowly for 1 hour.

Yield: 6 servings. Recipe may be doubled.

PRIZE PIZZA

1 pkg. active dry yeast	3 teaspoons olive or vegetable oil
¼ cup lukewarm water	Grated Parmesan cheese
1 tablespoon sugar	12 oz. Mozzarella cheese
1 teaspoon salt	1 (28-oz.) can tomatoes, drained
1 tablespoon shortening	Anchovies, pepperoni, chopped
1 cup boiling water	parsley
2¾ cups Five Roses All-purpose Flour	

Soften yeast in lukewarm water for 10 minutes. Place sugar, salt, shortening and boiling water in a large bowl; stir until sugar dissolves. Cool to lukewarm; add yeast. Add 1½ cups Five Roses Flour and beat until smooth. Add remaining flour or enough to make a dough just barely firm enough to handle; knead until smooth on lightly floured board. Divide in thirds; knead each piece into a smooth ball. Flatten, then roll with rolling pin until big enough to fit a lightly greased 9″ pie plate or pizza pan. Press up around edges to make a slight rim. Let rise 15 minutes; brush lightly with oil. Sprinkle with grated Parmesan cheese. Cover with slivers of Mozzarella cheese and pieces of drained canned tomatoes. Top with chopped anchovies, sliced pepperoni and chopped parsley, or one of the following variations or a combination of them. Bake in a moderate hot oven (425°F.) 20 to 25 minutes.

Yield: Three 9″ pizzas.

Toppings

The following ingredients are all sliced or chopped according to preference.
1. Green peppers and mushrooms—sprinkle with salt and pepper.
2. Ripe black olives, onions and green pepper.
3. Green peppers, pepperoni and onion rings.
4. Stuffed green olives, mushrooms and parsley.
5. Anchovies, ripe black olives and parsley.
6. Slightly cooked bacon and ripe black olives—sprinkle with salt.

7. Replace canned tomatoes with sliced tomatoes. Top with sliced cooked ham or salami and green pepper rings.

8. Cover Mozzarella cheese with cooked ground beef (about ⅓ lb. per pizza). Top with canned tomatoes and mushrooms—sprinkle with salt and pizza mix seasoning.

STUFFED GREEN PEPPERS

8 large green peppers	1 cup canned tomatoes
1 tablespoon butter	2 cups cooked rice
1 small onion, chopped	Salt and pepper to taste
1 lb. ground beef	⅓ cup fine dry bread crumbs

Cut green peppers in half; remove seeds and tough white membrane. Cover with boiling water; cook 5 minutes and drain. Sprinkle with salt; cool before filling. Sauté chopped onion and ground beef in butter. Add canned tomatoes and rice. Season with salt and pepper. Fill peppers with this mixture. Top with bread crumbs. Bake in a moderate oven (350°F.) 15 minutes; increase temperature to 400°F. and continue baking until tops are brown—about 10 minutes.

Yield: 8 stuffed peppers—allow 1 or 2 per person.

HAWAIIAN-STYLE TURKEY CASSEROLE

6 oz. noodles	2 cups chopped cooked turkey or chicken
2 tablespoons butter	1 (19-oz.) can drained, pineapple chunks
2 tablespoons green pepper	1 tablespoon chopped pimiento
1 tablespoon Five Roses All-purpose Flour	1 teaspoon Worcestershire Sauce
1 cup milk	1 teaspoon salt
1 (10-oz.) can condensed cream of mushroom soup	Few grains pepper
	1 cup blanched almond halves

Cook noodles according to directions on package. Melt butter in top of double boiler; sauté green pepper until soft, over direct heat. Remove green pepper and stir in Five Roses Flour; slowly add milk, stirring constantly. Cook, stirring constantly over boiling water, until mixture thickens. Stir in remaining ingredients, including the green pepper and half of the almonds. Place alternate layers of cooked noodles and creamed mixture (beginning with noodles and ending with creamed mixture) in a greased 2 quart casserole. Brown remaining almonds slightly in oven—then sprinkle over top of casserole. Bake in a moderate oven (350°F.) for 20 minutes.

Yield: 6 servings.

SHEPHERD'S PIE

3-4 cups hot mashed potatoes	1 cup leftover gravy
2 cups leftover cooked, diced beef	¼ teaspoon monosodium glutamate

Grease a 1½ quart casserole and spread ½″ thick with mashed potatoes. Fill with meat and gravy; sprinkle with monosodium glutamate. Garnish top with large spoonfuls of mashed potatoes. Bake in a moderate oven (375°F.) 20-25 minutes.

Yield: 6 servings.

Note: Cooked, diced beef may be substituted with leftover lamb or veal. Leftover vegetables may be added to meat.

SAVOURY CHICKEN ROLLS

1 recipe shortcake dough (page 92)	⅓ cup chopped onion
1½ cups chopped cooked chicken	Salt and pepper
⅓ cup finely chopped olives	1-2 tablespoons milk
½ teaspoon paprika	

Prepare shortcake dough and roll to ⅓" thickness. Combine chopped chicken, olives, paprika, chopped onion, salt and pepper to taste and a little milk to moisten the mixture slightly. Spread mixture evenly over dough and roll up tightly, jelly roll fashion. Cut in slices 1" thick. Place each slice, cut side down, in well greased muffin pans. Bake in a hot oven (450°F.) 15 to 20 minutes. Serve hot with gravy or with well seasoned White Sauce (or Cream Sauce (page 119).

Yield: 15 rolls.

Note: If desired, substitute chicken with any leftover cooked meat or flaked, canned fish.

BOSTON BAKED BEANS

4 cups white beans	½ teaspoon savory
½ lb. salt fat pork, cut in cubes	Few drops Worcestershire Sauce
1 large onion	¼ cup brown sugar
1 tablespoon salt	¼ cup ketchup
Dash of pepper	1 cup molasses
1 teaspoon dry mustard	6-8 cups boiling water
½ teaspoon sage	4 slices bacon

Wash beans and soak overnight in enough water to cover in an earthenware container. Drain. Add pork cubes and onion cut in half to beans, pushing into beans to distribute evenly. Combine remaining ingredients except boiling water and bacon; add to beans and stir well. Pour boiling water over beans and top with slices of bacon. Cover and bake in a slow oven (250°F.) 7 to 8 hours, adding more water if needed.

Yield: 8 to 10 servings.

CREAMED FOODS

Creamed dishes are wholesome and economical. Leftover fish, meat and vegetables, amounts too small to be used by themselves, may be combined with a good sauce to make an appetizing creamed dish suitable for luncheon or supper.

CREAMED PEAS AND EGGS

To 2 cups White Sauce (page 119) add a little chopped parsley, few drops onion juice, 1 cup cooked or canned peas and 3 chopped hard-cooked eggs. Heat thoroughly. Serve in toasted bread boxes, patty shells or on buttered toast. Serves 6.

CREAMED SALMON

To 2 cups White Sauce, Cream Sauce or Parsley Sauce (page 119) add flaked canned salmon. Heat thoroughly. Serve in toasted bread boxes, patty shells or on buttered toast. Serves 4 to 6.

CREAMED CHICKEN or TURKEY
See Turkey à la King, page 162.

EGGS À LA KING

2 cups White Sauce (page 119)	½ cup cooked peas
6 hard-cooked eggs, sliced	2 tablespoons chopped pimiento
1 cup sliced cooked mushrooms	6 slices buttered toast

Combine all ingredients together except the toast; heat thoroughly. Serve on toast. Garnish with tomato slices, if desired.
Yield: 6 to 8 servings.

ASPARAGUS IN PATTY SHELLS

12 asparagus spears	Dash of paprika
1 hard-cooked egg	1 cup Cream Sauce (page 119)
4 to 6 patty shells	

Cut asparagus into small pieces. Chop white of egg and add to the Cream Sauce with the asparagus. Fill patty shells. Press egg yolk through sieve and sprinkle over top. Garnish with paprika.
Yield: 4 to 6 servings.

SAVOURY TARTS AND PIES

TOURTIÈRE
(French Canadian Meat Pie)

½ lb. ground veal	1 teaspoon salt
½ lb. ground pork	¼ teaspoon pepper
⅓ cup chopped onion	1 pastry recipe
¼ cup water	

Prepare pastry; reserve some for top crust and line a 9″ pie plate with remainder. Combine all ingredients together in a saucepan. Cook over medium heat until meat has lost its pink colour but is still moist; cool. Roll out top crust; make slits in centre to allow steam to escape. Pour cooled meat mixture into pie shell; cover with top crust, seal and flute edges. Bake in a hot oven (425°F.) 20-25 minutes or until browned.
Note: Baked tourtières may be frozen and reheated before serving.

SAVOURY CHEESE TARTS

1 cup Cheese Sauce (page 119)	⅓ cup buttered soft bread crumbs
1 teaspoon onion juice	4 baked tart shells, 4" in diameter
2 hard-cooked eggs	

Season Cheese Sauce with onion juice. Chop eggs in coarse pieces. Place a layer of sauce, a layer of chopped egg, another layer of sauce, then a layer of crumbs in each tart shell. Place in a moderate oven (350°F.) to heat through and lightly brown the crumbs—about 10 minutes.
Yield: 4 servings.
Note: If desired, make 12 medium-size tarts and serve 2 to 3 per serving.

SALMON TARTLETS

1 pastry recipe	1 egg, beaten
1 (7¾ oz.) can salmon	1 (10 oz.) can peas
Salt and pepper to taste	1 cup White Sauce (page 119)
1 teaspoon parsley	¼ cup buttered bread crumbs
Few drops lemon juice	

Prepare pastry and make 12 medium-size tart shells. Flake salmon and season with salt, pepper, parsley and lemon juice. Stir in beaten egg. Place a spoonful of salmon mixture into each tart shell; cover with a layer of peas, then a layer of White Sauce. Top with buttered crumbs. Bake in a hot oven (450°F.) 10 minutes; reduce temperature to 325°F. and continue baking until mixture is heated through and crumbs are lightly browned—about 20 to 30 minutes.

Yield: 12 medium-size tarts. Serve 2 to 3 per person.

Note: Flaked tuna, lobster or leftover fish may be used instead of salmon.

WEST COUNTY PIE

1 pastry recipe	1 teaspoon onion juice
1 raw carrot, grated	1 teaspoon Worcestershire Sauce
2 raw potatoes, grated	Salt and pepper to taste
1-2 tablespoons butter	
2 cups chopped or ground cooked meat	

Prepare pastry and line a 9″ pie plate; reserve some for top crust. Sauté grated carrot and potato in butter; cool. Combine carrot, potato, meat and seasonings. (If necessary, moisten with a little water or gravy.) Place in pie shell. Roll out top crust and make slits to allow steam to escape. Cover pie and seal edges. Flute, if desired. Bake in a hot oven (450°F.) 15 minutes; reduce temperature to 350°F. and continue baking 20 to 25 minutes longer. Serve hot or cold.

Note: If raw ground meat is used, brown in melted fat and simmer until cooked; cool before using.

SCALLOPED ONION AND CHEESE PIE

1 pastry recipe	¼ cup grated cheese
4 large onions, sliced	½ cup White Sauce (page 119)

Prepare pastry and line a 9″ pie plate; reserve some for top crust. Parboil sliced onions for 10-15 minutes; drain and allow to become quite cold. Place alternate layers of onion and grated cheese in pie shell. Pour White Sauce over top. Roll out top crust and make slits to allow steam to escape. Cover pie and seal edges. Bake in a hot oven (450°F.) 10 minutes; reduce temperature to 350°F. and continue to bake until crust is done and onions are tender—about 30 to 35 minutes. Serve hot with cold or hot meat.

CHEESE AND EGGS

Cheese is a nutritious and appealing food either eaten as is, or when it is added to a variety of other foods. Both natural Cheddar cheese and process cheese are very popular for cooking. In general, process cheese melts more uniformly but a strong Cheddar will contribute more flavour.

The secret of cooking with cheese is not to overcook. Cheese cooking should be done at a low temperature or for a very short time at a higher temperature.

CHEESE SOUFFLÉ

¼ cup butter	Dash of pepper
¼ cup Five Roses All-purpose	Dash of basil
Flour	½ lb. process cheese, thinly sliced
1 cup milk	(or mild Cheddar)
¼ teaspoon salt	4 egg yolks
Dash of cayenne	4 egg whites, stiffly beaten

Melt butter in saucepan over medium heat; stir in Five Roses Flour gradually. Slowly add milk and stir until thick and smooth. Add salt, cayenne, pepper, basil and cheese; stir until cheese is melted and sauce is smooth. Remove from heat; add a little of the hot mixture to yolks, then stir yolks into cheese mixture. Cool; fold in stiffly beaten egg whites. Pour into a 2 quart soufflé dish. Bake in a slow oven (300°F.) 1 hour and 15 minutes, or until knife inserted in centre comes out clean. Serve immediately with a creamed sauce.

Yield: 6 servings.

CHEESE FONDUE

1½ cups milk	1 teaspoon salt
2 cups soft bread crumbs	⅛ teaspoon paprika
1½ cups grated Cheddar cheese	3 egg yolks, beaten
1 tablespoon butter	3 egg whites, stiffly beaten

Heat milk, bread crumbs, cheese, butter, salt and paprika in top of double boiler until cheese and butter are melted. Cool slightly; add to beaten egg yolks. Fold in stiffly beaten egg whites. Pour into buttered 1½ quart casserole and set in pan of hot water. Bake in a moderate oven (350°F.) until firm, 30-40 minutes. Serve immediately.

Yield: 6 servings.

WELSH RAREBIT

3 tablespoons butter
3 tablespoons Five Roses All-purpose Flour
2 cups milk
2 cups grated Cheddar cheese

1 teaspoon dry mustard
½ teaspoon salt
Few grains pepper
¼ teaspoon paprika
Toast or crackers

Melt butter in saucepan over medium heat. Blend in Five Roses Flour gradually and cook, stirring constantly, until mixture bubbles. Stir in milk gradually and cook until thickened. Add grated cheese and mustard; stir until cheese is melted. Add seasonings. Serve immediately over hot toast or crackers.

Yield: 4 to 6 servings.

BACON RAREBIT

Cook 1 cup diced bacon (4 strips) until crisp. Make Welsh Rarebit, using 3 tablespoons bacon fat in place of butter. Sprinkle crisp bacon over each serving.

CHEESE FRANKS

6 hot dog rolls
Butter
1 large onion, thinly sliced

Cheddar cheese, cut in 1" strips
Parsley

Cut 2 slices lengthwise in each roll to within ½" from bottom; butter both sides of cut slices. Sauté onion in butter until tender and lightly browned. Insert strips of Cheddar Cheese and onion slices in each cut. Bake in a hot oven (425°F.) 10 minutes or until cheese melts; sprinkle with snipped parsley.

Yield: 6 servings.

Note: These may be prepared ahead of time and baked when needed.

EGGS

Eggs are popular at any time—breakfast, lunch and as an addition to a supper dish or party fare.

The secret of cooking eggs is to cook them over low to moderate heat. Don't overcook as they will become tough.

Store leftover egg yolks in a jar covered with cold water. Place in refrigerator. Drain off the water before using the yolks.

Store leftover egg whites in a tightly covered jar and place in refrigerator.

Combine beaten eggs with hot mixtures by first adding a small amount of the hot mixture to the beaten eggs, then add them gradually to the hot mixture, stirring constantly.

SOFT-COOKED EGGS

Place eggs in a saucepan of cold water and heat slowly until boiling point is reached. Reduce heat so that water will not boil again and leave eggs in water 2 to 4 minutes, depending on desired softness of cooked eggs.

HARD-COOKED EGGS

Prepare as for soft-cooked eggs. When water boils, reduce heat to keep water just below simmering. Cover and cook eggs 15 to 20 minutes. Cool at once in cold water to prevent dark surface on yolks.

FRIED EGGS

Coat skillet with fat; place over medium heat. Add eggs and season with salt and pepper. When the whites of the eggs are set and edges cooked, cover and let cook until done to your liking.

POACHED EGGS

Have enough water in a saucepan to just cover eggs and let water come just to boiling. Stir the simmering water to make a swirl. Break egg into a saucer and slip egg right into the middle of the swirl. Be sure to follow the motion of swirl with dish so egg goes into the water in same direction. Repeat for each egg used. Turn heat down. It takes about 3 to 5 minutes for egg to cook, depending on the doneness you desire. Remove egg with a slotted spoon. Season with salt and pepper.

SCRAMBLED EGGS

6 eggs	**Few grains pepper**
⅓ cup milk	**1½ tablespoons butter**
½ teaspoon salt	

Beat eggs, milk, salt and pepper with a fork. Heat butter in a skillet until just hot enough to make a drop of water sizzle. Pour in egg mixture and turn heat low. Cook until eggs are just set, stirring as they thicken. Add more salt and pepper, if desired.

Yield: 3 to 4 servings.

BREAKFAST EGGS AND BACON

Line greased muffin tins with half-cooked bacon slices. Slip an egg into centre of each; sprinkle with salt and pepper. Place in a moderate oven (350°F.) and bake for 15 minutes or until eggs are firm.

EGG NESTS

3 tablespoons butter	**3 cups mashed potatoes**
1 tablespoon chopped onion	**6 eggs**
2 tablespoons chopped pimiento	**Few grains salt**
(optional)	**Grated cheese**
1 tablespoon chopped parsley	

Sauté onion and pimiento lightly in 1 tablespoon butter. Add chopped parsley, 1 tablespoon butter and mix with mashed potatoes; beat until creamy. Spread potato mixture in a buttered baking dish (8″ square or round). Make 6 hollow places with a spoon and drop an egg into each. Sprinkle with salt and grated cheese; dot with remaining butter. Bake in a moderate oven (375°F.) for 20-25 minutes.

Yield: 4 to 6 servings.

EGGS BENEDICT

6 English muffins	6 poached eggs
6 thin slices cooked ham	1 cup Hollandaise Sauce (page 120)

Split and toast the English Muffins. Top with sliced ham. Place a poached egg over the ham. Pour Hollandaise Sauce over top. Serve immediately. Allow 1 to 2 muffin halves per person.

Yield: 3 to 6 servings.

DEVILLED EGGS

6 hard-cooked eggs	Dash of onion powder
¼ teaspoon salt	Dash of pepper
¾ teaspoon prepared mustard	2 to 3 drops Worcestershire Sauce
2 tablespoons mayonnaise	Paprika, parsley or chives.

Cut hard-cooked eggs in half, lengthwise. Remove yolks carefully and force through a coarse sieve. Add next 6 ingredients and beat until smooth and fluffy. (Add more mayonnaise if necessary, as amount will depend on size of yolks.) Heap into egg whites. Do not pack or pat surface smooth. Sprinkle with paprika, parsley or chives. Chill.

Yield: 12 halves.

FRENCH TOAST

3 eggs	1 cup milk
½ teaspoon salt	6 slices bread
2 tablespoons sugar	

Beat eggs; add salt, sugar and milk. Mix well. Soak bread in mixture until soft. Cook in hot, well greased frying pan or griddle. Brown on one side, turn and brown other side. Serve hot, sprinkled with sugar and cinnamon or serve with maple syrup, molasses, jelly or honey.

Yield: 3 to 6 servings.

FRENCH OMELET

4 eggs	⅛ teaspoon pepper
¼ cup hot water	2 tablespoons butter
½ teaspoon salt	

Beat eggs slightly, just enough to blend yolks and whites. Add water and seasonings. Melt butter in a hot, heavy skillet; add eggs and reduce heat slightly. As omelet cooks, lift with spatula, letting uncooked part run underneath until whole is creamy; increase heat to brown slightly underneath. Fold double and turn onto hot platter.

Yield: 2 servings.

Note: Do not double recipe. Make several omelets instead.

Variations

Before folding omelet, spread with one of the following fillings or a combination: diced cooked bacon, chopped cooked or creamed chicken, flaked cooked or creamed fish, diced ham, cooked minced liver, creamed or sautéed mushrooms, chopped sautéed green peppers, cooked vegetables or grated cheese.

SOUFFLÉ SAUCE

3 tablespoons butter
3 tablespoons Five Roses All-purpose
Flour
½ teaspoon salt

Few grains pepper
Seasonings*
1 cup milk

Melt butter, stir in Five Roses Flour and seasonings. Cook over medium heat for 3 minutes after mixture begins to bubble, stirring constantly. Add milk gradually and stir constantly until sauce is smooth and thick. Remove from heat and use as directed.

Yield: 1 cup sauce.

*Some of the seasonings which may be added to the sauce are: parsley, celery salt, chopped celery, scraped onion, onion juice, minced red and green pepper, paprika, cayenne, etc. See also the seasonings used for the various Savoury Soufflés.

SAVOURY SOUFFLÉS

1 cup Soufflé Sauce
Soufflé Recipe (see below)

3 egg yolks
3 egg whites

Select Soufflé desired and add its ingredients to the Soufflé Sauce. Allow mixture to cool slightly. Beat egg yolks until thick and lemon coloured; add to sauce. Beat egg whites until stiff but not dry and fold in. Pour mixture into an ungreased 1 to 1½ quart baking dish or soufflé dish. Set dish in a pan containing 1″ of water. Bake in a moderate oven (350°F.) 50-60 minutes or until a knife inserted in centre comes out clean. Serve immediately. If soufflé is allowed to stand after it is taken from the oven, it will fall.

Yield: 4-6 servings.

Celery soufflé: Add 1 cup chopped cooked celery. Season with a few grains cayenne and 2 tablespoons grated cheese.

Spinach soufflé: Add 1 cup chopped cooked spinach, 1 teaspoon lemon juice and 1 teaspoon onion juice. Serve with fried bacon strips.

Chicken soufflé: Add 1½ cups minced cooked chicken, few grains paprika and 1 teaspoon onion juice.

Corn and cheese soufflé: Sauté 1 slice of onion, finely minced and 1 teaspoon chopped green pepper in butter before making the Soufflé Sauce. Add flour and finish making sauce as directed. Add ½ cup grated Cheddar cheese and 1 cup canned corn niblets.

Bacon soufflé: Add ½ cup cooked, crisp bacon bits.

Mushroom soufflé: Sauté 1 cup sliced mushrooms in butter; add ½ teaspoon salt, few grains pepper, ¼ teaspoon basil and add to Soufflé Sauce.

Many people find the Five Roses Guide to Good Cooking an excellent shower gift for the bride-to-be. Additional copies of this cook book may be obtained by clipping the coupons on pages 3 and 4.

FISH

With abundant supplies of fresh and frozen fish readily available, it is easy for us to enjoy a variety of fish dishes. Fish is an excellent, easily digested protein food. Cooked the right way, it soon becomes a favourite menu item.

BUYING

For top quality fish, look for fish that has been Government inspected.

Fresh Fish—buy when in season. Look for fresh characteristic odour or no odour, firm elastic flesh, bright eyes and gills, and sheen on scales. Fillets and steaks should have a fresh cut appearance.

Frozen Fish—buy all year round. Packages should be solidly frozen. Wrapping material should be moisture-vapour-proof and no air space between fish and package. The fish should have firm glossy flesh with no discoloration or parched white area and be free of frost and ice crystals.

Approximate Number of Servings per Pound

Whole or dressed	— 1 serving
Pan dressed (with head, tail and fins removed)	— 2 servings
Steaks	— 2 or 3 servings
Fillets	— 3 servings

STORING

Fresh Fish—use as soon as possible. Wash quickly in cold water and dry. Wrap in waxed paper and store in refrigerator.

Frozen Fish—store in freezer in the unopened package. Thaw in refrigerator and use immediately. Never refreeze thawed fish. Fat fish, such as salmon, mackerel and blue fish keep up to 2 months in freezer; lean fish, such as cod, haddock and halibut keep up to 3 months in freezer.

PREPARING FISH FOR COOKING

How to Scale—hold the tail firmly and with a dull knife or scaler held at a 45° angle, loosen scales by pushing the knife against the skin from tail to head. It is best to do this under running water so that scales won't scatter.

How to Clean—use a thin sharp knife or kitchen shears. Slit skin from vent to gills. Remove viscera and wash in running water to clean thoroughly. Remove head by cutting across base of gills. Cut off tail. Remove fins by cutting the flesh along both sides of the fins. Pull fin quickly towards head to remove root bones. Salt lightly and place in refrigerator until ready to use.

How to Fillet—cut through flesh along the centre of the back from the tail to head, then cut across just below head. Turn knife flat and starting at the head, cut flesh to the tail, easing the knife over the rib bones. Remove the fillet. Turn fish over and do other side.

How to Skin—place the fish, skin-side down, on the cutting board. Hold the tail end firmly with one hand and cut skin from the flesh with quick short strokes. A fresh fish is skinned easily.

How to Bone—continue beyond the slit made when cleaning the fish from vent to tail. Cut across from the slit to the back. Hold the tail and insert the sharp edge of knife flatly between tail and back bone. Press the knife towards the head, cutting the flesh from the ribs and backbone. Turn and cut bone from other side. Lift out bones, removing any flesh adhering to them.

COOKING

Cook fish quickly at high temperature—except where milk or cream are used in the baking sauce. The flesh of fish contains little connective tissue and therefore does not require a long cooking period.

Tips To Remember

1. Do not overcook fish—otherwise it becomes dry and tough.
2. Fish is cooked when the flesh becomes opaque, flakes readily and can be easily pierced with a fork.
3. Serve fish immediately after cooking while it is still hot, tender or juicy.
4. Do not thaw frozen fish before cooking except when necessary for ease in handling—such as panfrying or stuffing.

Cooking time is based on thickness of fish. Measure thickness at the thickest part of fish before cooking. Recommended time for baking, broiling, panfrying, boiling and steaming is:

10 minutes per inch thickness for fresh fish.

20 minutes per inch thickness for frozen fish.

Add an extra 5 minutes per inch thickness if fish is to be baked in a cream sauce.

How to Bake—for whole fish, steaks or fillets—fresh or frozen.

Season fish with salt and pepper. Brush with melted butter or top with a sauce. Fillets may be dipped in milk and rolled in bread crumbs. Place in a greased baking pan. Bake in a very hot oven (450°F.-500°F.) or 350°F. if a cream sauce is used. Allow 10 minutes cooking time per inch thickness. If fish is frozen, double the cooking time. Add an extra 5 minutes per inch thickness if fish is to cook in a sauce.

How to Broil—for steaks, fillets or small whole fish—fresh or frozen.

Season fish with salt and pepper. Brush with melted fat or French Dressing. Place on broiler pan in a preheated oven so that fish is 2" to 4" from heating unit. Place frozen fish lower to prevent over cooking surface before interior is cooked. If skin is left on fish, place skin-side down. Broil until fish is browned, then turn. Brush with melted fat and brown. Allow 10 minutes per inch thickness for fresh fish; 20 minutes for frozen. Thin cuts of fish may be broiled without turning.

How to Panfry—for fish steaks, fillets and small whole fish.

For easier handling, thaw or partially thaw frozen fish. Season with salt and pepper. Dip fish in milk or beaten egg, then roll in Five Roses Flour or dry bread crumbs. Place in hot frying pan that contains about ¼″ melted fat or oil. Do not use butter for frying as it smokes at high temperature. Fry until golden brown, turn and brown other side. Allow 10 minutes per inch thickness. Drain and serve piping hot.

How to Deep-fry—for fillets, smelts, fish cakes and some shellfish.

Partially thaw frozen fish first. Cut fillets into uniform size pieces about ½″ thick. Season fish with salt and pepper. Dip in batter (see page 169); or in milk or beaten egg and then in Five Roses Flour or fine dry bread crumbs. Place one layer of fish in frying basket and fry in hot deep fat at 375°F. until golden brown—about 3 to 4 minutes. Drain and serve piping hot. See Deep Fat Frying, page 168.

How to Boil—for whole fish, fillets or steak.

Fish that is to be used in salads, casseroles, fish cakes or creamed dishes may be cooked in this way. Season fish with salt and place on a piece of greased aluminum foil, cooking parchment paper or cheesecloth. Add about 1 tablespoon each of chopped onion and celery for flavour. Wrap fish and secure to make package watertight. Place in rapidly boiling water and cover. When water returns to the boil, time the cooking period. Boil 10 minutes per inch thickness for fresh fish; 20 minutes for frozen. When removing fish from package, save the juices for use in fish sauce.

How to Steam—for whole fish, fillets or steaks.

Season fish with salt and pepper. For easier handling, tie fish in cheesecloth. Place fish in upper part of steamer or in a sieve or colander and place over boiling water. Don't let water touch the fish. Cover and cook until tender. Allow 10 minutes cooking time per inch thickness for fresh fish; 20 minutes for frozen.

How to Oven Steam—for whole fish, fillets or steaks.

Season fish with salt and pepper. Wrap tightly in greased aluminum foil. Pinch folds and ends to seal tightly. Place on a shallow pan or cookie sheet and bake in a hot oven (450°F.). Allow 15 minutes per inch thickness for fresh fish; 30 minutes for frozen.

How to Poach in Milk—especially good for smoked fish fillets.

Place fish in enough milk to just cover. Cover pan and cook over medium heat until fish flakes easily when tested with a fork or bake in a moderate oven (350°F.). Allow 10 minutes per inch thickness for fresh fish; 20 minutes for frozen. Dot with butter and sprinkle with pepper. Serve with the milk.

BAKED STUFFED FISH

2-3 lbs. whole fish, fresh or thawed	1¼-1½ cups stuffing
Salt	2 tablespoons melted fat or oil

Sprinkle inside of cleaned fish with salt. Stuff loosely and truss with string. Place fish in greased pan and brush with melted fat or oil. Measure thickness of the stuffed fish at thickest part. Bake in a hot oven (450°F.). Allow 10 minutes per inch thickness. Cut in slices to serve.

Yield: 4 to 6 servings.

STUFFING FOR FISH

¼ cup butter
2 cups soft bread crumbs
2 teaspoons minced onion
¼ cup chopped celery

1 tablespoon lemon juice
½ teaspoon salt
Dash of pepper

Melt butter; stir in bread crumbs. Add remaining ingredients and mix thoroughly. If dressing seems dry, add a little water to moisten.

Yield: 1½ cups. Enough for a 3 lb. dressed fish.

Celery Stuffing—Follow above recipe, increasing celery to 1 cup.

Mushroom Stuffing—Follow above recipe, adding 1 cup chopped mushrooms.

SPENCER METHOD FOR FISH FILLETS

2-3 lbs. fish fillets, fresh or frozen
1 tablespoon salt
1 cup milk

Fine dry bread crumbs
Salad oil or melted fat

Cut fillets into serving portions and soak in salted milk for 3 minutes; roll in bread crumbs. Place in a pan and sprinkle with cooking oil or fat. Bake in a hot oven (500°F.) until fish flakes easily when tested with a fork. Allow 10 minutes cooking time per inch thickness for fresh fish; 20 minutes for frozen. Serve immediately, plain or top with grated Cheese or Cheese Sauce (page 119).

Yield: 6 to 8 servings.

FILLETS WITH LEMON BUTTER SAUCE

2 lbs. fish fillets, fresh or frozen
2 tablespoons lemon juice
¼ cup melted butter

2 tablespoons finely chopped
    parsley
½ teaspoon salt
⅛ teaspoon pepper

Arrange fillets in a greased baking dish. Combine remaining ingredients and pour over fillets. Bake in a hot oven (500°F.). Allow 10 minutes per inch thickness for fresh fish; 20 minutes for frozen.

Yield: 6 servings.

FISH LOAF WITH CREOLE SAUCE

2 cups flaked cooked fish or
1 (16 oz.) can fish
1 tablespoon lemon juice
¼ cup butter
¼ cup Five Roses All-purpose Flour
1 cup milk

½ cup fine dry bread crumbs
½ cup finely chopped celery
1 tablespoon chopped parsley
2 tablespoons chopped onions
¾ teaspoon salt
Few grains pepper

Drain flaked fish and sprinkle with lemon juice. Melt butter in medium-size saucepan; gradually stir in the Five Roses Flour, blending well. Slowly add milk and cook until mixture is smooth and thick, stirring constantly. Add fish and remaining ingredients; mix until well blended. Pour into a greased 9″ x 5″ x 3″ loaf pan. Bake in a moderate oven (350°F.) 45 minutes. Garnish with lemon slices and serve with Creole Sauce (page 122).

Yield: 4 to 5 servings.

SHELLFISH

WHAT YOU SHOULD KNOW ABOUT SHELLFISH

Lobster—may be purchased alive or cooked in the shell and as fresh, frozen and canned lobster meat. Live lobsters should be active when purchased. Colour of shell varies from deep blue to shades of green and turns bright red on cooking. Lobsters should be alive at moment of cooking. To test—straighten tail out; if it springs back into a curled position it was alive and healthy when cooked.

Shrimps—may be purchased as fresh, frozen or shelled, cooked and canned. They vary in size and in colour, from grey and green to pink. All turn pink on cooking. Before cooking, lift out the dark sand vein that runs the length of the body. Most frozen and some canned shrimp come deveined. 1 lb. fresh yields ½ lb. cooked and shelled and will give 3 to 4 servings.

Crab—may be purchased fresh, frozen, cooked in the shell or canned (crab meat). Live crab is sold only in areas close to fishing centres as they must be cooked and refrigerated promptly.

Clams—may be purchased alive in the shell or as shucked meat in fresh, frozen and canned forms. Shells of live clams are tightly closed. These may be steamed or pried open with a knife.

Oysters—Atlantic coast oysters are generally sold in the shell. Pacific coast or Japanese oysters tend to have brittle shells and are sold as shucked meat— either as fresh, frozen, canned or smoked canned oyster meat. Make sure shells are tightly closed. Gaping shells indicate that the oysters inside are dead and no longer edible. Store in refrigerator (between 34°F. and 40°F.) in a damp atmosphere. Do not freeze in the shell. Good months for purchasing oysters are September to April.

Scallops—may be purchased shucked, either fresh or frozen. Wipe scallops with a damp cloth before using. Always thaw frozen scallops before using.

BOILED FRESH LOBSTER

Plunge live lobsters, head first, into boiling salted water (¼ cup salt per quart of water). Cover and simmer 15 to 20 minutes—time from moment of plunging. Remove from water. Cool quickly under cold water and drain. Place lobster on its back. Split lengthwise down the centre with sharp knife or scissors. Remove the dark sand vein, small sac back of head and spongy grey-green tissue on either side of the back. The bright green liver and red roe (if present) are delicious. Crack large claws. Serve hot with melted butter and lemon slices.

COLD LOBSTER

Cool cooked lobster under cold water. Drain and refrigerate. Prepare for serving as above. For salads and main dishes, remove all meat from claws, tails and legs and break into bite-size pieces.

LOBSTER À LA NEWBURG

1 tablespoon butter	1 tablespoon grated onion
1 tablespoon Five Roses All-purpose Flour	2 cups (10 oz. can) flaked, cooked or canned lobster
1¼ cups thin cream	1 egg, slightly beaten
1½ tablespoons chopped pimiento	1 pastry recipe
1½ tablespoons chopped green pepper	

Make a 9″ pie shell or 12 individual tarts; bake at 450°F. 12-15 minutes or until lightly browned. Melt butter in small saucepan; gradually add Five Roses Flour and stir until mixture bubbles. Add cream slowly, stirring constantly and bring to boiling point. Stir in remaining ingredients and cook 3 minutes longer. Serve in pastry shell, tarts or on toast.

Yield: 5 to 6 servings.

Note: Other types of canned fish may be substituted for lobster.

SEAFOOD SCALLOP

1 lb. fish fillets	6 tablespoons butter
1 lb. scallops, fresh or frozen and thawed	½ cup Five Roses All-Purpose Flour
5 cups milk	1 can condensed mushroom soup
1 (10 oz.) can lobster	1⅓ cups cooked rice
2 (6 oz.) cans oysters, drained	1½ cups dry bread crumbs
	¼ cup melted butter

Place fillets and scallops in a large saucepan; cover with milk and cook slowly— about 8 minutes. Drain and reserve milk. Reserve juice from lobster and set aside. Break fillets into bite-size pieces and combine with scallops, lobster and drained oysters. Melt butter in saucepan and blend in Five Roses Flour. Stir in reserved milk gradually. Add mushroom soup and juice from lobster. Stir constantly over medium heat until thick and smooth. Pour a layer of sauce into a buttered 3-quart casserole. Add a layer of cooked rice, then a layer of fish. Repeat, ending with a layer of sauce. Sauté bread crumbs in melted butter; sprinkle on top. Heat in a moderate oven (350°F.) 1 hour before serving.

Yield: 15 to 18 servings.

STEAMED CLAMS

Scrub clams under running water to remove the sand. Place in steamer or large kettle containing ½″ of water. Cover tightly and steam for 10 minutes or until shells are partially open; remove. Detach top shells, if desired. Serve hot with side dishes of strained clam liquid and melted butter. Dip clams in liquid then in melted butter before eating.

OYSTERS ON THE HALF SHELL

Scrub shells clean under cold running water. Hold shell with deep half down. Insert a strong blunt oyster knife between the shells near the hinge. With a twisting motion, pry open. Sever the muscle which holds the shells together and the one holding the oyster to the shell. Retain as much juice as possible. Serve the oysters on their shells. Have shells embedded in finely crushed ice in shallow dishes. Garnish with lemon wedges. If desired, sink a small glass of Seafood Cocktail Sauce (page 123) in centre of each dish. Allow about 6 oysters per serving.

MEATS

Meat is an important food for good nutrition. Make sure you buy wisely, know how to store it and how to cook your various cuts of meat for optimum results.

BUYING

Recognize Quality—Meat should be firm, velvety and fine grained with streaks of fat through it. As yet, beef is the only meat which consumers can generally purchase by grade. Canada Choice (Red Brand) is the highest quality beef with a high proportion of meat to bone. It has a good covering of fat and the lean is well marbled with fat. Canada Good (Blue Brand) is a good quality beef with a slightly lower proportion of meat to bone and less fat than Red Brand.

Beef—Outside fat is creamy white and firm. The meat is a uniform rich red colour, varying from light red to dark red.

Veal—Outside fat is creamy white or tinged with pink. Young veal is greyish pink and older veal is pinkish brown.

Lamb—Outside fat is creamy white or slightly pink in colour. Mutton is more brittle and white in colour. The meat varies from a light pink to a dark pink and in mutton from light to dark red.

Pork—Outside fat should be firm and white and there should be a good proportion of lean to fat. The meat varies from greyish pink to a deep rose colour (older animals).

Amount to Buy—The number of servings per pound will vary depending on the amount of bone, fat, gristle, cooking loss and size of servings.

Approximate Number of Servings per Pound

Boneless roasts	— 3 to 4	Chops	— 2 to 3
Bone-in roasts	— 2 to 3	Stew meat (boneless)	— 3
Steaks	— 2 to 3	Stew meat (bone-in)	— 2
Ground meat	— 3 to 4	Kidneys	— 3
Cold cuts	— 8	Heart	— 3 to 4
Liver	— 3 to 4	Tongue	— 2

STORING

Remove store wrappings and wipe with a damp cloth. Place on a shallow plate and cover loosely with waxed paper. Store in refrigerator. Cured meats may be left in store wrappings.

To freeze: See Freezing Foods (page 194).

Approximate Storage Time in Refrigerator (40°F.)

Roasts—2 to 3 days
Steaks and chops—2 to 3 days
Ground meat—1 to 2 days
Liver, heart, kidney, etc.—1 day
Cured, smoked meats—1 week
Sausages—1 to 2 days

Wieners—2 to 3 days
Cooked meats—3 to 4 days
Leftover casseroles, stews—
  2 to 3 days
Jellied meats—1 to 2 days

COOKING

Tender cuts: roasting, panfrying (or panbroiling) and broiling is recommended.

Less tender cuts: pot roasting, braising and stewing is recommended

How to Roast—Roast meats in a moderate oven (325°F.). Place roast, fat side up, on a rack in an uncovered roasting pan in centre of oven. Insert meat thermometer, if used, in centre of meatiest part of roast so that the tip is not touching bone or fat. Baste occasionally during roasting. Season halfway through cooking. Roast to desired stage of doneness or until meat thermometer registers required internal temperature. DO NOT sear meat, cover pan or add water. Let roast stand at least 10 minutes to make carving easier. Make gravy from drippings in pan (see page 121).

Timetable for Roasting Meats at 325°F.

	Minutes per Pound		
	RARE	MEDIUM	WELL DONE
Beef	20 to 25 (130°F.-140°F.)*	25 to 30 (140°F.-150°F.)*	35 to 40 (150°F.-170°F.)*
Veal	—	—	35 to 40 (180°F.)*
Lamb	—	—	30 to 35 (180°F.)*
Pork **Fresh**	—	—	40 to 50 (185°F.)
Cured or Smoked	—	—	25 to 40 (170°F.)

*Indicates internal temperature of meat thermometer. Allow the longer times for lighter weight roasts and the shorter times for heavier roasts.

How to Panfry (or Panbroil)—Use a heavy frying pan and add a small amount of fat or fat cut from the meat. Snip fat edges of meat to prevent curling. Brown meat on both sides, over medium heat, cooking to desired doneness. DO NOT cover pan unless indicated in recipe and do not prick meat. Season only after browning, using salt, pepper and monosodium glutamate. If cooking fat meat, do not add fat. Pour off excess fat as it accumulates in pan.

BEEF CHART

RED BRAND ← *Officially graded beef is branded to indicate quality* → BLUE BRAND
indicates
"CHOICE"
grade.

indicates
"GOOD"
grade.

RETAIL CUTS   **WHOLESALE CUTS**   **DIAGRAM OF CUTTING**

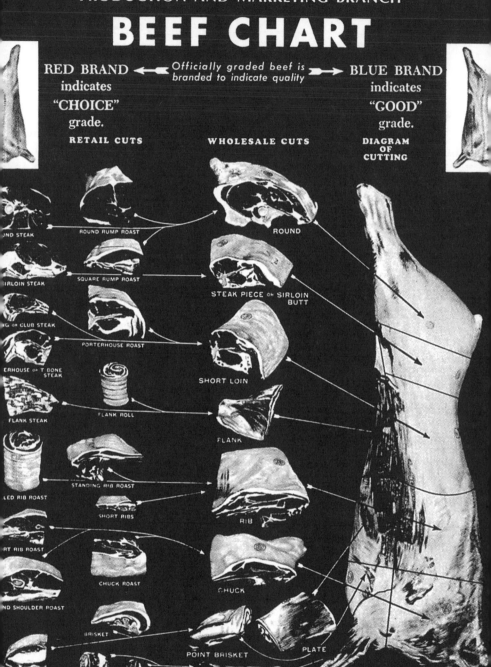

UND STEAK — ROUND RUMP ROAST — ROUND

SIRLOIN STEAK — SQUARE RUMP ROAST — STEAK PIECE or SIRLOIN BUTT

NG or CLUB STEAK — PORTERHOUSE ROAST — SHORT LOIN

ERHOUSE or T BONE STEAK — FLANK ROLL

FLANK STEAK — FLANK

LED RIB ROAST — STANDING RIB ROAST — RIB

RT RIB ROAST — SHORT RIBS — CHUCK

ND SHOULDER ROAST — CHUCK ROAST

BRISKET — POINT BRISKET — PLATE

RISKET POINT — SOUP MEAT — SOUP BONE — SHANK

CANADA DEPARTMENT OF AGRICULTURE
PRODUCTION AND MARKETING BRANCH
LAMB CHART

RETAIL CUTS   WHOLESALE CUTS   DIAGRAM OF CUTTING

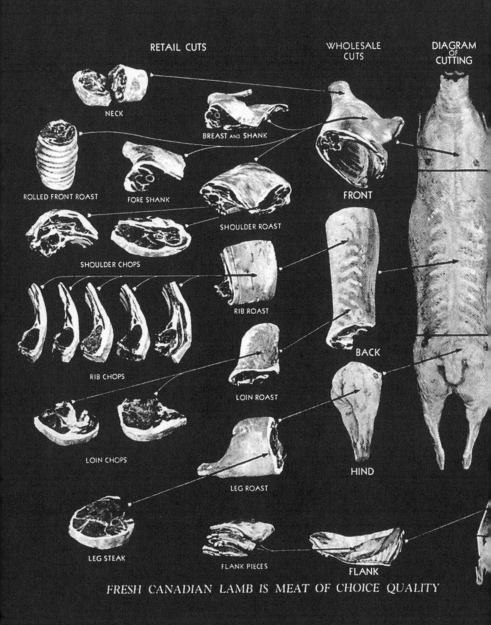

NECK

BREAST AND SHANK

ROLLED FRONT ROAST

FORE SHANK

SHOULDER ROAST

FRONT

SHOULDER CHOPS

RIB ROAST

RIB CHOPS

LOIN ROAST

BACK

LOIN CHOPS

LEG ROAST

HIND

LEG STEAK

FLANK PIECES

FLANK

FRESH CANADIAN LAMB IS MEAT OF CHOICE QUALITY

CANADA DEPARTMENT OF AGRICULTURE
PRODUCTION AND MARKETING BRANCH
PORK CHART

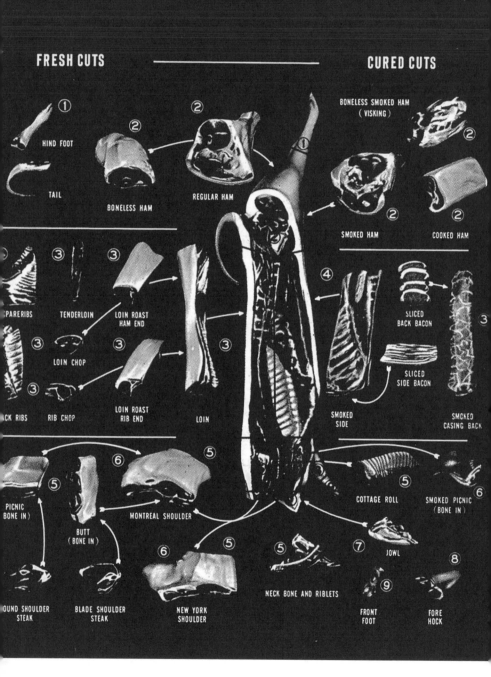

FRESH CUTS ——————— **CURED CUTS**

HIND FOOT

TAIL

BONELESS HAM

REGULAR HAM

BONELESS SMOKED HAM (VISKING)

SMOKED HAM

COOKED HAM

SPARERIBS

TENDERLOIN

LOIN ROAST HAM END

LOIN CHOP

CK RIBS

RIB CHOP

LOIN ROAST RIB END

LOIN

SLICED BACK BACON

SLICED SIDE BACON

SMOKED SIDE

SMOKED CASING BACK

PICNIC (BONE IN)

BUTT (BONE IN)

MONTREAL SHOULDER

COTTAGE ROLL

SMOKED PICNIC (BONE IN)

OUND SHOULDER STEAK

BLADE SHOULDER STEAK

NEW YORK SHOULDER

NECK BONE AND RIBLETS

JOWL

FRONT FOOT

FORE HOCK

How to Broil—Directions will vary with type of broiler used, thickness, kind of meat and degree of doneness desired. Preheat broiler and leave door slightly open. Place meat on cold rack of broiler pan at recommended distance from heat— usually 3 to 5 inches. Broil meat on one side until browned, season and do other side.

How to Pot Roast—Brown meat well on all sides in hot fat, in a heavy kettle or Dutch oven. Season well with salt, pepper and monosodium glutamate. Cool kettle slightly and slip a rack under meat. Add a small amount of water or soup stock— about 2 to 3 tablespoons. Cover tightly and cook over low heat on top of stove or in a moderate oven (325°F.) until tender and well done. Allow about 30 to 35 minutes per pound for bone-in roasts, and 40 to 45 minutes for boneless roasts. Add vegetables, if desired, during the last hour of cooking. Uncover oven cooked pot roast last half hour of cooking for better browning. Use pan juices to make gravy.

How to Braise—Score or pound the meat to break down coarse fibers. Season and flour meat and brown in hot fat in heavy frying pan. Add liquid, cover and cook slowly over low heat or in a moderate oven (325°F.) until tender and well done.

How to Stew—Trim off excess fat and gristle. Cut meat in 1″ cubes. Flour meat and brown in hot fat, in a heavy kettle or Dutch oven. Add seasonings and enough liquid (water or stock) to half cover the meat, stir well. Cover kettle tightly and simmer meat slowly over low heat until meat is tender. Add vegetables about 30 minutes before meat is done. For a thicker stew, add flour mixed with a little water. When Dumplings are to be served, see page 149 for full directions.

BEEF

SWISS STEAK

2 lbs. round steak (½″-¾″ thick)	1 small onion, sliced
1 teaspoon salt	2 cups tomato juice
⅛ teaspoon pepper	1 teaspoon Worcestershire Sauce
2 tablespoons Five Roses All-Purpose Flour	1 tablespoon chopped celery
	1 tablespoon chopped green pepper
2-3 tablespoons fat	¼ cup sliced mushrooms

Leave steak in one piece or cut into serving pieces. Season with salt and pepper; sprinkle with Five Roses Flour. Heat a heavy frying pan and melt the fat. Brown meat on both sides; brown onions. Add remaining ingredients; stir well. Cover and cook slowly on top of stove or bake in a moderate oven (325°F.) 1¼ to 1½ hours or until tender. Add more liquid if necessary, to keep meat from sticking.

Yield: 4 to 6 servings.

BARBECUED SHORT RIBS

3 lbs. short ribs of beef	1 clove garlic, minced
3 tablespoons fat	2¼ cups Barbecue Sauce (page 123)

Brown ribs in fat. Transfer meat and drippings to deep baking dish. Add garlic and Barbecue Sauce. Cover and bake in a moderate oven (350°F.) 1½ to 2 hours or until tender. Stir carefully after 1 hour. Remove excess fat, if necessary.

Yield: 6 servings.

BEEF STROGANOFF

¼ cup shortening
1½ cups sliced onions
½ lb. sliced mushrooms
1½ lbs. round or boneless chuck
    steak, sliced ¼" thick
2 tablespoons Five Roses
    All-purpose Flour

3 medium tomatoes, peeled
1½ teaspoons salt
⅛ teaspoon pepper
¼ teaspoon Worcestershire Sauce
½ cup sour cream

Sauté onions in shortening 10 minutes; add mushrooms, cover and continue cooking 5 more minutes. Remove onions and mushrooms. Cut meat into 1" strips; brown meat slowly and sprinkle with Five Roses Flour and stir until well blended. Cut tomatoes into bite-size pieces; add to meat along with seasonings. Cover and simmer very slowly for 1 hour, stirring occasionally. Add mushrooms, onions and sour cream; simmer again for ½ hour or until meat is tender. Serve with cooked noodles.

Yield: 5 to 6 servings.

MEATLOAF

1 egg, slightly beaten
1 tablespoon sweet relish
1 tablespoon ketchup or chili sauce
½ onion, grated
1 teaspoon salt

¼ teaspoon pepper
1 teaspoon parsley
½ teaspoon onion flakes
2½ lbs. ground beef
½ cup Oglivie Quick Oats

Combine slightly beaten egg with relish, ketchup, onion and seasonings. Add ground beef and Quick Oats; mix thoroughly. Pack into a 9" x 5" x 3" loaf pan. Bake in a moderate oven (350°F.) for 1 hour.

Yield: 6 to 8 servings.

MEATBALL KABOBS

1½ lbs. ground beef
1 cup fine bread crumbs
1 teaspoon salt
¼ teaspoon pepper
1 egg

Barbecue Sauce (page 123)
4 tomatoes
2 green peppers
16 small onions
2 tablespoons melted butter

Mix ground beef, bread crumbs, salt, pepper and egg together. Shape in 1" meatballs and fry over medium heat until brown and cooked. Marinate in Barbecue Sauce for 1 hour or longer. Wash tomatoes and green peppers; cut into bite-size pieces. Prepare onions and parboil 10 minutes. Thread Kabob skewers alternately with meat and vegetables, allowing 3 meatballs per skewer. Brush with melted butter. Place Kabobs on grill; barbecue, turning frequently until meat seems hot and vegetables begin to brown. (Or broil in oven 2-3 minutes.) Serve hot with remaining Barbecue Sauce.

Yield: 10 Kabobs.

Note: For a picnic, prepare everything ahead of time. Place meatballs and Barbecue Sauce in a large jar. Wrap prepared vegetables in Saran Wrap or aluminum foil.

LAMB

LAMB STEW WITH DUMPLINGS

1½ lbs. lean boneless shoulder
    lamb, cut in cubes
¼ cup Five Roses All-purpose Flour
2 tablespoons fat
3 cups water
2 teaspoons salt
¼ teaspoon pepper

4 carrots, chopped
3 small onions
3 small potatoes, halved
1 pkg. (12 oz.) frozen peas
2 tablespoons minced parsley
⅓ cup chopped green pepper

Flour meat and brown in fat in deep kettle. Add water, salt and pepper. Cover and simmer 1½ hours. Add carrots, onions and potatoes and cook until done—about 20 to 30 minutes. Add peas, parsley and green pepper and cook 5 minutes longer. Add more seasonings if necessary. Serve with Dumplings.

Yield: 6 to 8 servings.

DUMPLINGS

2 cups Five Roses All-purpose Flour
4 teaspoons baking powder
½ teaspoon salt

2 tablespoons shortening
1 cup milk

Stir Five Roses Flour, baking powder and salt together. Work in shortening with tips of fingers or pastry blender. Add milk gradually and mix with a fork to a soft dough. Drop spoonfuls of the dough onto hot stew mixture, allowing space for dumplings to rise. Cover pot closely. Boil hard for 12 to 14 minutes. Do not lift cover during cooking. Serve hot.

Yield: 6 to 8 servings.

LAMB CURRY

2 lbs. boneless stewing lamb,
    cut in 1″ cubes
1 cup finely chopped onion
2 tablespoons fat
1 tablespoon salt
⅛ teaspoon pepper
1 cup hot water
1 tablespoon parsley

¼ teaspoon thyme
1 clove garlic, minced (optional)
2 tablespoons Five Roses
    All-purpose Flour
1 tablespoon curry powder
¼ cup cold water
¼ cup seedless raisins
2 cups tart apples, sliced

Brown lamb and onion in fat in deep frying pan or skillet. Drain off any excess fat. Sprinkle lamb with salt and pepper. Add hot water, parsley, thyme and garlic. Cover and simmer 1 hour or until meat is tender. Combine Five Roses Flour and curry powder with cold water to make a smooth paste. Blend with a little of the hot cooking liquid, then gradually add to the meat mixture. Stir well. Add raisins and apples; cook 15 minutes longer. Serve with cooked rice.

Yield: 6 servings.

PORK

SAVOURY PORK CHOPS

8 pork chops	1 tablespoon sugar
Cooking fat	¼ teaspoon sage
2 tomatoes, cut in ¼'s	½ teaspoon salt
2 garlic cloves, minced (optional)	⅛ teaspoon pepper
1 green pepper, thinly sliced	½ cup sliced black olives
1 medium-size onion, thinly sliced	2 tablespoons chopped parsley

Brown pork chops in hot fat. Add tomatoes, garlic, green pepper, onion, sugar, sage, salt and pepper. Cover and cook over medium heat 25 to 30 minutes or until pork chops are done. Add olives and parsley; cook 10 more minutes.

Yield: 4 servings.

STUFFED SPARERIBS

4 tablespoons butter or drippings	1 teaspoon salt
1 cup chopped onion	1 cup water
1 cup chopped celery	2 cups tomato sauce
4 cups soft bread cubes	2 lbs. spareribs
⅛ teaspoon pepper	

Sauté onion in butter until golden brown. Stir in celery, bread cubes, salt, pepper and water. Place dressing in a baking pan and top with spareribs; cover with tomato sauce. Bake uncovered in a moderate oven (350°F.) 1½ to 2 hours.

Yield: 4 servings.

BAKED GLAZED HAM

Bake ham fat-side up in roasting pan in a moderate oven (325°F.) 25 to 40 minutes per pound or until meat thermometer registers 170°F. Half an hour before cooking time is up, remove ham from oven and pour off fat drippings. Score fat surface in diamond shapes, cutting only ¼" deep. Stud with whole cloves. Spoon one of the following glazes over the ham until evenly coated. Return to oven and continue baking the remaining half-hour, brushing occasionally with remaining glaze.

Peach Glaze

1 cup brown sugar	½ teaspoon ground cloves
⅓ cup syrup from canned peaches	¼ teaspoon cinnamon
3 tablespoons white vinegar	

Mix all ingredients together.

Yield: 1 cup.

Ham Glaze

⅓ cup molasses	2 tablespoons ham drippings
⅓ cup prepared mustard	

Mix all ingredients together.

Yield: ⅔ cup.

VEAL

BREADED VEAL CUTLETS

2 lbs. veal cutlets, ½" thick
Salt and pepper
½ cup Five Roses All-purpose Flour
1 egg

1 tablespoon water
½-¾ cup dry bread crumbs
¼ cup fat, melted

Cut cutlets into serving pieces; sprinkle with salt and pepper, then roll in Five Roses Flour. Beat egg slightly with water; dip floured cutlets into egg, then roll in crumbs. Chill ½ hour; sauté slowly in melted fat until well browned and tender, allowing 15 minutes for each side.

Yield: 4 to 6 servings.

VEAL PAPRIKA

2 lbs. veal shoulder chops, ½" thick
2 tablespoons fat
Salt and pepper
¼ teaspoon thyme

¼ teaspoon marjoram
1 cup commercial sour cream
½ cup milk
1 teaspoon paprika

Brown veal chops in hot fat in deep frying pan; season with salt, pepper, thyme and marjoram. Mix sour cream and milk and pour over chops. Sprinkle with paprika. Cover closely and cook slowly, 18 to 20 minutes each side.

Yield: 5 to 6 servings.

VEAL SCALLOPINI

1½-2 lbs. veal cutlets
1 cup French Dressing
1 small onion, sliced
2 tablespoons hot fat
Salt and pepper
2 tablespoons Five Roses
   All-purpose Flour

2 tablespoons chopped green pepper
1½ cups consomme or chicken broth
5 to 6 sliced olives
½ lb. sautéed mushrooms
2 tablespoons chopped parsley

Flatten veal cutlets and marinate in French Dressing for 15 minutes. Brown meat and sliced onion in hot fat in deep frying pan or skillet. Season with salt and pepper. Sprinkle both sides of meat with Five Roses Flour and brown again slightly. Add chopped green pepper and consomme; stir well. Cover closely and cook slowly 18 to 20 minutes on each side. Add sliced olives, mushrooms and parsley just before serving.

Yield: 5 to 6 servings.

Many people find the Five Roses Guide to Good Cooking an excellent shower gift for the bride-to-be. Additional copies of this cook book may be obtained by clipping the coupons on pages 3 and 4.

VARIETY MEATS

Liver, Heart, Kidney, Sweetbreads, Brains and Tongue

These meats are perishable, spoil more quickly than other kinds. Storage time in refrigerator is 1 day, therefore cook promptly.

LIVER

Liver is a tender meat but tenderness and flavour vary in the different types. Beef and pork liver will have a milder flavour if covered with milk and allowed to soak for 2 hours in refrigerator before cooking. Allow ¼ to ⅓ pound per serving.

TO PREPARE

Wipe liver well. Remove skin by inserting a sharp knife under it and pulling or scraping the skin away from the meat. Carefully cut out tubes with sharp pointed scissors. If liver is to be ground for liver loaf, scald it for 5 minutes in boiling water to make grinding easier.

Panfry—for beef, veal, pork, lamb liver. Use ¼″ to ½″ slices. Season and flour liver slices. Brown in a small amount of fat for 1 minute over high heat. Turn and cook over moderate heat—2 to 3 minutes on each side. After browning, partly cover to make liver more juicy.

Broil—for calf or baby beef liver. Use ¼″ to ½″ slices. Brush liver slices with melted fat. Place 3″ from heat in pre-heated broiler unit. Broil 4 to 5 minutes each side.

CALF'S LIVER CREOLE

3 tablespoons butter
1 medium-size onion, sliced
2 tablespoons chopped green pepper
2 cups canned tomatoes
1 tablespoon chopped pimiento
½ cup chopped mushrooms

1 clove garlic (optional)
1 teaspoon salt
½ teaspoon pepper
6 slices calf's liver
Five Roses All-purpose Flour
Melted fat or cooking oil

Melt butter; add onion and green pepper and sauté until golden brown—about 10 minutes. Add tomatoes, pimiento, mushrooms, garlic, salt and pepper. Cook slowly for 1 hour; remove garlic clove. Dredge liver with Five Roses Flour. Panfry in melted fat until cooked. Place on hot platter; cover with hot sauce.

Yield: 4 to 6 servings.

BRAISED LIVER

1 lb. calf's liver	2 medium onions, chopped
½ teaspoon salt	1 cup finely chopped celery
⅛ teaspoon pepper	2 cups finely chopped carrots
¼ cup Five Roses All-purpose Flour	1 can tomato soup
4 tablespoons shortening	

Cut liver in 2″ squares; sprinkle with salt and pepper, then roll in Five Roses Flour. Melt the shortening in a large skillet and brown the liver pieces. Place liver in a 1½ quart casserole or 8″ square baking dish. Brown the chopped vegetables in the same fat and place on top of the liver; top with the tomato soup. Cover the casserole and bake in a moderate oven (375°F.) for 45 minutes; uncover and continue baking 15 more minutes.

Yield: 4 servings.

LIVER LOAF WITH PAN GRAVY

1½ lbs. beef liver	2 eggs, slightly beaten
1½ cups boiling water	1 teaspoon salt
2 slices salt pork, ¼″ thick	¼ teaspoon pepper
1 small onion, chopped	2 tablespoons Five Roses
¼ cup chopped parsley	All-purpose Flour
2 cups soft bread crumbs	1½ cups cold water

Rinse liver, cover with boiling water and let stand 10 minutes; drain. Grind liver and salt pork together. Add onion, parsley, bread crumbs, eggs, salt and pepper; mix together. Press into an 8″ x 4″ loaf pan. Bake in a moderate oven (350°F.) 1 hour or until browned. Remove liver loaf to hot platter, leave drippings in pan. Mix Five Roses Flour with a small amount of the cold water; stir into drippings and brown. Add remaining water gradually and cook 5 minutes, until thickened; season and pour over loaf.

Yield: 6 servings.

KIDNEY

Kidneys vary in flavour and tenderness and all are not cooked the same way.

TO PREPARE

Remove the membrane and cut lobes away from the fat and tubes with sharp pointed scissors. Cut kidneys crosswise in ¼″ slices, ½″ slices or pieces. They may be cut in half lengthwise for panfrying or broiling. Beef and pork kidneys have a milder flavour if they are covered with cold salted water and allowed to soak for 1 hour in the refrigerator. Brown only a small amount at a time for best colour. Kidney is well done when the red colour has disappeared in the centre. Do not overcook or it will become tough. Allow ⅓ pound per person.

Panfry—for veal, lamb, pork kidney. Brown in small amount of fat over high heat 1 to 2 minutes. Continue cooking over medium heat, turning often.
3 to 5 minutes for ¼″ or ½″ slices.
7 to 9 minutes for halved kidneys.

Broil—for pork, veal, lamb kidney. To prevent halved kidneys from curling, run a skewer through them. Place on cold rack of broiler pan so that kidneys are 3" from heat. Brush with melted fat. Broil.

3 to 4 minutes for ¼" or ½" slices.
5 to 7 minutes for halved kidneys.

Braise—for beef, pork kidney (cut ¼" or ½" slices). Season and flour kidney. Brown in a small amount of fat over high heat 1 to 2 minutes. Add liquid (water or tomato juice)—about ⅔ cup per pound of kidney. Cover tightly and cook slowly on top of stove or in a moderate oven (325°F.) 35 to 40 minutes.

STEAK AND KIDNEY STEW OR PIE

1½ lbs. cubed stewing beef	3 cups boiling water or stock
¾ lb. beef kidney, cut in pieces	1 bay leaf
Five Roses All-purpose Flour	1 cup diced carrots
Salt and pepper	1 cup chopped celery
3 tablespoons butter	½ cup sliced mushrooms (optional)
1⅓ cups chopped onion	½ pastry recipe (for pie)

Prepare beef and kidney; dredge in Five Roses Flour, seasoned with salt and pepper. Melt butter; add onions and sauté until golden. Remove onions and add stewing beef and brown. Return onions to pan. Add boiling water or stock; cover and simmer 2 hours—or until tender. Brown kidneys and add with bay leaf, carrots, celery and mushrooms last 30 minutes of cooking. If necessary, thicken with Five Roses Flour and season with salt and pepper. Remove bay leaf before serving.

Yield: 6 to 8 servings.

Pie: Cook stew as above and place in deep baking dish (1½ quarts). Cover with pastry or tea biscuit dough. Bake at 400°F. for 20 minutes or until topping is done. Make slits in pastry to allow steam to escape.

HEART

Hearts should be plump and well rounded in appearance, with a smooth shiny finish. All types of heart (beef, veal, pork and lamb) require long cooking at a low temperature.

TO PREPARE

Wash heart thoroughly and wipe with a damp cloth. Trim off coarse fibers, tubes and excess fat. Allow ¼ to ⅓ pound per serving.

BAKED STUFFED HEART

Trim hearts, as directed, and trim out heart cavity. Season cavity with salt and pepper. Fill with well seasoned bread stuffing. Fasten with skewers and lace with string. Place suet or fat trimmings over surface. Place on rack in a shallow pan and bake in a moderate oven (325°F.). Baste several times during cooking.

Beef (3 to 4 pounds)—2½ to 3 hours	Pork (½ to ¾ pound) —2 to 2½ hours
Veal (¾ to 1 pound) —1½ to 2 hours	Lamb (¼ to ⅓ pound)—1 to 1¼ hours

For 6 servings use: 1 beef heart, or 2 or 3 veal hearts, or 3 pork hearts, or 6 lamb hearts.

STUFFING FOR HEART

2 slices bacon	1 egg, beaten
2 tablespoons chopped onion	½ teaspoon salt
4 slices day-old bread	Few grains pepper

Brown bacon; remove from pan and chop finely. Sauté chopped onion in hot bacon fat until golden. Break bread into coarse crumbs and add to onion with beaten egg, salt, pepper and chopped bacon. Mix well.

Yield: Approximately 1 cup.

STEWED CALF'S HEART

2 calf's hearts	2 tablespoons Five Roses
Water	All-purpose Flour
1 bay leaf	2 tablespoons butter
1 teaspoon salt	¼ lemon, thinly sliced
⅛ teaspoon pepper	

Prepare hearts as directed. Place in boiling water, using just enough to cover; simmer 1½ hours. Remove from water and cut off any remaining fat; set aside to cool. Cut lean portions of heart in small pieces and place in saucepan. Add 2½ cups water, bay leaf, salt and pepper; simmer 10 minutes. Rub Five Roses Flour and butter together; add to heart with sliced lemon. Stir thoroughly and cook 5 minutes. Serve hot.

Yield: 6 servings.

TONGUE

Tongue may be from beef, veal, lamb or pork and may be fresh, pickled, corned or smoked.

TO PREPARE

Wash tongue thoroughly in warm water. Smoked or pickled tongue should be soaked in cold water for 2 hours before cooking.

TO COOK

Tongue should be cooked at a simmering temperature until tender. When tongue is tender, remove skin, excess fat, glands and bones from thick end of tongue while still hot. Strain cooking liquid and reheat tongue in cooking liquid if it is to be served hot. Allow about ½ pound per person.

TONGUE WITH RAISIN SAUCE

1 beef tongue	1 cup raisins
1 cup cider vinegar	1 lemon, thinly sliced
1 cup dark brown sugar	2 dozen whole cloves

Simmer tongue, in enough water to just cover, for 4-5 hours or until tender. Remove from water and remove skin while still hot (as directed). Place tongue in baking pan. Prepare sauce by combining remaining ingredients; pour over tongue. Bake in a moderate oven (375°F.) 40 minutes, basting with the sauce several times.

Yield: 6 to 8 servings, depending on size of tongue.

JELLIED TONGUE

1 tongue (beef, veal, lamb or pork)	1 tablespoon gelatin
Water	¼ cup cold water
1 tablespoon white vinegar	

Simmer tongue, in enough water to cover, for 4-5 hours or until tender. Remove skin while still hot. Strain cooking liquid and re-heat 4 cups; add vinegar. Soften gelatin in ¼ cup cold water and add to boiling liquid. Press whole or chopped tongue into a cold wet 1½ quart mould; cover with liquid. Chill until set. Unmould and cut in slices to serve.

SWEETBREADS AND BRAINS

Sweetbreads are from the thymus gland of young beef and calves and are pinkish white. Brains are pinkish grey, very tender, delicately flavoured. Both are considered a great delicacy.

TO PREPARE

Since they are very perishable, they are usually sold frozen. After thawing, wash and soak them for 30 minutes in cold, salted water—using enough to just cover. Drain. Cover with hot, salted water and 1 tablespoon vinegar. Simmer 15 minutes; drain. Cover with cold water. When cool, remove membrane and fat and dry. Panfry or broil. Allow ½ pound per person for Sweetbreads. Allow ¼ to ½ pound per person for Brains.

Panfry—Cook slowly in a small amount of melted butter. Turn often. If desired, crumb before frying—coat with flour, dip in egg, then roll in crumbs.

Sweetbreads—10 to 12 minutes

Brains   —13 to 16 minutes

Broil—Place on cold rack of broiler pan so that sweetbreads or brains are 6″ from heat. Season and brush with melted butter. Allow 6 to 8 minutes for each side. If desired, wrap in bacon and secure with toothpick. Then broil. Serve with Cream Sauce (page 119) or Tomato Sauce (page 120) and garnish with lemon wedges.

SWEETBREADS (OR BRAINS) VICTORIA

1 pair sweetbreads	2 tablespoons butter
2 teaspoons lemon juice	2 tablespoons Five Roses
½ teaspoon salt	All-purpose Flour
⅛ teaspoon pepper	1 cup milk
Few grains nutmeg	1 egg yolk
1 teaspoon chopped parsley	Patty shells

Parboil sweetbreads as directed. Remove membranes and cut into small pieces. Add lemon juice, salt, pepper, nutmeg and parsley. Melt butter, slowly stir in Five Roses Flour. Add milk gradually, stirring until sauce is thickened and smooth. Remove from heat and stir in egg yolk. Add seasoned sweetbreads; mix lightly. Serve in patty shells or on toast.

Yield: 4 to 6 servings.

POULTRY

Domestic fowl such as chicken, turkey, duck and goose are classified under poultry.

BUYING

Recognize Quality—Look for the grade mark. Canada Grade A (Red) is the best quality. Canada Grade B (Blue) is second in quality. These are not as well fatted and fleshed as Grade A and may have a few tears in the skin and a few pinfeathers. Poultry is sold either fresh or frozen, although frozen is more common.

Fresh Poultry—available in two forms:
1. Eviscerated (sometimes called Oven-Ready or Ready-to-Cook) refers to poultry which has had its feathers, head, feet and viscera removed. The giblets and neck may be enclosed in the bird.
2. Dressed refers to poultry that has been slaughtered, bled and has had its feathers removed but still has its feet, head and viscera.

Frozen Poultry—is eviscerated. All poultry should be thawed completely before cooking except for stewing. Thawed poultry is cooked the same way as fresh. DO NOT REFREEZE poultry after it has thawed. For more information on frozen poultry, see page 194.

STORING

Remove any pinfeathers with tweezers and any body hair by singeing over a low gas flame or candle. Remove any bits of lung, windpipe, etc. that may have been left in. Pull out any large leg tendons. Unwrap the giblets and wash carefully. Wipe the bird inside and out with a damp cloth or rinse well in cold water and dry thoroughly. Wrap loosely in waxed paper and store in refrigerator. DO NOT STORE STUFFED POULTRY. Stuff poultry only **just before** roasting.

Approximate storage time in refrigerator (40°F.)

Fresh poultry — 2 to 3 days.
Thawed poultry — up to 24 hours.
Cooked poultry — 3 to 4 days (remove stuffing and store separately).

TO EVISCERATE

Make an incision lengthwise from the tail piece to the breast bone. Loosen and remove entrails, giblets, kidneys and lungs. Be careful not to break the small green gall bladder. Check and remove all the lung tissue along the back bone. Loosen (or slit) the skin at the neck and remove crop and windpipe. Cut off neck close to body but leave neck skin intact. Cut out oil sac above the tail, being careful not to break it. Wash the bird thoroughly under cold running water, then pat dry with a cloth.

Giblets—Remove thin membrane, arteries, veins and blood around heart. Cut fat and membrane from gizzard and make a long gash along edge through thickest part, cutting it as far as inner greyish lining and being careful not to pierce it. Pull gizzard open and discard inner lining. Separate gall bladder carefully from liver, removing any liver that has a greenish tinge. Wash giblets thoroughly and use in stuffing, gravy or as desired.

COOKING

Roasted poultry may be stuffed or unstuffed. Stuff **just before roasting;** do not store with stuffing in.

How to stuff: Allow about ½ to ¾ cup stuffing for each pound of eviscerated bird (see page 124). Sprinkle inside of bird with salt. Fill neck cavity with stuffing but do not pack tight as stuffing swells. Fold neck skin over opening and fasten to back with a metal skewer. Fold wing tips (chicken and turkey) over back to anchor the neck skin. Fill body cavity with stuffing. Close opening with thread or metal skewers.

How to truss: Chicken or Turkey—Lie bird on its back, tie drumsticks to tail with a string. Bring string up firmly between drumsticks and body, then over wing tips to centre back and tie securely.

Duck or Goose—Tie a string around drumstick ends, pulling them close to body.

CLASSIFICATION	EVISCERATED WEIGHT	AMOUNT TO BUY (PER SERVING)	HOW TO COOK
Chicken broilers and fryers	up to 4 lbs.	¾ to 1 lb.	Broil-bake, fry or barbecue
Chicken roasters	over 4 lbs.	¾ to 1 lb.	Roast
Chicken capons	5 to 8 lbs.	¾ lb.	Roast
Fowl (mature hens)	3 lbs. and over	¾ lb.	Braise, stew, oven-brown or pressure-cook
Turkey broilers	up to 10 lbs.	¾ to 1 lb.	Broil-bake, roast or barbecue
Young turkeys	10 to 12 lbs. over 12 lbs.	¾ to 1 lb. ½ to ¾ lb.	Roast
Mature turkeys	10 to 12 lbs. over 12 lbs.	¾ to 1 lb. ½ to ¾ lb.	Roast, braise or oven-brown
Young ducks	4 to 6 lbs.	1 to 1¼ lbs.	Roast or braise
Young geese	9 to 12 lbs.	¾ to 1 lb.	Roast

CHICKEN

How to Roast—Place stuffed and trussed chicken, breast side up, on a rack in a shallow roasting pan. Brush skin all over with butter or vegetable oil. Sprinkle with salt and pepper. **Do not add water.** If desired, cover loosely with aluminum foil (dull side out). To brown the chicken, remove foil ½ hour before roasting time is up. Roast in a moderate oven (325°F.) according to the following timetable. Baste occasionally. For unstuffed chicken, deduct 5 minutes per pound. See test for doneness.

TIMETABLE FOR ROASTING CHICKEN AT 325°F.

EVISCERATED WEIGHT	ROASTING TIME (STUFFED BIRD)
4 to 5 lbs.	2¾ to 3½ hours
5 to 6 lbs.	3½ to 4½ hours
6 to 7 lbs.	4½ to 5 hours

Timetable approximates 41 to 42 minutes per pound for all weights.

For unstuffed chicken, deduct 5 minutes per pound.

Test for doneness—Drumstick should twist easily. If using a meat thermometer, insert it into thickest part of thigh muscle (do not touch bone). When chicken is cooked, thermometer reads 190°F.

How to Broil-bake—Chicken (and turkey) pieces often become dry before completely cooked. To avoid this, partially cook by broiling and finish by baking. Brush chicken with butter or vegetable oil; sprinkle with salt and pepper. Place skin-side down in a greased shallow pan about 6″ to 8″ from heating unit. Broil until brown—about 10 minutes. Turn to do other side—about 5 minutes. Bake at 325°F. until tender.

How to Panfry—Season Five Roses Flour (about ¼ cup per pound of chicken) with salt and pepper. Coat chicken pieces evenly. Cook chicken, turning once or twice, in hot melted fat or oil in a heavy frying pan until lightly browned—about 15 minutes. Reduce heat, cover pan tightly and cook slowly for another 15 or 20 minutes.

How to Ovenfry—Flour and lightly brown chicken pieces as in the panfry method. Arrange pieces skin-side up, in a single layer, in a shallow baking pan. For each pound of chicken, spoon a mixture of 1 tablespoon of melted butter and 1 tablespoon broth. (Use chicken broth or chicken bouillon cube dissolved in water.) Bake in a moderate oven (350°F.) turning once or twice to crisp evenly, until chicken is tender—about 1 hour.

How to Deep Fry—Coat raw chicken pieces with seasoned flour (as for panfried chicken). Dip in egg beaten with water—2 teaspoons per egg. Roll in fine bread crumbs or dip in batter (page 169). Heat 1 quart vegetable oil in deep fryer to 375°F. Dip frying basket into fat first before adding chicken. This prevents the chicken from sticking to it. Lower chicken, a few pieces at a time into pre-heated fat. Do not overcrowd frying basket. Cook until tender—15 to 20 minutes. Temperature will drop to 325°F. when chicken is added, so continue cooking at this temperature. Precooked chicken is prepared the same way for frying as raw chicken. Time of frying is 5 minutes. Precook by placing chicken in boiling salted water; reduce heat and simmer until tender—about 30 to 40 minutes.

Note: For batter-coated chicken, use broilers weighing less than 2 pounds. Otherwise the batter will be too brown before the chicken is cooked. If larger, precook first.

How to Barbecue—Brush grill and chicken pieces with butter or vegetable oil. Sprinkle chicken with salt and pepper. Place skin-side down on grill—about 3″ from fire—brown for 3 minutes; turn and brown other side. Raise grill to 4″ to 6″ from fire and continue to barbecue until chicken is tender—about 20 to 45 minutes. Turn frequently and baste each time with butter, oil or French Dressing. With Barbecue Sauce—do not brush on until 7 or 8 minutes before chicken is done. This helps to avoid scorching. See page 123 for recipe.

CURRY OF FRIED CHICKEN

1 boiling chicken (3 to 4 lbs.)	¼ cup butter
½ cup Five Roses All-purpose Flour	2 cups chopped tart apples
2 teaspoons salt	1 small onion, chopped
1 teaspoon curry powder	½ cup shredded coconut
½ teaspoon paprika	2 cups chicken broth or water
¼ teaspoon ginger	½ cup light cream
¼ teaspoon pepper	

Cut chicken into serving pieces and wipe dry. Blend Five Roses Flour and seasonings together; pour into small paper bag. Place one piece of chicken at a time into bag and shake vigorously until well coated. Continue process until all pieces are coated. Melt butter in large skillet. Add chicken pieces and brown evenly. Lower heat to medium and cover. Cook gently for 30 minutes until chicken is tender. Remove chicken and set aside in a warm place. Prepare gravy as follows: add apples, onion and coconut to skillet drippings; cook 5 minutes. Meanwhile, blend ¼ cup of the seasoned Five Roses Flour and chicken broth; stir until smooth. Add to ingredients in skillet; stir well and add cream. Cook until thickened, stirring constantly—about 5 minutes. Replace chicken pieces and heat thoroughly. Serve piping hot with steamed rice.

Yield: 6 servings.

CHICKEN CACCIATORA

1 cut-up chicken (3 to 4 lbs.)	1 teaspoon salt
¼ cup Five Roses All-purpose Flour	1 teaspoon oregano
¼ cup olive oil	½ teaspoon celery seed
2 medium-size onions, sliced	¼ teaspoon pepper
1 clove garlic, minced	1 bay leaf
2½ cups canned tomatoes	¼ cup dry white wine (optional)
1 can (5½-oz.) tomato sauce	

Coat chicken pieces with Five Roses Flour; brown in olive oil. Remove chicken from skillet. Add onions and garlic; sauté until tender but not brown. Combine remaining ingredients (except wine). Return chicken to skillet and pour sauce on top. Cover and simmer 45 minutes; stir in wine, if used. Cook uncovered, turning chicken occasionally, about 20 minutes or until chicken is tender and sauce is thick. Skim off excess fat and remove bay leaf. Serve with rice or noodles.

Yield: 4 to 6 servings.

BOILED CHICKEN

1 chicken or fowl (4 to 5 lbs.)	2 celery tops
Boiling water	½ teaspoon salt
1 large onion, sliced	1 bay leaf

Leave chicken whole or cut in pieces; place in large kettle. Half cover with boiling water; add onion, celery tops and seasonings. Cover and simmer until tender—2 to 3 hours. Remove chicken from broth. Remove bay leaf. Cool chicken and broth before storing in refrigerator. To skim fat off broth, see page 116. Use as cold sliced chicken or in many recipes calling for cooked chicken.

Yield: 4 to 6 servings or 4 cups chopped.

TURKEY

Cooked in much the same way as chicken. Most recipes are interchangeable.

How to Roast—Turkey is roasted in the same way as chicken. See previous pages.

TIMETABLE FOR ROASTING TURKEY AT 325°F.	
EVISCERATED WEIGHT	ROASTING TIME (STUFFED BIRD)
6 to 8 lbs.	3 to 4 hours (30 minutes per lb.)
8 to 10 lbs.	4 to 5 hours (27-30 minutes per lb.)
10 to 16 lbs.	5 to 6 hours (22½-27 minutes per lb.)
18 to 22 lbs.	7 to 8½ hours (22½ minutes per lb.)

For unstuffed bird, deduct 5 minutes per pound.

TURKEY PIE

1 pastry recipe (double crust)	½ cup milk
1 cup thinly sliced onions	2 cups chopped, cooked turkey or
1 tablespoon chopped green pepper	chicken
2 tablespoons butter or margarine	¾ cup cooked vegetables
1 can (10 oz.) condensed cream of	½ teaspoon salt
mushroom soup	Few grains pepper

Prepare pastry and line a deep 9″ pie plate; reserve some for top crust. Sauté onions and green pepper in butter until tender. Add remaining ingredients. Pour mixture into pie shell. Roll out top crust; make slits to allow steam to escape. Place over pie and seal edges. Flute, if desired. Bake in a moderately hot oven (425°F.) 20-25 minutes or until pastry is done.

Yield: 6 servings.

Country Style Turkey Pie

Make filling as above. Pour into an 8″ square baking dish. Prepare Tea Biscuit dough (page 32) for topping; roll ½″ thick. Cut in small rounds and place close together to cover pie. Bake in a hot oven (450°F.) 15-20 minutes or until tea biscuits are done.

Yield: 6 servings.

QUICK TURKEY À LA KING

2 tablespoons butter
¼ cup chopped green pepper
1 tablespoon Five Roses All-purpose Flour
1 cup milk

1 can (10 oz.) condensed cream of mushroom soup
2 cups chopped, cooked turkey or chicken
Salt and pepper to taste
¼ cup chopped pimiento

Sauté green pepper in butter until tender. Remove green pepper; blend in Five Roses Flour, then slowly stir in milk. Add cream of mushroom soup; heat slowly, stirring constantly. Add remaining ingredients and green pepper; cook 10 minutes longer. Serve on patty shells, toast, boiled rice or noodles.

Yield: 5 to 6 servings.

GOOSE

Prepare goose for roasting as indicated in the previous pages. It may be roasted stuffed or unstuffed.

How to Roast—Prick the skin all over with a table fork. Place goose, breast-side down, on a rack in a shallow roasting pan. Sprinkle with salt. Do not add water. Roast for 1 hour in a moderate oven (325°F.). Turn goose breast up and finish roasting according to timetable, pricking the skin once or twice. **Do not baste.** Remove excess fat as it accumulates in the pan. As bird begins to brown, cover loosely with aluminum foil, removing it near end of cooking time so that skin will be crisp. Drumstick should twist easily when done. Serve with gravy (page 121). Garnish with Cinnamon Apples.

Roasting time at 325°F. — 22½ to 30 minutes per lb.

8 to 12 lbs. goose — about 3 to 5 hours.

CINNAMON APPLES
(An attractive garnish for Roast Goose)

1 cup apple cider
1 cup sugar
1 teaspoon cinnamon

6 to 10 small, tart apples
6 to 10 teaspoons currant jelly
Few sprigs of parsley

Combine cider and sugar; bring to boiling point and simmer 5 minutes. Add cinnamon. Pare and core apples; place in skillet. Pour sauce over apples and cook over medium heat, basting from time to time, until apples are tender—about 25 minutes. Drop a spoonful of jelly in centre of each apple. Arrange apples around goose on platter with sprigs of parsley. Pour remaining sauce over goose.

Yield: Enough for 10 small apples. Use only number of apples desired.

DUCK

Because it has more fat, duck should be roasted in a moderate oven (350°F.) or at 425°F. for 20 minutes and then at 350°F. for remaining cooking time. Prepare duck for roasting as indicated on the previous pages. It may be stuffed or unstuffed.

How to roast at 350°F.—Prick skin all over with a table fork. Place duck, breast-side down, on a rack in a shallow roasting pan. Sprinkle with salt. Roast uncovered for 45 minutes. Do not add water or fat. Turn duck breast up and roast until tender —about 1¾ hours. Remove excess fat as it accumulates in pan—baste sparingly once and prick the skin twice more. When tender, drumstick should twist easily.

Roasting time —30 to 36 minutes per lb.

4 to 5 lbs. duck —about 2½ hours.

How to Roast at 425°F. and 350°F.—Prepare duck for roasting as mentioned above except start with breast-side up. Roast at 425°F. for 10 minutes; turn breast-side down and roast 10 minutes longer. Reduce heat to 350°F. and continue cooking for 25 minutes; turn breast-side up for remainder of cooking time. Serve with gravy (page 121).

Roasting time —30 to 36 minutes per lb.

4 to 5 lbs. duck —about 2½ hours.

ROAST DUCK À L'ORANGE

1 duck (about 5 lbs.)	½ cup water
½ teaspoon salt	1 cup orange juice
½ teaspoon curry	2 teaspoons cognac (optional)
Rind of 2 oranges	½ cup dry white wine or apple juice
2 peeled apples, cut up	1 tablespoon cornstarch
2 oranges, sliced	1 tablespoon water

Prick skin of duck all over. Mix salt, curry, rind of 1 orange and apples together; place in cavity of duck. Place duck, breast-side up on rack in shallow roasting pan. Arrange a few orange slices on duck and put remainder in pan. Add water and roast at 425°F. for 20 minutes, turning twice. Reduce temperature to 350°F. and roast for 45 minutes; turn and continue cooking until done— about 1 hour. Remove excess fat as it accumulates in pan—baste sparingly. At end of cooking, remove duck and place on hot platter; set aside. Remove orange rind mixture from duck. Strain juice in pan and pour back ½ cup; place pan on top of stove over medium heat. Add orange juice, orange slices from pan, cognac, dry white wine or apple juice, and rind of 1 orange. Bring to boiling point, stirring constantly. Combine cornstarch and water to make a paste. Slowly add to the sauce, stirring constantly until thickened. Serve hot with duck. Garnish with fresh orange slices, if desired.

Yield: 4 to 5 servings.

Note: If sauce is too strong in flavour, dilute with boiling water.

We appreciate the fact that from time to time certain problems may arise with regard to home cooking and baking. For this reason we are pleased to remind you that our Five Roses Kitchens will always be most pleased to help you. Address all inquiries to:

PAULINE HARVEY, *Director*
FIVE ROSES KITCHENS
BOX 6089
MONTREAL, P.Q.

WILD GAME COOKERY

All recipes in this chapter courtesy of Edith Adams' Cottage, The Vancouver Sun.

Wild game, properly prepared and cooked, is truly gourmet fare. Follow the few basic rules for birds and wild game and your hunter's labours will be truly rewarded.

WILD BIRDS
(Duck, Geese, Partridge, Quail, Grouse, Pheasant)

1. Clean immediately after shooting. See Poultry (page 157).

2. Pluck as soon as convenient.

3. Refrigerate 2 to 3 days before cooking or freezing.

4. Strong flavoured birds such as Mallards, which may have a "fishy" taste, should be soaked in a marinade or milk or overnight in salted water.

5. Follow general directions for cooking duck and goose (page 162).

6. Other game birds may be prepared and cooked as for chicken.

ROAST PARTRIDGE

4 small partridges	¾ cup chicken broth, fresh or
4 slices bacon (about 2″ long)	canned but clear
Salt and pepper	¾ cup commercial sour cream
4 thin slices lemon, seeded	Bread Sauce (page 121)

Clean partridges very carefully and tie a slice of bacon over the breast of each. Rub partridges, inside and out, with salt and pepper; place a slice of lemon inside. Arrange in buttered baking dish with broth and roast in moderate oven (350°- 375°F.) 25 to 30 minutes, basting frequently. When birds and gravy are a rich brown, pour the sour cream over them. Let cream bubble up in the pan for one minute, basting twice. Serve with the gravy from the pan, Bread Sauce and a side dish of tart jelly.

Yield: 4 servings.

PARTRIDGE STEW

1 large partridge	4 onions, sliced
2 tablespoons butter	Salt and pepper
3 slices bacon	2 tablespoons parsley
½ cabbage, chopped	2 quarts water

Sauté partridge in butter; then tie the bacon around the bird with thread. Put the other ingredients in pan used to sauté partridge, and place bird on top of vegetables. Cook slowly 10 minutes, then add 2 quarts of water and cook slowly 2 hours. Stir occasionally. Serve on buttered toast.

Yield: 3 to 4 servings.

PHEASANT

To roast, leave skin on but pluck bird. If cooked in a sauce, you may skin it. Pheasant has a flavour all its own. If you wish to avoid this characteristic flavour, use only the breasts. They may be rolled in crumbs and fried like chicken.

ROAST PHEASANT

1 plump young pheasant, 2 to 3 pounds (dressed weight)	1 slice lemon
Salt and pepper	4 slices bacon
1 bay leaf	Melted butter
1 clove garlic, crushed	1 large onion, sliced
Few celery leaves	2 (4 oz.) cans mushrooms
	1 cup chicken broth

Sprinkle pheasant inside and out with salt and pepper. Place bay leaf, garlic, celery leaves and lemon in cavity. Tie legs together with string. Turn wings under. Cover breast with bacon and cheesecloth soaked in melted butter. Place pheasant breast up in baking pan. Arrange onion slices and mushrooms with liquid around pheasant. Pour chicken broth (canned or made with 1 chicken bouillon cube and 1 cup hot water) over pheasant. Roast in a moderate oven (350°F.) 30 minutes per pound or until tender, basting frequently with liquid in pan. Remove cheesecloth and string. Serve with wild rice, baked tomatoes, greengage plums and beverage.

Yield: 3 to 4 servings.

FRIED GROUSE AND ONIONS

1 grouse (cut in pieces)	½ cup thinly sliced onions
Five Roses All-purpose Flour	1½ cups milk
⅔ cup melted butter or shortening	Salt and pepper

Soak grouse in a weak solution of salted water the night before. Drain well and roll each piece in Five Roses Flour. Heat shortening and fry until golden brown on all sides, sprinkle with salt and pepper. Cook until tender then take from pan and keep in warm oven. Add sliced onions to fat and cook until brown. Stir in 1 tablespoon Five Roses Flour and blend well. Add milk, stirring all the while, bring to boil and season with salt and pepper. Arrange grouse on platter and pour sauce over it. Serve with a tart jelly.

Yield: 1 to 2 servings.

VENISON

1. Avoid puncturing bladder, stomach or intestines when cutting up game animals.

2. Edible organs are highly perishable. Prepare and cook as soon as possible.

3. Let carcass hang 1 to 2 weeks in a cool airy place (35°-40°F.) before cutting up for cooking or freezing.

4. To prevent a "gamey" flavour, trim off most of fat before cooking and soak for 24 hours (in refrigerator) in a marinade. This applies particularly to older animals.

5. Cook venison in the same manner as beef. If it is a young animal, it may be cooked by the same methods as tender beef—dry heat. If it is an older animal or age is uncertain, cook by moist heat such as braising or stewing to ensure tender meat.

6. If fat is trimmed off, prevent dryness by "larding". This is done by piercing meat in several places and inserting thin strips of chilled salt pork into the slits or fastening strips of fat around the meat with a string.

7. Venison may be served rare, medium or well-done.

VENISON MARINADE

⅔ cup burgundy wine or apple juice　　1 clove garlic, crushed
⅓ cup white vinegar　　　　　　　　　4 crushed peppercorns
¼ cup salad oil　　　　　　　　　　　1 crumbled bay leaf

Combine all ingredients and use to marinate fat-trimmed venison—the tougher cuts and roasts, steaks, chops from older animals. Marinate stews and small cuts for 6 to 24 hours and larger pieces 2 to 3 days. After marinating, cook cuts as you would corresponding beef cuts.

BEAR

1. Cook in the same manner as beef.

2. Cook until well-done as there is danger of trichinosis.

3. Bear meat is not marbled with fat as is beef, therefore it needs "larding". See instructions for Venison.

4. Bear meat may be marinated in the same way as Venison. However, connoisseurs prefer to cook bear meat without high seasonings or marinades as the meat flavour is so delicious.

RABBIT

Wild or domesticated rabbit may be prepared as you would chicken. Young animals may be roasted or fried while older animals should be braised or cooked in liquid.

HASSENPFEFFER

2 rabbits, cut in serving pieces
1 tablespoon salt
2 medium onions, sliced
3 whole cloves
1 bay leaf
6 whole allspice

1 cup white vinegar
Water
2 tablespoons butter
2 tablespoons Five Roses All-purpose
  Flour
Pepper

Place pieces of rabbit in casserole and sprinkle with salt. Heat, but do not boil, onions, cloves, bay leaf and allspice in vinegar and pour this over the rabbit. Let cool and set in refrigerator for 2 days, turning pieces occasionally. Put in a Dutch oven with the marinade, adding water to cover. Cover pan and simmer until rabbit is tender (1-1½ hours). Melt butter and stir in Five Roses Flour. Add strained rabbit broth and cook 5 minutes, stirring constantly. Pour over rabbits. Serve with potato balls fried to a golden colour and cole slaw.

Yield: 6 to 8 servings, depending upon size of rabbits.

WILD GAME ACCOMPANIMENTS

The favourite accompaniment for game is Wild Rice or Brown Rice, mixed with buttered toasted crumbs or chopped nuts. Cinnamon Apples (page 162) are also very popular. See also Apple Stuffing for Goose or Duck (page 124).

WILD RICE

1 cup wild rice
1 tablespoon butter
1 tablespoon minced onion

1 teaspoon salt
2½ cups water or chicken broth

Wash rice thoroughly, changing water several times. Melt butter in saucepan. Add onion and sauté until tender. Add rice, salt and liquid. Bring to boil. Stir once; reduce heat. Cover tightly and cook over very low heat about 45 minutes, until liquid is absorbed. Transfer to buttered, shallow baking dish and place in slow oven (250°F.) 10 to 15 minutes, or until rice grains are separate and dry.

Yield: 3 cups or 4 servings.

GOURMET GAME SAUCE

1 cup red currant jelly
2 tablespoons prepared mustard
¼ teaspoon grated onion
⅛ teaspoon ginger

Grated rind of 1 orange
½ cup orange juice
Grated rind of 1 lemon
2 tablespoons lemon juice

Combine jelly and mustard in small saucepan; mix well. Add onion, ginger and grated rind. Gradually stir in orange and lemon juices and cook over low heat until sauce is blended. Use as a basting when broiling or roasting game birds or serve hot or cold as a sauce for roast venison.

Yield: 1½ cups.

DEEP FAT FRYING

Foods fried in deep fat should never be greasy. If they have been prepared and cooked in the proper manner, they will be as light and as delicate as foods cooked in the oven.

Fats best suited for deep frying are vegetable oils (such as peanut oil, corn oil or cottonseed oil) or hydrogenated vegetable shortenings.

Temperature of oil for frying is most important. Most foods are fried at 375°F. unless indicated otherwise. It is best to use a deep fat frying thermometer or an electric deep fat fryer. If you have neither, the fat has reached 375°F. when a 1″ cube of bread turns golden brown in one minute. Be sure fat is heated to the correct temperature before adding food. **Too low a temperature** will not cook food properly, allows fat to be absorbed and causes food to be soggy. **Too high a temperature** will cook the outside of the food before inside is completely cooked, causes fat to smoke and develop off flavours. This fat cannot be used again and must be discarded. Never allow fats to reach a temperature higher than 390°F. or 400°F.

Fill deep fryer with oil or shortening to about one-third depth of pan. A certain amount of bubbling takes place when food is added. If fat comes too near the top of the pan, there is danger of it bubbling over and becoming ignited.

Cook only a few pieces of food at a time. Do not crowd or overload the fryer. A wire frying basket or tongs are useful for lifting foods from fat. If basket is used, dip it in the hot fat before adding the food. This prevents food from sticking. Drain cooked food on absorbent paper. Keep warm in a slow oven (300°F.) until all food pieces are cooked.

TO CLARIFY FAT

Heat fat slowly and add four or five slices of raw potato. Let the potato cook until it becomes brown. This will absorb leftover flavours. Remove the potato, strain the fat through several layers of cheesecloth and refrigerate for future use.

HOW TO CRUMB FOODS

Coating foods with crumbs prevents fat from being absorbed by the food. Egg forms a protective coating through which fat cannot enter. Beat an egg until yolk and white are well blended and add 1 tablespoon water. Use fine dry bread crumbs for crumbing. Roll or dip foods in Five Roses Flour first to form a dry surface to which the egg will cling, then dip in beaten egg and then in crumbs.

FRENCH FRIED POTATOES

8 potatoes   **1 qt. vegetable oil**

Peel potatoes and cut into ½″ strips. Rinse in cold water; drain well and pat dry with paper towel. Fry a few at a time, in deep fat that has been heated to 375°F., until golden brown—about 8 minutes. Drain on absorbent paper. Sprinkle with salt before serving.

Yield: 6 servings.

Note: If desired, cut potatoes into cubes, curls, thin slices or "shoestrings". Fry as above.

FRENCH FRIED ONION RINGS

2 medium-size onions   **1 egg**
½ cup Five Roses All-Purpose Flour   **1 qt. vegetable oil**
½ cup milk

Peel onions. Cut in ¼″ slices and separate into rings. Mix Five Roses Flour, milk and egg together. Dip onion rings in this mixture. Fry in deep fat that has been heated to 375°F. Takes about 2 minutes on each side. Drain on absorbent paper. Sprinkle with salt, if desired.

Yield: 4 servings.

FISH OR CHICKEN BATTER

1 cup Five Roses All-purpose Flour   **½ cup milk**
1 teaspoon baking powder   **½ cup water**
½ teaspoon salt

Mix Five Roses Flour, baking powder and salt together. Add milk and water slowly and beat until batter is smooth. Use as directed for fish (page 138) or chicken (page 159).

Yield: Enough for 2 lbs. fish fillets or 2 to 3 lbs. chicken pieces.

CROQUETTES

Croquettes are a delightful and appetizing food. An excellent way to use up left-over meat or fish. The foundation of these croquettes is a thick white sauce.

TO SHAPE CROQUETTES

Round balls—Roll 1 rounded tablespoon of the mixture between the hands.

Cone-shaped—Make round balls; flatten one end and shape other end to form a point.

Flat cakes—Pat mixture into flat round cakes, 1″ thick.

Note: Crumb all croquettes before frying.

CROQUETTE SAUCE

3 tablespoons butter
3 tablespoons Five Roses All-purpose
   Flour
½ teaspoon salt

Few grains pepper
Seasoning*
½ cup milk

Melt butter, stir in Five Roses Flour and seasonings. Cook over medium heat for 3 minutes, after mixture begins to bubble, stirring constantly. Add milk gradually and stir constantly until sauce is smooth and thick. Remove from heat and use as directed.

Yield: ⅔ cup sauce.

*Some of the seasonings which may be added to the Croquette Sauce are: parsley, celery salt, chopped celery, scraped onion, onion juice, minced red and green pepper, paprika, cayenne, etc.

CHICKEN CROQUETTES

Make Croquette Sauce as directed; add few grains cayenne, ¼ teaspoon paprika and ¼ teaspoon celery salt. When cooked, add few drops onion juice, 1 teaspoon lemon juice, 1 egg yolk and 2 cups chopped or minced cooked chicken; mix well. Chill. Shape, crumb and fry as directed. Serve with Cream Sauce, Curry Sauce or Velouté Sauce (page 119).

Yield: 12 to 15 croquettes.

HAM CROQUETTES

Make Croquette Sauce as directed. Add 2 cups chopped or minced cooked ham, 3 finely chopped shallots, 1 tablespoon brown sugar, 1 slightly beaten egg yolk and 1 cup soft bread crumbs; mix well. Chill. Shape, crumb and fry as directed. Serve with Raisin Sauce (page 122) or Egg Sauce (page 119).

Yield: 15 to 20 croquettes.

LOBSTER CROQUETTES

Make Croquette Sauce as directed. Add a little of the warm sauce to 1 egg yolk, then return to sauce and cook 1 minute longer. Remove from heat. Add 1 teaspoon lemon juice and 2 (5 oz.) cans flaked lobster; mix well. Chill. Shape, crumb and fry as directed. Serve with Tartar Sauce (page 122). Use flaked salmon in place of lobster, if desired.

Yield: 12 to 14 croquettes.

EGG CROQUETTES

Make Croquette Sauce but sauté 2 tablespoons chopped onion in the butter first; continue as directed. Add a little of the warm sauce to 1 egg yolk, then return to sauce and cook 1 minute longer. Remove from heat. Add 4 coarsely chopped hard-cooked eggs, 1 tablespoon grated cheese and 1 cup soft bread crumbs; mix well. Chill. Shape, crumb and fry as directed. Serve with Cream Sauce or Cheese Sauce (page 119).

Yield: 12 to 15 croquettes.

FRITTERS

Like Croquettes, Fritters are light and crisp and provide an interesting change from every day foods.

FRITTER BATTER

1½ cups Five Roses All-purpose Flour	Few grains pepper
2 teaspoons baking powder	¾ cup milk
¾ teaspoon salt	2 eggs
	1 tablespoon sugar

Mix all ingredients together and beat until smooth.

Yield: Enough for 2 dozen fritters.

TO FRY FRITTERS

Heat fat in deep fryer to 375°F. Dip fritter mixture into batter. Fry only a few fritters at a time. Drop by scant tablespoons into hot fat. As soon as they rise to the top, turn them over. Turn frequently during cooking. When fritters are a rich brown shade, lift from the fat and drain on absorbent paper before placing them on serving dishes. Fritters are normally irregular in shape and this adds to their appeal.

BANANA FRITTERS

Peel and cut 6 bananas into rounds about ½" thick. Sprinkle with 2 tablespoons sugar and 1 tablespoon orange juice; let stand 20 minutes. Dip banana rounds into Fritter Batter and entirely coat each piece. Drop one by one into hot fat and fry as directed. Sprinkle with icing sugar and serve immediately. Makes about 2 dozen.

APPLE FRITTERS

Peel and core 6 firm, medium-size apples and cut into ½" slices. Sprinkle with 3 tablespoons icing sugar and 2 tablespoons lemon juice. Dip into Fritter Batter and coat pieces completely. Fry as directed. Sprinkle with icing sugar, if desired, and serve immediately. Delicious with maple syrup. Makes about 2 dozen.

CORN FRITTERS

1½ cups Five Roses All-purpose Flour	2 tablespoons milk
2 teaspoons baking powder	1 tablespoon sugar
1¼ teaspoons salt	2 egg yolks, well-beaten
Few grains pepper	2 egg whites, stiffly beaten
	1 cup cream-style corn

Mix first 7 ingredients together and beat until smooth. Fold in stiffly beaten egg whites. Fold in corn. Use only 1 tablespoon batter per fritter and drop into hot fat. Fry as directed. Serve hot. Delicious with maple syrup.

Yield: About 20 small fritters.

VEGETABLES

In addition to their valuable nutritive elements, vegetables add colour, texture and flavour to any meal.

THE SECRET OF COOKING VEGETABLES is not to overcook. Cook just until barely tender and still colourful. Use smallest amount of water possible.

PREPARATION

Wash vegetables thoroughly before cooking, scrubbing if necessary. If wilted, freshen by soaking in cold water. Roots and tubers may be pared, peeled or scraped according to kind. Cauliflower, cabbage, broccoli and Brussels sprouts should be soaked head down in cold salted water (1 teaspoon salt to 1 quart water) for 30 minutes before cooking to draw out any insects.

COOKING

To Boil: Add vegetables to boiling salted water (1 teaspoon salt to 1 quart water). Use small amount of water and cover or cook uncovered in enough water to just cover. Bring water back to boil and start timing. Cook at a gentle boil until just tender.

To Steam: Place vegetables in collander or steamer over rapidly boiling water. Cover tightly and steam just until tender.

To Bake: Leave skins on for potatoes and squash. Pare other vegetables. Pared vegetables can be cut up or left whole and placed in shallow baking dish with a small amount of water, season, cover and bake, in a moderate oven. Remove from oven when done.

To Fry: Preparation varies. See individual recipes.

To Cook Frozen Vegetables: Follow directions on package. Do not thaw before cooking except for corn on the cob which should be partially thawed.

To Heat Canned Vegetables: Pour liquid from can into saucepan; boil to reduce liquid to half. Add vegetables. Heat and season to taste with salt, pepper and butter.

EASY WAYS TO VARY VEGETABLES

Creamed Vegetables

Allow 1 cup White Sauce (page 119) or one of the variations to 2 cups cooked vegetables.

Au Gratin Vegetables
Place creamed vegetables in a baking dish, cover with grated cheese and buttered bread crumbs. Bake in a moderate oven (350°F.) until cheese is melted — about 15 to 20 minutes.

Scalloped Vegetables
Place creamed vegetables in a baking dish with alternate layers of buttered bread crumbs. Sprinkle top with crumbs and bake in a moderate oven (350°F.) until brown—about 15 to 20 minutes.

ASPARAGUS

Trim off hard stalks and scales. Tie in bunches and stand upright in boiling salted water to within one inch of tips; boil for 10 minutes. (Use about 1½ teaspoons of salt per quart of water.) Add more water to cover tips and boil another 5 minutes. If the pan is covered, the second addition of water need not be added. Season with salt, pepper and butter. Serve plain or with Cheese Sauce (page 119) or Drawn Butter Sauce (page 120).

2 lbs. serves 4.

FRENCH ARTICHOKES

Choose smooth, dark green, tightly closed heads. Cut off stems close to leaves; remove outside leaves and cut off 1″ from top. Tie with string to keep in place. Soak ½ hour in cold water. Cook in boiling salted water 25 minutes to 1 hour, depending on size. Test tenderness by piercing with a fork. Drain by turning upside down. Cut out choke (thistle-like part in centre). Serve hot with melted butter or Hollandaise Sauce (page 120). Or serve cold with mayonnaise, seasoned highly with lemon juice and prepared mustard.

BOILED GREEN OR WAXED BEANS

Select beans as nearly stringless as possible. Remove ends and strings; wash. Cut in desired lengths or leave whole. Cook in boiling water 20 to 30 minutes or until tender. Drain; season with salt, pepper and butter.

1 lb. serves 4.

BEANS WITH ALMONDS

Arrange cooked and seasoned green beans in a buttered casserole. Add thin White Sauce (page 119). Cover with slivered, blanched almonds. Bake at 400°F. 15 to 20 minutes until almonds are browned.

BOILED BEETS

Wash and cut off leaves, leaving 1″ of stem. Cook whole in boiling salted water. Drain, drop in cold water for a minute and skin. Leave whole, slice or quarter. Season with salt, pepper and butter.

 Young beets require 30 minutes to cook.
 Old beets require 1½ hours to cook.

2 lbs. serves 4.

BOILED BROCCOLI

Cut off only the hard end of stalk; wash. Insert broccoli, stem first, into boiling salted water. (The heads should not be submerged.) Cook from 15 to 20 minutes. Season with salt, pepper and butter. Serve plain or with Cheese Sauce (page 119) or Lemon Butter (page 123).

1 lb. serves 2 to 4.

BOILED BRUSSELS SPROUTS

Select light green, compact heads with no yellow spots. Remove wilted leaves, cut off stems, and soak 15 minutes in cold, salted water. Drain. Cook, covered, in boiling salted water 10 to 20 minutes or until just tender. Drain. Serve with butter or Hollandaise Sauce (page 120).

1 lb. serves 4.

BOILED CABBAGE

Remove outside leaves; wash. Cut in quarters and remove tough centre core. Slice into shreds. Cook quickly in a covered saucepan, using just enough boiling water to keep from burning. Cook just until tender but still crisp. Drain. Season with salt, pepper and butter. Serve plain or with Egg Sauce or Hollandaise Sauce (pages 119-120).

Green or white cabbages require 5 to 15 minutes to cook.
Red cabbage requires 20 to 25 minutes to cook.

1 medium-size head serves 4 to 6.

BOILED CARROTS

Wash and scrape or thinly pare. Leave whole or dice, slice or cut in fingers. Cook in boiling salted water until tender. Season with salt, pepper and butter. Serve plain or with Cream Sauce (page 119).

Young carrots require 15 to 20 minutes to cook.
Old carrots require 30 to 45 minutes to cook.

1 lb. serves 4.

BOILED CAULIFLOWER

Select white head with fresh green leaves. Remove leaves and cut off stalk. Soak, head down, for 30 minutes in cold water; drain. Leave whole or break into flowerets. Cook in boiling salted water until tender. Drain and season with salt, pepper and butter. Serve plain or with Cheese Sauce, Hollandaise or White Sauce (pages 119-120).

Flowerets require 10-15 minutes to cook.
Whole head requires 20 to 30 minutes to cook.

1 medium-size head serves 4.

BOILED CELERY

Wash and scrape celery stalks; cut in 1″ pieces. Steam or cook in boiling salted water, 15 to 20 minutes; drain. Serve with salt, pepper and butter or with White Sauce (page 119).

1 bunch celery makes 2 to 3 servings.

BOILED CORN ON THE COB

Remove husks and silky threads. Place in deep kettle of boiling water. Let water return to boiling point again and boil 15 minutes. Boil only enough for first serving. If you are boiling a large quantity, the corn will be done as soon as water returns to boiling point. Serve with butter and salt.

ROAST OR BARBECUE CORN

Husk ears. Butter corn liberally, sprinkle with salt. Wrap each ear loosely with aluminum foil. Let foil lap over seam—about ½-inch—don't seal, but twist ends. Cook corn on grill over hot coals 15 to 20 minutes or until tender, turning frequently. If desired, place under broiler, 5" to 6" from heat and broil 50 to 60 minutes. Have extra butter and salt on hand for serving.

FRIED EGG PLANT

Cut egg plant into ½" slices, remove skin if desired. Sprinkle each slice with salt; lay slices on top of one another and let stand 2 hours. (The salt will draw out any bitter flavour.) Half an hour before serving, wipe each slice dry, dip in beaten egg and then in bread crumbs; fry in hot fat. Drain each piece on absorbent paper and serve crisp and hot.

A medium-size egg plant (about 1½ lbs.) serves 4.

MUSHROOMS SAUTÉED

Clean mushrooms; slice crosswise or leave whole. Dredge with Five Roses Flour. Melt butter in frying pan; add mushrooms. Sprinkle lightly with salt and paprika. Sauté for 5 minutes; add water or stock (⅔ cup per lb.) and cook 5 minutes longer. Serve on toast or with meat.

1 lb. serves 4 (or 2 if used as a main dish).

CREAMED MUSHROOMS

Follow above recipe but use cream or milk instead of water.

BOILED ONIONS

Remove skins from onions and trim off some of the root. Do not remove root completely if you want onion to stay whole. Place in cold water and boil gently, uncovered, for 15-30 minutes or until tender. Drain; season with salt, pepper and butter. If desired, add a little milk or cream and cook 5 minutes longer.

1½ lbs. serves 4.

Fried Onion Rings—See Deep Fat Frying Section, page 169.

BOILED PARSNIPS

Wash and scrape parsnips. Leave whole if small, or cut lengthwise in 3-inch strips. Cook in boiling salted water for 30 minutes or until tender. Serve with salt, pepper and butter.

1½ lbs. serves 4.

BOILED PEAS

Choose peas with bright shiny pods. Shell and add just enough water to keep from burning. Cook until soft in boiling water—about 15 to 20 minutes. Drain and season with butter, salt and pepper. One sprig of mint for every 2 cups of peas adds flavour. Serve plain or with Cream Sauce (page 119), Onion Sauce (page 120) or Mushroom Sauce (page 120).

1 lb. unshelled peas serves 2.

BOILED POTATOES

Wash, pare (if desired), and drop into cold salted water. Bring water to boil and cook in boiling salted water 15 to 20 minutes or until tender. Drain thoroughly. Sprinkle with chopped parsley or paprika, if desired.

MASHED POTATOES

Mash boiled potatoes. Add butter (about 2 tablespoons for 4 potatoes), salt and pepper to taste. Beat well until creamy. Add a little milk, if desired.

BAKED POTATOES

Use firm, smooth potatoes with no blemishes. New potatoes will not bake very well. Scrub with vegetable brush and dry. Puncture skin with a fork or knife in one or two places. Place directly on oven rack and bake at any convenient temperature ranging from 350°F. to 425°F. 50-60 minutes or until soft. To test for softness, prick with a fork or pick up one potato in a folded towel and squeeze gently. If it feels soft, the potato is done.

BAKED STUFFED POTATOES

Select potatoes of medium size and bake as above. Cut a lengthwise slice from the flat side of each potato and remove contents from shells, being careful not to break shells. Mash potatoes, add hot milk, butter, salt and pepper and beat until light and fluffy. Pile potatoes into shells; sprinkle with paprika or chopped parsley. Place in oven to reheat, and bake until the tops of the potatoes are lightly browned. If desired, a well-beaten egg, grated cheese, well seasoned chopped meat, bacon, ham or chicken may be added to the potato mixture before it is piled back into the shells.

OLD-TIME HASHED BROWN POTATOES

Chop cold left-over potatoes and season with salt. Add 3 tablespoons milk and a few bits of bacon, ham or sausage (if desired). Heat bacon drippings or other fat in frying pan. Add potatoes, stir for a moment, then press lightly. Allow potatoes to become a rich, golden brown on bottom; turn to do other side.

DUCHESS POTATOES

Beat 2 egg yolks, then add them to 3 cups mashed potatoes; whip well until light and creamy. Spread on top of any baked meat or fish dish, then set in oven to brown. Serves 3 to 4.

SCALLOPED POTATOES

6-7 medium-size potatoes	Few grains pepper
3 tablespoons butter	2 cups scalded milk
3 tablespoons Five Roses All-purpose Flour	¼ cup chopped onion
	Few grains paprika
1 teaspoon salt	Grated cheese (optional)

Wash and peel potatoes; slice thinly. Spread about ⅓ of the slices in a buttered 1½ quart casserole. Melt butter in a saucepan; slowly blend in Five Roses Flour, salt and pepper. Gradually add hot milk, stirring constantly. Sprinkle potatoes with half of the onions and ⅓ of the sauce. Cover with another layer of potatoes and remaining onions. Place remaining potatoes on top, then cover with remaining sauce. Sprinkle with paprika and grated cheese, if desired. Bake, uncovered, in a moderate oven (375°F.) 1 hour or until done and potatoes are lightly browned on top.

Yield: 6 servings.

CANDIED SWEET POTATOES

6 sweet potatoes	Salt and pepper to taste
1 cup brown sugar	1 tablespoon butter
¼ cup water	

Wash sweet potatoes and cook in boiling water until tender—about 30 to 35 minutes. Drain and peel off skin. Make a syrup by boiling together the brown sugar and water. Cut potatoes in half and dip each piece into the syrup. Place potatoes in a greased 9″ square baking dish. Dot with butter and season to taste with salt and pepper. Pour remaining syrup on top. Bake in a hot oven (450°F.) 20 minutes or until slightly brown.

Yield: 6 servings.

BOILED SPINACH

Wash spinach carefully, cutting off root ends, tough stems and yellow leaves. Drain well. Put in saucepan (without water); cover and cook over medium heat 10 to 15 minutes. Serve with butter, pepper and salt.

1 lb. serves 2 or 3.

BOILED WINTER SQUASH

Acorn (or Pepper), Butternut and Hubbard are considered Winter Squash. Cut in pieces, remove seeds and stringy portion and pare. Cover and cook in boiling salted water until tender—about 20 to 30 minutes. Drain. Mash and season with salt, pepper and butter. If desired, a small amount of brown sugar may be added if squash lacks sweetness.

1 Acorn Squash serves 2.
1 lb. Hubbard or Butternut serves 2.

BOILED SUMMER SQUASH

Yellow crooknecks, dark green zucchini and striped vegetable marrow are considered summer squash. Wash, quarter or cut in thick slices. Do not peel unless rough and old. Add just enough water to keep from burning. Cover and cook until tender—about 10 to 20 minutes. Drain. Mash and season with butter, salt and pepper.

1 lb. serves 3.

BAKED ACORN SQUASH

Wash. Cut in half and remove seeds and stringy portion. Sprinkle with salt. Brush with melted butter and place cut side down on baking sheet. Bake in a hot oven (400°F.) 30-45 minutes or until tender. Turn cut side up. Put 1 teaspoon butter in each cavity and brush rims with butter; sprinkle with brown sugar. Continue baking until browned.

TO PEEL TOMATOES

Dip tomatoes in boiling water for 1 minute; remove. Cut out stem end, peel and chill.

CRUMB STUFFED TOMATOES

4 fresh tomatoes	1 teaspoon sugar
1 cup fine dry bread crumbs	1½ teaspoons salt
1 tablespoon minced onion	Dash of pepper
3 tablespoons melted butter	1 tablespoon grated cheese

Wash tomatoes and cut off thin slices from top; scoop out pulp and reserve. Cut tomato pulp into small pieces and combine with the juice from tomatoes and bread crumbs. Sauté onion in 2 tablespoons of butter until soft and add to crumb mixture with sugar, salt and pepper. Stuff tomatoes with this mixture, sprinkle tops with grated cheese and pieces of butter. Place in a shallow baking dish and bake at 375°F. for 20 minutes or until crumbs appear brown.

Yield: 4 servings.

MASHED TURNIPS

Wash turnips and pare. Slice, dice or quarter. Cook in boiling salted water, covered, 15 to 30 minutes or until tender. Drain off liquid. Mash turnips and cook a minute or two to dry thoroughly. Season with salt, pepper and butter.

2 lbs. serves 4.

FLUFFY TURNIPS

2 tablespoons butter	1 tablespoon sugar
1 tablespoon chopped onion	⅛ teaspoon pepper
4 cups mashed yellow turnips	⅛ teaspoon paprika
½ teaspoon salt	2 eggs, separated

Melt butter in medium size saucepan; sauté onion. Add turnip, salt, sugar, pepper and paprika; mix well. Beat egg yolks and add to turnip mixture. Beat egg whites until stiff but not dry and fold into mixture. Place in a greased 8″ pie plate and bake in a moderate oven (375°F.) 20 to 25 minutes.

Yield: 4-6 servings.

SALADS

Salads usually consist of cold foods, cooked or uncooked and served with a dressing. They are made from meat, fish, poultry, vegetables, eggs, fruit, nuts or any combination of foods having harmonious flavours. They may be used as an appetizer, an accompaniment to the main course, as the main course and even as a dessert.

The garnish determines to a large extent the attractiveness of a salad. The best effects are produced by a few materials which contrast pleasantly in colour. As a rule, the garnish should be edible.

A Guide to Perfect Salads

1. Use fresh, crisp greens, vegetables that are in season and full-flavoured fruits. If vegetables are wilted, they will regain some of their crispness by soaking in cold or ice water for a short time.

2. Thoroughly wash all uncooked vegetables. Drain before using. Dry greens so that dressing can cling.

3. Use a variety of greens in addition to head and leaf lettuce. Romain, endive, escarole, water cress and tender spinach leaves add colour and flavour.

4. Break or slice ingredients into generous bite-size pieces. If cut too small, the salad is unattractive. Fish should be flaked; meat and poultry should be trimmed of all skin and fat, and cut into neat cubes. Vary the shape of the fruit by cutting it into balls, cubes, spears or sections.

5. Dip slices of apple, peach, pear, banana and avocado in lemon juice to prevent discolouring.

6. Make use of the shells of fruits for interesting containers, e.g. honey dew, coconut, fresh pineapple.

7. Never put salad dressing on lettuce or other salad greens until just before serving as it makes them limp and wilted.

8. For added flavour, marinate cooked vegetables, meat and fish in French Dressing for at least an hour.

9. Keep salad simple and casual.

10. Toss ingredients lightly or arrange on lettuce just before serving. Use simple garnishes.

11. Chill salad bowls or plates ahead of time.

Preparation of Head Lettuce for Salads

Cut out core; remove coarse, outside leaves. Hold head, cut part up, under cold running water to open leaves. This exposes the best of the lettuce for immediate use. Wash each leaf thoroughly and dry by pressing lightly on a towel. Place in a moist cloth or plastic bag. Keep in crisper part of refrigerator.

FAVOURITE POTATO SALAD

5 cups cooked potatoes, cut in cubes (about 6 medium)	½ teaspoon paprika
	1 small onion, grated
¼ cup white vinegar	⅓ cup mayonnaise
¼ teaspoon salt	2 tablespoons chopped parsley

While potatoes are still warm, add vinegar, salt, paprika and grated onion; chill. Just before serving, mix in mayonnaise and parsley. (Add mayonnaise carefully as potatoes vary in quality and therefore amount of mayonnaise may vary.)

Yield: 6 to 8 servings.

STUFFED TOMATO SALAD

Scoop out tomatoes of uniform size and shape and fill with any desired salad mixture or one of the following fillings:

1. A mixture of sliced cucumbers, chopped celery, tomato pulp and mayonnaise.
2. A mixture of chopped celery, nuts and a thick salad dressing.
3. Any cabbage salad mixture.
4. Cottage cheese.

COLE SLAW

Combine finely shredded cabbage, chopped pimiento (optional), grated raw carrot and toss with French Dressing. For tender cabbage, soak cabbage in boiling water for 5 minutes, then rinse under cold water before adding other vegetables.

TOSSED SALAD WITH ALMONDS

Prepare crisp salad greens and chill. Just before serving, toss with Italian Dressing (page 185) and sprinkle with slivered, blanched almonds.

FRUIT SALAD

Arrange lettuce leaves in cups on individual plates. In each cup, arrange canned peach and pear halves, bananas (quartered, dipped in lemon juice and rolled in coconut), pineapple rings and spoonful of cottage cheese. Top with a maraschino cherry.

Other fruit combinations:
1. Sectioned oranges and grapefruit combined with avocados and served with Fruit French Dressing (page 185).
2. Orange slices, bananas, grapes and dates, cut up and combined with mayonnaise. Serve with Fruit French Dressing or Cream Fruit Dressing (pages 185-186).

FRESH PINEAPPLE SALAD

Cut fresh pineapple in half, keeping leafy top intact. Hollow out, leaving shells ½" thick. Cut out core and discard. Dice remaining pineapple and mix with orange sections and fresh strawberries. Refill shells. Chill. Garnish with mint leaves. Serve with Fruit French Dressing (page 185). Serves 8.

MARGUERITE SALAD

Cut hard-cooked eggs in half, lengthwise. Remove yolks and mix with salad dressing. Cut whites to form long petals and arrange the yolks as centre of "flowers". Serve on bed of crisp lettuce.

WALDORF SALAD

2 cups diced tart apples	1 cup chopped celery
1 tablespoon sugar	½ cup broken walnuts
½ teaspoon lemon juice	½ cup whipping cream
Dash of salt	¼ cup mayonnaise

Sprinkle diced apples with sugar, lemon juice and salt. Add celery and nuts. Whip cream; fold mayonnaise into cream. Gently fold into apple mixture. Chill. Serve in lettuce lined bowl.

Yield: 4 to 6 servings.

MEAT SALAD

2 cups chopped cooked meat or poultry	1 teaspoon salt
¾ cup finely chopped celery	Few grains pepper
1 hard-cooked egg, chopped	Mayonnaise or salad dressing
	Stuffed olives

Mix chopped meat, celery, hard-cooked egg and seasonings together. Moisten with mayonnaise or salad dressing and let stand in a cold place for 1 hour or until ready to serve. Serve on lettuce leaves; garnish with stuffed olives and mayonnaise.

Yield: 4 to 6 servings.

CRAB LOUIS

½ cup mayonnaise	4 large lettuce cups
¼ cup whipped cream	2 (6½ oz.) cans crab meat
¼ cup chili sauce	1 tomato
¼ cup chopped green pepper	2 hard-cooked eggs
½ medium-size onion, chopped	Paprika
1 teaspoon lemon juice	

Combine first 6 ingredients for dressing; chill. Line 4 large salad plates with lettuce cups; arrange flaked crab meat on top, reserving claws for garnishing. Circle with wedges of tomato and eggs. Pour dressing over top. Sprinkle with paprika. Top with claw meat.

Yield: 4 servings.

MOULDED SALADS

More festive in appearance, moulded salads should be prepared a day ahead and refrigerated. Never freeze. Ingredients should be chopped or sliced into small, uniform pieces. In some salads, the gelatin mixture requires partial setting and in others it is chilled only until it is the consistency of an unbeaten egg white before other ingredients are added. This helps to keep the ingredients evenly distributed throughout the mould.

To fill mould: Rinse mould with cold water or brush with salad oil to make unmoulding easier. Fill mould to the top. Allow at least 6 to 12 hours for salads to set. Time will depend on size of mould.

To unmould: Run a knife around edge of mould to a depth of about ½″ only in order to loosen the bottom edge. Dip mould quickly into a pan of warm water, then place the serving plate over the mould and invert plate and mould. Remove mould with care. If mould does not loosen after first dipping, repeat procedure. Do not leave the mould in the warm water too long as the gelatin will melt.

JELLIED CABBAGE SALAD

1 pkg. lemon jelly powder	12 stuffed olives, sliced
1½ cups boiling water	2 tablespoons minced onion
½ cup white vinegar	¼ teaspoon salt
1½ cups chopped cabbage	Few grains pepper
⅓ cup chopped celery	Few grains paprika

Dissolve jelly powder in boiling water; cool to lukewarm and add vinegar. Chill in refrigerator until mixture begins to thicken; stir in remaining ingredients, mixing well. Pour into cold wet 8″ ring or individual moulds. Chill until firm; serve unmoulded on crisp lettuce or cabbage leaves. Garnish as desired.

Yield: 6 to 8 servings.

JELLIED CHICKEN SALAD

1 tablespoon unflavoured gelatin	½ cup chopped celery
¼ cup cold water	¼ cup chopped olives
¾ cup Boiled Salad Dressing or	2 tablespoons chopped pimiento
mayonnaise	Dash of salt
1 cup chopped cooked chicken	Dash of paprika

Soak gelatin in cold water and dissolve over hot water; add to dressing. Fold in chicken, celery, olives and pimiento. Season to taste with salt and paprika. Place in a cold wet 1 pint mould or individual moulds and chill until firm. Unmould on bed of lettuce. Garnish with olives or radish roses.

Yield: 6 servings.

VARIATIONS:

Jellied Veal Salad: Substitute chicken with 1 cup chopped cooked veal.

Jellied Salmon Salad: Substitute chicken with 1 cup flaked canned salmon (7¾ oz. can).

Jellied Tuna Salad: Substitute chicken with 1 cup flaked canned tuna (7¾ oz. can).

MOULDED CHEESE SALAD

1 can condensed tomato soup	1 cup mayonnaise
1 tablespoon unflavoured gelatin	1½ cups finely chopped raw
½ cup cold water	vegetables (celery, onions,
8 oz. cream cheese	green pepper and pimiento)

Heat soup to boiling. Soak gelatin in cold water and add to hot soup; stir until dissolved. Add cheese and beat with rotary or electric beater until blended. Stir in remaining ingredients and pour into a cold wet 8″ square pan or individual moulds. Chill until firm. Serve on a bed of lettuce.

Yield: 8 to 10 servings.

TOMATO ASPIC

1 tablespoon unflavoured gelatin	½ bay leaf (optional)
¼ cup cold water	Few grains salt, cayenne and paprika
2 cups canned tomatoes	1 tablespoon white vinegar
½ cup chopped celery	1 tablespoon onion juice

Soften gelatin in cold water. Combine tomatoes, celery, bay leaf, salt, cayenne and paprika in a saucepan. Bring to boil and simmer 10 minutes. Add softened gelatin and stir until dissolved. Stir in vinegar and onion juice. Strain. Turn into cold wet 8″ ring mould or individual moulds. Chill until firm. Unmould and serve on lettuce. Place dressing in small cup and place the cup in centre of aspic. Garnish.

Yield: 6 to 8 servings.

TOMATO ASPIC WITH CHICKEN

Make Tomato Aspic in cold wet 8″ ring mould. When firm, turn out on crisp lettuce leaves. Fill centre of ring with a mixture of: 2 cups chopped cooked chicken, ¾ cup chopped celery, 1 teaspoon salt, few grains pepper, 1 chopped hard-cooked egg and 4 chopped olives. Marinate this mixture in ¾ cup French Dressing for 1 hour in refrigerator before serving. Garnish with mayonnaise. Makes 6 servings.

A CHRISTMAS SALAD

Make Tomato Aspic and Jellied Cabbage Salad (coloured with a few drops of green food colouring). Mould each salad into cold wet 8″ square pans. To serve, cut each salad into rectangular shapes. Garnish red jelly with strips of green pepper and green jelly with strips of pimiento to simulate the ribbon on a Christmas package. Sprigs of holly may be placed where strips of garnish cross. Serve on bed of lettuce with salad dressing or mayonnaise. Serves 9 to 10.

SALAD DRESSINGS

There are 3 types of salad dressings in common use: cooked or boiled dressing, mayonnaise and French. Each have variations to give us a wide variety of dressings that complement our salads. As a rule, add the dressing just before serving the salad.

French Dressing is a basic oil and vinegar (or lemon juice) dressing varied by the choice of vinegars and seasonings.

Mayonnaise combines an oil, an acid (vinegar or lemon juice) and egg. The secret of success is to add the oil very slowly to the egg mixture.

Boiled Salad Dressing calls for milk rather than oil. It is basically a cream sauce mixture with eggs, vinegar and seasonings.

MAYONNAISE

¼ teaspoon dry mustard
½ teaspoon salt
Few grains pepper
⅛ teaspoon paprika

1 egg yolk
2 tablespoons white vinegar or
    lemon juice
1 cup salad oil

Mix mustard, salt, pepper and paprika together. Add egg yolk and mix well. Stir in 1 tablespoon of vinegar or lemon juice. Add salad oil, a few drops at a time, beating constantly. As mixture thickens, oil may be added more quickly. Add remaining tablespoon of vinegar or lemon juice.

Yield: 1 cup. RECIPE MAY BE DOUBLED.

VARIATIONS

Russian Dressing: To 1 cup mayonnaise, stir in ½ cup chili sauce and 1 tablespoon lemon juice. Chill.

Cranberry Dressing: To 1 cup mayonnaise, stir in ⅓ cup cranberry juice and dash of salt. Chill. Just before serving, fold in 2 tablespoons toasted chopped almonds.

Blue Cheese Dressing: To ½ cup mayonnaise, stir in 4 oz. softened cream cheese, ½ cup crumbled blue cheese, ½ cup light cream and 1 tablespoon lemon juice. Chill.

Herb Dressing: To 1 cup mayonnaise, add 2 tablespoons lemon juice, ⅓ cup chopped onion, ½ teaspoon grated lemon rind, 1 clove garlic, minced (optional), 2 teaspoons Worcestershire Sauce and ½ teaspoon dried mixed herbs. Chill.

Thousand Island Dressing: To 1 cup mayonnaise, add ¼ cup chili sauce, 2 tablespoons chopped green pepper, 1 chopped hard-cooked egg and 2 tablespoons chopped stuffed olives. Chill.

BOILED SALAD DRESSING

2 tablespoons Five Roses All-purpose Flour	2 egg yolks
2 tablespoons sugar	½ cup evaporated milk
1½ teaspoons dry mustard	¼ cup milk or light cream
1 teaspoon salt	⅓ cup white vinegar
	2 tablespoons butter

Mix Five Roses Flour, sugar, mustard, salt and egg yolks together in top of double boiler. Add evaporated milk and mix well. Cook over lightly boiling water, stirring constantly, until mixture is heated. Add cream (or milk) and vinegar alternately, a few drops at a time. Stir and beat mixture until thick and smooth. Remove from heat and stir in butter. When butter is melted, strain dressing and store in scalded glass jars. Dilute with more cream as required.

Yield: 1 cup. RECIPE MAY BE DOUBLED.

VARIATIONS

Green Pepper Dressing: To 1 cup Boiled Dressing, add ¼ cup chopped green pepper.

Cheese Dressing: To 1 cup Boiled Dressing, add 1 cup grated Cheddar cheese.

SOUR CREAM DRESSING (Eggless)

½ cup commercial sour cream	½ teaspoon salt
2 tablespoons white vinegar	1 teaspoon onion juice
½ teaspoon paprika	

Combine all ingredients and beat until thick and smooth. Good with potato, cucumber, cabbage or lettuce salad.

Yield: ½ cup.

FRENCH DRESSING

¼ teaspoon pepper	1 teaspoon fruit sugar
½ teaspoon salt	3 tablespoons lemon juice
⅛ teaspoon paprika	6 tablespoons white vinegar
⅛ teaspoon dry mustard	1 cup salad oil

Put all ingredients in a glass jar; cover and shake thoroughly. Store in refrigerator; shake well before using.

Yield: About 1½ cups.

VARIATIONS

Italian Dressing: Make French Dressing omitting paprika, sugar and lemon juice. Add 1 clove garlic, minced, ¼ teaspoon cayenne and a dash of Tabasco sauce. Increase mustard to ¼ teaspoon.

Fruit French Dressing: Make French Dressing omitting pepper and mustard. Increase sugar to ⅓ cup; paprika and salt to 1 teaspoon each. Decrease vinegar to 1 tablespoon. Add ¼ cup orange juice and 1 teaspoon grated onion.

CREAM FRUIT DRESSING

⅔ cup sugar
2 tablespoons Five Roses All-purpose
    Flour
Few grains salt
2 eggs, beaten slightly

1 tablespoon butter
3 tablespoons lemon juice
¼ cup orange juice
1 cup pineapple juice
½ cup whipping cream

Mix sugar, Five Roses Flour and salt together. Stir in remaining ingredients except cream. Cook in double boiler until thickened. Chill. Whip cream and fold into chilled mixture. Good with fruit salads.

Yield: 2 cups.

FAVOURITE CHEESE DRESSING

4 tablespoons salad oil
1 teaspoon salt
¼ teaspoon pepper

2 tablespoons white vinegar
1 teaspoon Worcestershire Sauce
½ cup grated Cheddar cheese

Mix all ingredients together in order given; shake thoroughly. Good with green salads.

Yield: About ¾ cup.

BACON DRESSING

2 slices bacon, diced
1 tablespoon white vinegar

Few grains pepper
¼ teaspoon sugar

Fry diced bacon; measure fat in pan (about 3 tablespoons) and add ⅓ as much vinegar (about 1 tablespoon), while fat is still hot. Season with pepper and sugar; add bacon pieces. Pour on salad while hot. Good with potato salad or green salads.

Yield: ½ cup.

LOW CALORIE DRESSING

¼ teaspoon gelatin
1 tablespoon cold water
¼ cup boiling water
1 tablespoon sugar
½ teaspoon salt
2 tablespoons lemon juice

2 tablespoons chili sauce
⅛ teaspoon dry mustard
¼ teaspoon paprika
Few grains cayenne
Few grains pepper
¼ teaspoon onion juice

Soak gelatin in cold water; dissolve mixture in boiling water. Stir in sugar and salt; cool. Add remaining ingredients; shake. Chill. Shake before serving.

Yield: ½ cup.

Many people find the Five Roses Guide to Good Cooking an excellent shower gift for the bride-to-be. Additional copies of this cook book may be obtained by clipping the coupons on pages 3 and 4.

FREEZING FOODS

Freezing is one of the simplest and most effective methods for preserving foods. Colour, flavour, texture and much of the original food value are retained. When thawed, the product resembles the fresh food.

What Not To Freeze

Salad greens and vegetables that are eaten crisp and raw—such as celery, radishes, cucumbers, tomatoes.

Mayonnaise—but salad dressing may be frozen.

Gelatin salads and desserts unless they are whipped.

Custard pies, cream puddings, cream fillings.

Cream—but whipped cream may be frozen.

Cream cheese alone.

Boiled potatoes.

Whites of hard-cooked eggs.

A GUIDE TO FREEZING FOODS

1. **Select** only fresh foods of high quality. Fruits and vegetables should be in their prime, ripe and firm. Quality of foods taken from the freezer can be no better than that which you put in.

2. **Prepare** foods quickly and carefully. Waste no time between picking or buying and freezing. If unable to process immediately, refrigerate the food until ready to use.

3. **Package** in moisture-vapor-proof freezer containers or wrappings to prevent the food from drying out and to protect it from absorbing flavours. Seal tightly.

4. **Label and date** all packages for quick identification. On each package, include type of food, weight or number of servings and date of freezing.

5. **Freeze** foods at 0°F. or lower as soon as possible after packaging. If a delay is unavoidable, refrigerate sealed packages.

6. **Store** frozen foods at 0°F. or lower with as little variation in temperature as possible. Keep frozen until ready to use.

7. **Use** frozen foods regularly in order to have a complete turnover of frozen foods each year.

8. **Cook** frozen foods carefully according to directions. Cook thawed meat and poultry in the same way as fresh. Do not overcook frozen vegetables.

9. **Do not refreeze** thawed foods. Use foods as soon as possible after thawing. In an emergency, foods can be refrozen if still firm and ice crystals remain. Relabel and use as soon as possible. Thawed foods may be cooked and then refrozen.

PACKAGING

Special freezer containers and wrappings are available on the market and should be used to prevent foods from drying out in the freezer. They should be moisture-vapor-proof, odourless and tasteless.

FREEZER WRAPPINGS

1. Moisture-vapor-proof plastic films—cellophane, polyethylene, Saran.
2. Freezer aluminum foil.
3. Laminated papers, locker papers.
4. Heavily waxed freezer paper—for short storage of not more than 2 weeks.

To prevent puncturing of foil, plastic and other thin wrappings, an outer covering of heavy paper should be used.

How to wrap: Place food in centre of paper and bring the two edges together over the food. Fold these edges over two or three times until the wrapping fits closely around the food, forming a tight seal and leaving as little air space as possible. Force air out at the ends of the parcel by pressing the hand outward to the edges and folding the ends under the parcel. This method is called the "drugstore wrap". Aluminum foil does not require the drugstore wrap but is shaped around the food.

How to seal: Secure package with freezer tape, string or rubber or metal bands. Parcels wrapped in cellophane or plastic films may be "heat sealed". This is done by using a hand iron set on "rayon" or "synthetic". Place a piece of paper between plastic film and iron. Allow seal to set for a few minutes before folding ends under package.

FREEZER BAGS

Plastic bags are available in assorted sizes. They are good for packaging poultry, some cuts of meat, dry-pack fruits and vegetables and some prepared foods such as bread, cakes, cookies. **To seal:** Press out as much air as possible, twist top several times and secure tightly with a metal closure or rubber band. For long storage, plastic bags containing frozen food should be placed in a cardboard box or wrapped in heavy paper.

FREEZER CONTAINERS

These are available in several shapes, sizes and materials. Select the size that will hold only enough of a fruit or vegetable for one meal. Square and rectangular shapes with flat tops take up less space and may be stacked easily.

1. Folding cartons with replaceable liners. Some liners may require heat-sealing (see freezer wrappings).
2. Rigid containers—made of heavy aluminum foil, glass, plastic, tin or heavily waxed cardboard.
3. Baking dishes—heat and freezer proof glassware, aluminum pie plates, cake and roasting pans or special foil containers.

Headspace: When using liquid pack, it is essential to leave a headspace of 1″ in glass jars and ¼″ to ½″ in other containers.

FREEZING FRUITS AND VEGETABLES

Freeze only high quality fruits and vegetables of proper maturity. Always use garden-fresh vegetables and freeze within a few hours of gathering. Select varieties of fruits and vegetables that are recommended for freezing. Check with your Provincial Department of Agriculture for this information.

PREPARATION

In general, clean and cut up fruits and vegetables as for eating or cooking. Prepare and pack quickly and carefully, working with only enough fruits or vegetables to fill 3 or 4 containers at a time. All vegetables must be blanched (see page 191) before freezing to retard enzyme action and thus retain colour, flavour and texture. To remove insects that may be present in broccoli, Brussels sprouts or cauliflower, immerse prepared vegetables for 30 minutes in a brine made from about 1 tablespoon salt to 5 cups water. Rinse thoroughly and blanch.

PACKAGING

Pack fruits and vegetables in freezer cartons or containers, freezer bags (dry pack) or freezer wrappings.

Storage time for fruits and vegetables is 1 year.

PACKING FRUITS

1. **Dry Pack** is for those fruits which can be frozen without any preparation other than washing, draining, discarding imperfect ones and packing (e.g. blueberries, cranberries, currants, gooseberries, rhubarb.)

2. **Dry Sugar Pack** is for those fruits which can be combined with sugar, packaged and frozen. Fold recommended amount of sugar gently into the fruit. (See chart page 190.)

3. **Syrup Pack** is for those fruits which are packed in a syrup of a strength best suited to tartness of the fruit. (See chart page 190.) Slice or cut fruits directly into container. Leave berries whole, if desired. Be sure that syrup covers fruit and that headspace (page 188) is left for expansion. To keep fruit under syrup, especially apricots and peaches, place a crumpled piece of waxed paper or cellophane on top.

To make syrup: Add sugar to boiling water and stir until dissolved. Chill. **Do not cook or heat.**

TYPE OF SYRUP	SUGAR	WATER	YIELD
Thin	1 cup	2 cups	2½ cups
Moderately thin	1 cup	1½ cups	2 cups
Medium	1 cup	1 cup	1½ cups
Heavy	1 cup	¾ cup	1¼ cups

Allow ⅔ to 1 cup syrup for each 16 fluid ounce container.

TO PREVENT DISCOLOURATION OF FRUITS

Syrup Pack (for apricots and peaches)—add ¼ teaspoon powdered or crystalline ascorbic acid (Vitamin C) to 4 cups cold syrup and stir to dissolve.

Dry Sugar Pack (for apples, apricots and peaches)—dissolve ⅛ teaspoon ascorbic acid in 2 tablespoons cold water per 2 cups of prepared fruit; sprinkle over fruit and mix gently.

SERVING FROZEN FRUITS

To thaw—leave in unopened container in refrigerator for about 6 hours or at room temperature for about 2 hours.

To use in pies, muffins or cobblers—thaw in unopened package just until fruit can be separated. Continue as with fruit that has not been frozen.

To use in sauces, jams, jellies or preserves—place frozen fruit directly in saucepan and continue as for fruit that has not been frozen.

To use as a fresh fruit—serve when partially thawed. A few ice crystals should remain.

FRUITS

FRUIT	PREPARATION	TREATMENT AND RECOMMENDED PACK	FOR YIELD OF 4 CUPS FROZEN, YOU WILL NEED
Apples	Wash, pare, core, cut into slices.	Treat to prevent discolouration. Syrup Pack—use thin syrup. Dry Sugar Pack—use ¼ cup sugar to 4 cups prepared apples.	2½-3 lbs. sliced apples.
Applesauce	Prepare as usual.	Chill thoroughly and pack.	2½-3½ lbs. apples.
Apricots	Wash, peel if desired. Leave whole, halve or cut in quarters. Remove pits.	Treat to prevent discolouration. Syrup Pack—use moderately thin syrup. Dry Sugar Pack—use ⅔ cup sugar to 4 cups prepared apricots.	1⅓-2 lbs.
Blueberries	Sort out imperfect berries, wash, stem and drain.	Dry Pack—without sugar or syrup. Dry Sugar Pack—use ⅔ cup sugar to 4 cups prepared berries.	1 quart.
Cherries (Sour)	Sort out imperfect ones, wash, stem and pit.	Dry Sugar Pack—use 1 cup sugar to 4 cups prepared fruit. Syrup Pack—use heavy syrup.	2½-3 lbs. unpitted.

FRUIT	PREPARATION	TREATMENT AND RECOMMENDED PACK	FOR YIELD OF 4 CUPS FROZEN, YOU WILL NEED
Currants Cranberries	Stem and wash.	Dry Pack—without sugar or syrup.	1 lb.
Peaches	Dip in boiling water 1 minute, then in cold water. Remove skins and pits, then slice. Slice fruit directly into sugar or syrup.	Treat to prevent discolouration. Syrup Pack—use moderately thin syrup. Dry Sugar Pack—use ⅔ cup sugar to 4 cups prepared fruit.	2-3 lbs.
Plums	Wash, halve and pit.	Treat to prevent discolouration. Dry Sugar Pack—use ⅔ cup sugar to 4 cups prepared fruit. Syrup Pack—use thin syrup.	2-3 lbs.
Raspberries	Sort out imperfect ones, wash.	Dry Sugar Pack—use ½ cup sugar to 4 cups prepared fruit. Syrup Pack—use thin syrup.	1½-2 qts.
Rhubarb	Wash and cut into 1″ lengths or make into sauce.	Dry Pack—without sugar or syrup Dry Sugar Pack—use 1 cup sugar to 4 cups prepared fruit. Sauce—sweeten to taste and pack cold.	1½-2 lbs.
Strawberries	Sort out imperfect ones. Wash, sort and hull. Slice if desired.	Dry Sugar Pack—use ½ cup sugar to 4 cups whole berries or ⅔ cup sugar to 4 cups sliced berries. Syrup Pack—use medium syrup.	1-1⅓ qts.

BLANCHING (PRE-COOKING) VEGETABLES

Vegetables contain enzymes which if not controlled by blanching will cause undesirable changes in flavour, colour and texture of the vegetables when frozen. Place vegetables in a wire basket, colander or cheesecloth bag. Lower into vigourously boiling water (a gallon or more per pound of vegetable); cover kettle and immediately start counting the blanching time (see chart page 192). Keep heat on high so that water will quickly return to boiling. As soon as water returns to a vigourous boil, remove cover and move vegetable container up and down to ensure uniform blanching. **It is important that you follow the exact blanching time.** Chill immediately by placing in cold running water. Drain thoroughly. Do not allow the vegetables to remain in the cold water any longer than necessary. Blanch only 1 pound of vegetables at a time.

PACKING VEGETABLES

Pack the blanched and chilled vegetables in freezer containers (page 188). Pack dry. Label and freeze as soon as possible. Do not allow to stand at room temperature.

TO COOK FROZEN VEGETABLES

Cook most vegetables without thawing. Vegetables requiring partial or complete thawing should be thawed in the unopened freezer container. Thaw asparagus, broccoli and spinach just enough to break apart. Corn on the cob should be thawed completely before cooking. Pumpkin or squash can be thawed completely and used as you would for cooked or canned. In general, frozen vegetables are cooked by the same methods as fresh except that cooking time is reduced to about ½ the time of the corresponding fresh vegetable. **To boil:** For each pint container of frozen vegetable, use ¼ to ½ cup boiling water and ½ teaspoon salt. Cook corn on the cob in enough water to cover. Add vegetables, cover saucepan and bring to a boil. As vegetables thaw, break apart with a fork to allow all parts to cook evenly. **Begin counting the cooking time** as soon as water returns to a boil and cook gently until vegetables are just tender (see chart). For other methods of cooking vegetables, see page 172.

VEGETABLES

VEGETABLE	PREPARATION	BLANCHING TIME	COOKING TIME BEFORE SERVING	FOR YIELD OF 4 CUPS FROZEN, YOU WILL NEED
Asparagus	Select young tender stalks and remove tough ends and scales. Wash, trim, cut in 1″ pieces or leave whole.	small - 3 min. large - 4 min.	5 - 8 min.	2 - 3 lbs.
Beans, Green or Wax	Select young tender beans. Wash, trim, cut in uniform pieces or leave whole.	Cut - 3 min. Whole - 4 min.	Green, 7-10 min. Wax, 5 - 8 min.	1½ - 2 lbs.
Beans, Lima	Select young tender beans. Shell and wash.	small - 2 min. large - 4 min.	10 - 15 min.	4 - 5 lbs.
Broccoli *	Select dark green, compact heads. Trim off woody stalk. Cut through heads and stalk so that pieces are about 1″ across. Wash carefully.	medium - 3 min. large - 4 min.	5 - 8 min.	2 lbs.

VEGETABLE	PREPARATION	BLANCHING TIME	COOKING TIME BEFORE SERVING	FOR YIELD OF 4 CUPS FROZEN, YOU WILL NEED
Brussels * Sprouts	Select deep green, compact heads. Trim, removing coarse outer leaves. Wash carefully.	small - 3 min. medium - 4 min. large - 5 min.	5 - 9 min.	2 lbs.
Carrots	Select young tender carrots. Remove tops, wash and scrape. Slice, dice or leave small carrots whole.	Cut - 3 min. Whole - 5 min.	4 - 8 min.	2½ - 3 lbs. (without tops)
Cauliflower *	Select compact, white tender heads. Break into flowerets about 1″ in diameter. Wash carefully.	3 min.	3 - 6 min.	2 - 3 lbs.
Corn, whole kernel	Select freshly picked corn and prepare immediately. Husk, remove silk, trim. Cut kernels from cob **after** blanching.	4 min.	4 - 5 min.	4 - 5 lbs.
Corn, on the cob	Husk, remove silk, trim. Sort for size.	small - 7 min. medium - 9 min. large - 11 min.	3 - 6 min.	4 - 5 lbs.
Peas	Select young tender peas. Shell and wash.	2 min.	4 - 7 min.	4 - 5 lbs. (in pod)
Spinach, Chard and other greens	Select only tender leaves. Discard tough stems and bruised leaves. Wash very thoroughly.	2 min.	4 - 6 min.	2 - 3 lbs.
Squash, Pumpkin	Select well matured pumpkin or squash. Remove seeds and stringy portion. Cut in small pieces and boil until tender. Cool quickly and remove rind. Mash or sieve. Pack and freeze.	None	As a vegetable—reheat. For pies—thaw and use as canned or cooked.	2 - 3 lbs.

*Broccoli, Brussels sprouts and cauliflower are immersed in a brine solution (1 tablespoon salt to 5 cups water) for ½ hour to remove insects. Drain and rinse thoroughly before blanching.

FREEZING MEATS, FISH AND POULTRY

Use good quality meat, fish or poultry. Prepare as for table use in cuts of the size and weight to suit the needs of the family.

PACKAGING

Package roasts individually in freezer wrappings or bags, covering sharp bones with small pieces of crumpled aluminum foil to prevent puncturing of wrappings. Package steaks, chops, patties, chicken pieces, fish fillets, etc., in freezer wrappings or bags with double layer of waxed paper between pieces so that they can be easily separated while still frozen. Only freshly caught or cooked shellfish should be frozen. Use freezer cartons for bulk minced meat, stew meat, leftover meats, stew, gravy, etc. **Do not stuff poultry before freezing.** Wrap giblets and freeze separately. Label each package clearly with date, cut and weight. Freeze quickly at low temperature (below 0°F.).

STORAGE

Store at 0°F. or lower with as little temperature fluctuation as possible.

MAXIMUM STORAGE TIMES AT 0°F.

Bacon—1 to 2 months
Beef roasts, steaks—10 to 12 months
Cooked meats or poultry (stews, etc.)
— 1 to 2 months
Cooked roasts—2 to 3 months
Fish (lean)—up to 3 months
    (fat) —up to 2 months
Gravy (unthickened)—3 to 4 months
Ground meat (raw)—3 to 4 months
Lamb chops—4 to 5 months
Lamb roasts—6 to 8 months
Lobster, crabmeat—up to 2 months

Pork chops—3 to 4 months
Pork (cured)—1 to 2 months
Pork roasts—4 to 5 months
Poultry (whole)—up to 12 months
    (cut-up)—up to 6 months
    (giblets)—up to 3 months
    (geese, duck)—up to 3 months
Sausages, wieners—2 to 3 weeks
Shrimp, oysters, clams—up to 6 months
Variety meats—3 to 4 months
Veal roasts, chops—4 to 5 months

THAWING

Thaw meats and poultry in freezer wrapper at room temperature or in refrigerator. Frozen meat may be cooked thawed or in the frozen state. Variety meats may be partially or completely thawed before cooking. All poultry used for roasting or frying should be thawed completely whether birds are whole or cut in pieces. Cut up portions for stewing or braising may be cooked from the frozen state. Do not thaw fish before cooking except for frying and stuffing. **Do not refreeze** meat, fish or poultry that has been thawed. Cook promptly to prevent spoilage. After cooking fresh or frozen meat or poultry, it may be frozen and stored for a short period of time as for leftover meats (see chart above). If meat or poultry has only partially thawed, it may be safely refrozen. Use cooked poultry as soon as thawed, heating if desired.

COOKING

Thawed meat, fish and poultry are cooked in the same way as fresh. For unthawed meat, cooking time is longer. Cook frozen meats as follows:

Roasts—roast uncovered at 325°F. Increase cooking time by approximately half that required for fresh roasts.

Beef Steaks, Lamb Chops—panfry or broil. Increase cooking time by approximately twice that required for fresh.

Pork Chops—panfry or bake. Increase cooking time by half that required for fresh.

Veal Chops—panfry or bake. Increase cooking time by 5 to 10 minutes over that required for fresh.

Stewing Chicken—braise or stew. Usually not necessary to increase cooking time. For further recipes, see Meats (page 142) and Poultry (page 157). For cooking times of frozen fish, see Fish (page 136).

FREEZING PREPARED FOODS

Fill your freezer with a variety of baked goods to take care of special occasions and emergencies such as an unexpected guest.

BREADS, QUICK BREADS, CAKES, COOKIES

Preparation

Bake these in the usual manner. Cool quickly to room temperature before packaging. Freeze cookies either baked or unbaked. Macaroons and meringues do not freeze very well. Freeze cakes un-iced unless an uncooked butter icing is used.

Packaging

Package in freezer wrappings or bags. For easier handling, freeze iced cakes and fancy cookies first and then wrap them. Place wrapped cakes and cookies in cardboard boxes to prevent damage during storage. Unbaked cookie or'pastry dough may be wrapped in freezer wrappings or packaged in freezer cartons.

Thawing

Thaw in freezer wrapper at room temperature. If foil wrapped, they may be thawed in a slow oven (300°F.). Thaw only in the amounts needed as they soon become stale. Waffles, pancakes and sliced bread may be thawed in toaster if desired. Thaw unbaked cookies at room temperature for about 1 hour and use as fresh. To give freshness to breads, rolls, muffins or biscuits thawed at room temperature, wrap in foil and heat them in a slow oven (300°F.) 5 to 15 minutes.

Storage Time

Yeast Breads—3 months; Quick Breads and Cakes—4 to 5 months; Fruit Cakes— 1 year; Baked Cookies—12 months; Unbaked Cookie Dough—6 to 8 months.

PIES

Best pies for freezing are mince pies and double crust fruit pies. Never freeze cream or custard pies.

Preparation

Prepare pies in usual way. For best results, freeze unbaked in either regular or aluminum foil pie plates. Do not make slits in top crust before freezing. Add ⅓ more thickener to fruit pies that are to be frozen.

Packaging

Freeze pies and then package in freezer wrappings or bags. Place wrapped pie in cardboard box or cover with a cardboard plate to prevent damage during storage. Do not thaw pies before baking. Wrap unbaked pastry dough in freezer wrapping or package in a freezer carton; thaw at room temperature and use as for fresh.

Cooking

Cut slits in top crust. Place unbaked pie in hot oven (425°F.) and bake 60-75 minutes.

Storage Time

3 months. Unbaked pastry dough—6 to 8 months.

FREEZING SANDWICHES

Only a few ingredients are unsuitable to use in fillings for frozen sandwiches (see page 111). Fillings made of meat, fish, cheese or nuts freeze well.

Preparation

Prepare in usual way but do not trim crusts. Wrap at once and freeze.

Packaging

For 1 or 2 weeks of storage, wrap in double thickness of waxed paper. For longer storage, wrap in moisture-vapor-proof wrappings or freezer bags. Pack canapés and fancy sandwiches on trays or in boxes with double thickness of waxed paper between layers. Do not wrap different kinds of sandwiches in the same package as flavours of fillings will intermingle. Wrap sandwiches in small packages for speedier and even thawing.

Thawing

Thaw in freezer wrapper at room temperature. Trim crusts and cut sandwiches just before serving. Use promptly. Do not refreeze. At room temperature, open face sandwiches will take ½ hour to thaw; small packages of sandwiches will take 1 to 3 hours; large packages will take 4 to 6 hours.

Storage Time

3 to 4 weeks. Party type sandwiches—about 1 week..

JAMS, JELLIES, CONSERVES AND PRESERVES

Rules for Making Jelly

1. Use hard-ripe fruits when NOT ADDING PECTIN; use fully ripe fruits, if using pectin. Apples, currants, crab apples, grapes and sour plums, do not need added pectin.

2. Wash fruits; discard all bruised and spoiled portions.

3. Remove hulls (caps), stems, pits or seeds according to recipe instructions; leave whole, slice, chop or crush as stated in recipe.

4. Measure fruits after preparing, using a scale or liquid measuring cup.

5. Prepare juice as directed in recipe.

6. Measure sugar accurately; use cane or beet sugar. When not using pectin, usually ¾ cup sugar to 1 cup juice is added.

7. Juice which does not have a tart taste is not acid enough and needs lemon juice added to it, about 1 tablespoon per cup of juice.

8. Cook in small batches. Do not double recipes.
   With Pectin—follow manufacturer's instructions exactly.
   Without Pectin—sugar should be stirred until it dissolves, and then mixture is boiled, without stirring to the jellying point.

9. Quickly skim to remove foam, spoon boiling hot into hot sterilized jars. Use wide opening jars and spoon in jelly carefully to avoid air bubbles.

10. Let jars stand upright to cool.

TYPES OF JARS

Canning or Freezing Jars—Do one jar at a time. Leave ⅛" head space. Wipe jar with clean damp cloth. Place lid on jar immediately; screw band tight. Invert jar for 30 seconds (to destroy any mould or yeast which may have settled on the lid). Stand jar upright, then fill next jar. Remove band about 12 hours after. Check for seal. If seal is not perfect, leave bands on to keep jars tightly closed.

Jelly Glasses—Leave ¼" head space. Cover immediately with ⅛" hot paraffin wax. Prick any air bubbles that form on paraffin. Allow jars to stand undisturbed overnight or until cool. Cover with paper or metal lids.

STERILIZING JARS AND LIDS

Check jars for cracks, nicks and sharp edges on sealing surface. Wash jars and lids; rinse well. Cover with hot (not boiling) water and bring to a boil—no further boiling is necessary. Keep hot until ready to use. While jams or jellies are cooking, remove jars and lids from hot water and invert them to drain. Jars should be hot and dry when filled.

Test for Seal—Grasp lid and lift jar. If lid supports the weight of the jar, the seal is perfect.

JELLYING POINT TEST

Thermometer—Check boiling point of water with candy thermometer. Boil jellies etc. until the temperature reaches 8°F. above the boiling point of water; 9°F. for jams.

Spoon Test—Dip a cool metal spoon into boiling syrup; raise and tilt spoon until syrup runs from side. When jellying point is reached, liquid will not flow in a stream, but will divide into distinct drops which run together and fall off the spoon as one sheet.

MINT JELLY

1½ cups packed mint leaves
    and stems
2½ cups water
3½ cups granulated sugar
3 tablespoons lemon juice

Green food colouring
½ bottle (6 oz.) commercial
    liquid pectin
¼ teaspoon mint flavour extract

Wash 1½ cups of packed mint leaves. Place in a large saucepan and crush thoroughly with a wooden masher; add 2½ cups water and bring quickly to a boil. Remove from heat, cover and let stand 10 minutes; strain. Measure 1¾ cups in a saucepan; add sugar and lemon juice, mixing well. Stir in green food colouring until desired colour is obtained (about 10-15 drops). Place over high heat and bring to a boil, stirring constantly; add liquid pectin immediately. Taste and add mint flavour if necessary. Bring to a full rolling boil and boil hard for 1 minute; remove from heat. Skim quickly and pour hot into hot sterilized jars; seal.

Yield: 2 (8 oz.) jars.

APPLE OR CRABAPPLE JELLY

3½ quarts tart, ripe apples
7½ cups granulated sugar
Cold water

Do not peel or core apples; remove stems and leaves and cut in small pieces. Add 3 cups of water; bring to a boil, cover and simmer 10 minutes. Crush apples, cover and simmer 5 more minutes. Place in a jelly cloth or bag and squeeze out juice. Strain this juice once more in a jelly bag WITHOUT SQUEEZING. Measure 5 cups of juice into a large saucepan; add sugar and mix well. Bring to boil over high heat, stirring constantly, until jelly point; remove from heat. Skim quickly and spoon carefully and quickly into hot sterilized jars; seal.

Yield: 3 (8 oz.) jars.

Rules for Jams, Marmalades, Conserves and Preserves

1. Select firm, ripe but never over-ripe, fruit.
2. Wash fruit in cold running water.
3. Remove hulls (caps), cores, pits, seeds or skins; leave whole, slice or chop as stated in recipe, discarding all spoiled portions.
4. Weigh or measure fruit and sugar accurately. Cane or beet sugar may be used.
5. Cook in small batches, do not double recipe unless indicated.
6. Combine fruit and sugar and cook over low heat until sugar dissolves, stirring occasionally.
7. When sugar is dissolved, cook rapidly (boil); stir frequently to prevent sticking.
8. Jams, marmalades, conserves and preserves thicken as they cool. Cook until jelly point is reached. (See below.)
9. Pour hot jam, marmalade, conserves or preserves into hot, sterilized jars, leaving a ½" head space. Jars should be hot and dry when filled.
10. Seal all fruit products air tight in home canning jars. If ordinary household jars are used, seal with melted, hot paraffin wax. Use only enough paraffin to make a layer about ⅛" thick. Prick any air bubbles that form in the paraffin wax.
11. Store in dark, dry, reasonably cool area.

STERILIZING JARS AND LIDS

Check jars for cracks, nicks and sharp edges on sealing surface. Wash jars and lids; rinse well. Cover with hot (not boiling) water and bring to a boil—no further boiling is necessary. Keep hot until ready to use. While jams or jellies are cooking, remove jars and lids from hot water and invert them to drain. Jars should be hot and dry when filled.

JELLYING POINT TEST

Thermometer--Check boiling point of water with candy thermometer. Boil jams, etc. until the temperature reaches 9°F. above the boiling point of water for jams—8°F. for jellies.

Spoon Test—Dip a cool metal spoon into boiling syrup; raise and tilt spoon until syrup runs from side. When jellying point is reached, liquid will not flow in a stream, but will divide into distinct drops which run together and fall off the spoon as one sheet.

DRIED APRICOT JAM

4 cups (½ lb.) dried apricots
4 cups boiling water
7 cups granulated sugar
3 tablespoons lemon juice
¼ cup packed, slivered, blanched almonds
1 bottle (6 oz.) commercial liquid pectin

Wash dried apricots; drain and put through food chopper, using a coarse blade or cut coarsely with scissors. Pour 4 cups boiling water over apricots and let stand 48 hours. Simmer 30 minutes or until mixture measures 4 cups; add sugar slivered almonds and lemon juice. Bring to full boil and boil rapidly for 1 MINUTE. Remove from heat; add pectin and stir. Skim quickly and pour into hot sterilized jars; seal. Jam is slow in setting but becomes quite firm in a week or two.

Yield: 7 (8 oz.) jars.

SPICED PEACH JAM

2 cups crushed, peeled peaches	¼ teaspoon whole cloves
2 tablespoons water	⅛ teaspoon whole allspice
1½ cups granulated sugar	¼ cinnamon stick

Combine crushed peaches and water; cook gently for 10 minutes. Add sugar and slowly bring to boiling, stirring occasionally until sugar dissolves. Add whole cloves, whole allspice and cinnamon stick, tied in a cheesecloth bag, to jam during cooking; remove just before pouring jam into jars. Cook rapidly until thick, about 15 minutes, stirring frequently to prevent sticking. Pour boiling hot into hot sterilized jars; seal.

Yield: 2 (8 oz.) jars. RECIPE MAY BE DOUBLED.

RASPBERRY JAM

9 cups crushed raspberries	6 cups granulated sugar

Combine crushed raspberries and sugar; bring slowly to boiling, stirring occasionally until sugar dissolves. Cook rapidly to, or almost to, jellying point, depending on whether a firm or soft jam is preferred. Pour boiling hot into hot sterilized jars; seal.

Yield: 3 to 4 (16 oz.) bottles.

Note: Recipe is good for blackberries, blueberries, boysenberries, gooseberries, loganberries.

YELLOW PLUM JAM

6 cups chopped yellow plums (about 3 pounds)	3 tablespoons lemon juice
4½ cups granulated sugar	1 cup water

Combine all ingredients. Bring slowly to boiling point, stirring occasionally until sugar dissolves. Cook rapidly almost to jellying point—takes about 20 minutes. Stir frequently to prevent sticking. Pour boiling hot into sterilized jars; seal.
Yield: 4 (8 oz.) jars.

PEACH AND CHERRY MARMALADE

6 lbs. peaches	1 bottle (6 oz.) commercial
3 oranges	liquid pectin
5 lbs. granulated sugar	1 jar (8 oz.) maraschino cherries
½ cup lemon juice	

Peel and slice peaches; slice oranges thinly using skin and pulp. Combine peaches, oranges and sugar. Tie peach stones in a cheesecloth bag and add to peaches with syrup from cherries. Simmer 3 hours; add lemon juice and simmer 5 more minutes. Remove peach stones and add chopped cherries and pectin. Stir and let stand for 5 minutes. Pour into sterilized jars; seal.

Yield: 6 (16 oz.) jars.

CITRUS MARMALADE

1½ cups thinly sliced grapefruit peel (about 2)	1½ cups finely chopped grapefruit pulp
½ cup thinly sliced orange peel (about 2)	1 cup finely chopped orange pulp
6 cups water	½ cup thinly sliced lemon
	6½ cups granulated sugar

Peel the skin from grapefruits and oranges, allowing a small portion of the white underskin to remain. Save seeds from fruit pulp and place in a small cheesecloth bag. Add water to fruit peel, pulp, lemon slices and seeds; cover and let stand 12-18 hours in a cool place. Remove seeds and add sugar. Bring slowly to boiling point, stirring until sugar dissolves. Cook rapidly to jelling point, about 30 minutes, stirring frequently. Pour, boiling hot, into sterilized jars; seal.
Yield: 4 (8 oz.) jars.

CHERRY-APPLE PINEAPPLE CONSERVE

2 cups chopped, cored, pared tart apples	6 cups sugar
	½ cup coarsely chopped walnuts
5 cups pitted sweet cherries (about 2 pounds)	¼ cup lemon juice
¾ cup canned, drained pineapple chunks	

Combine fruits and sugar; let stand 1 hour. Bring slowly to boiling point, stirring occasionally until sugar dissolves. Cook rapidly until thick, about 25 minutes, stirring frequently to prevent sticking. Add nuts and lemon juice the last 5 minutes of cooking. Pour, boiling hot, into sterilized jars; seal.

Yield: 3 (16 oz.) jars.

PINEAPPLE AND PEACH CONSERVE

2½ cups diced peaches	2 cups sugar
1 cup canned pineapple chunks	Juice and rind of 1 orange

Wash and blanch peaches; cut into cubes to measure 2½ cups. Mix peaches and pineapple and sugar; add grated orange rind and juice. Slowly bring to boil, stirring occasionally until sugar dissolves; cook rapidly until thick and clear—about 20 minutes, stirring frequently. Pour, boiling hot, into hot sterilized jars; seal.

Yield: 3 (8 oz.) jars.

WATERMELON PRESERVES

7 cups watermelon pieces	1 tablespoon ground ginger
4 tablespoons coarse salt	4 cups granulated sugar
Cold water	¼ cup lemon juice

Use the firm light pink watermelon flesh; cut in 1″ pieces. Dissolve salt thoroughly in 8 cups cold water and pour over watermelon pieces; let stand 5 to 6 hours. Drain, rinse well and drain again. Cover with cold water and let stand 30 minutes; drain. Sprinkle with ginger, cover with water and cook until fork tender; drain. Combine sugar and lemon juice and 7 cups water. Bring slowly to boiling and boil 5 minutes; add watermelon pieces and boil gently for 30 minutes, then simmer until watermelon is clear, about 3 hours. Pack, boiling hot, into cleaned jars, leaving ¼″ head space; adjust caps. Process jars about 20 minutes at 180°F. in hot water bath.

Yield: 3 (8 oz.) jars.

Note: Good with ice cream and as a sweet relish with meat.

PICKLES AND RELISHES

Rules for Pickles and Relishes

1. Select fresh, firm fruits and vegetables that are free of decayed spots. Slightly underripe fruits are best for pickling. Cucumbers and green tomatoes should be small to medium size and should be pickled within 24 hours of picking.

2. Use coarse salt for pickling. If table salt is used, use measures as given in recipe. However, table salt tends to cloud the brine.

3. Use the best vinegar. Cider vinegar gives the best flavour but white vinegar gives the best colour.

4. Use fresh spices and herbs. When left in pickles too long, spices cause pickles to become dark and strong-flavoured.

5. Use white granulated sugar unless specified otherwise.

6. Use enamel ware, glass, aluminum, stainless steel or stoneware utensils for pickling. Brass, copper, iron and galvanized utensils are apt to cause undesirable colour changes or they will react with the acid or salt to produce unwholesome substances.

7. Pack, while hot, in sterilized jars or bottles. Remove air bubbles by running a rubber bottle scraper between jar and food. If needed, add more liquid to cover. The condition of the fruit or vegetable and the manner of packing the food product will determine how much liquid is needed.

8. Fill one jar and adjust cap before next jar.

9. Stand filled jars, right side up, away from drafts to cool.

10. Check for seal 12 hours later.
    Test for Seal—Grasp lid and lift jar. If lid supports the weight of the jar, the seal is perfect.

11. Store in dark, dry, reasonably cool place.

STERILIZING JARS AND LIDS

Check jars for cracks, nicks and sharp edges on sealing surface. Wash jars and lids; rinse well. Cover with hot (not boiling) water and bring to a boil—no further boiling is necessary. Keep hot until ready to use. While pickles or relishes are cooking, remove jars and lids from hot water and invert them to drain. Jars should be hot and dry when filled.

CORN RELISH

18 ears of corn	2 tablespoons dry mustard
4 onions	3 cups sugar
2 green peppers	1 cup Five Roses All-purpose Flour
5 cups white vinegar	1 tablespoon tumeric
¼ cup salt	Water

Cut corn from cob; place in large kettle and just cover with water; bring to boil and simmer for 15 minutes then pour off all the water. Chop onions and green peppers and mix with corn. Add 4 cups vinegar and boil for 15 minutes, timing from when the mixture begins to boil. Mix salt, mustard, sugar, Five Roses Flour and tumeric in top of double boiler. Gradually add remaining vinegar and cook over boiling water for 10 minutes. Add this mixture to vegetables and cook for another 10 minutes until thoroughly mixed, **stirring constantly.** Seal in sterilized jars while relish is hot.

Yield: 7 pint (16 oz.) jars.

Note: This is a sweet and sour type relish. Excellent with ham, pork, veal or beef.

PRIZE FRUIT SAUCE

30 large ripe tomatoes	1 large bunch celery
6 onions	4 cups sugar
6 pears	2 tablespoons salt
6 peaches	4 cups cider vinegar
3 green peppers	½ cup mixed pickling spices
3 red sweet peppers	

Wash, prepare and chop fruits and vegetables; place in large kettle. Mix sugar, salt and vinegar with fruits and vegetables. Tie the pickling spices in a muslin bag and add to mixture; discard before bottling. Bring to boil and simmer slowly until thick —about 2½ to 3 hours. Store in sterilized air-tight jars, while hot. As we cannot control the juices from the fruits, the mixture may be still juicy at the end of 2½ hours simmering. If this happens, drain off the excess liquid.

Yield: 11 to 12 (16 oz.) jars.

Note: Excellent with roast beef, steak or pork.

HOME-MADE TOMATO SAUCE

24 ripe tomatoes	2 tablespoons salt
6 onions, chopped	1 cup brown sugar
2 red sweet peppers, chopped	2 tablespoons dry mustard
1 cup chopped celery	1 cup malt vinegar
1 teaspoon allspice	

Mix tomatoes, chopped onions, chopped red peppers, chopped celery, allspice and salt together and simmer until soft; strain through a sieve. Add brown sugar, mustard and vinegar; bring to boil and simmer for 30 minutes. Seal hot in sterilized bottles.

Yield: 5 to 6 - 1 pint (16 oz.) jars.

PEPPER HASH

12 red sweet peppers
12 green peppers
12 onions, medium size
½ cup salt

2 cups cider vinegar
4 cups sugar
Cold water

Remove seeds and white inside part from pepper; peel onions. Put peppers and onions through food chopper or chop very finely; cover with boiling water and let stand 15 minutes then drain well. Put in large saucepan and add salt; cover with cold water and bring quickly to boiling point. Boil 5 minutes; drain well. Add cider vinegar and sugar; bring to boil and boil 12 minutes. Pack in sterilized jars, while hot.

Yield: 10 (8 oz.) jars.

INDIA RELISH

1 peck (13 lbs.) green tomatoes
1 small cabbage, finely chopped
6 onions, chopped
3 red sweet peppers, chopped
2 green peppers, chopped
1½ cups salt

5 cups cider vinegar
8 cups sugar
2 tablespoons celery seeds
2 tablespoons mustard seeds
2 tablespoons coriander seeds
1 tablespoon whole cloves

Chop tomatoes; add salt and let stand over night. Drain tomatoes; add finely chopped cabbage and boil in cider vinegar. Add chopped onions, chopped red and green peppers, sugar, celery, mustard and coriander seeds. Tie the cloves in a muslin bag; boil together until onions are tender. Remove muslin bag and bottle relish while hot in sterilized jars.

Yield: 8 to 9 (16 oz.) jars.

PRIZE MUSTARD PICKLES

2 green peppers
2 red sweet peppers
3 pints (6 cups) silverskin onions
2 quarts (8 cups) small firm gherkins
2 small heads cauliflower
1½ cups coarse salt
Cold water

1 cup Five Roses All-purpose Flour
2½ cups sugar
2 tablespoons tumeric
1 tablespoon mustard seed
1 cup water
5 cups cider vinegar
½ cup dry mustard

Remove seeds from peppers and cut in strips; peel onions and wash gherkins. Break cauliflowers into small flowerets; mix with peppers, onions and gherkins. Place in scalded crock or other large earthenware receptacle. Sprinkle vegetables with coarse salt and cover with cold water; let stand over night. Drain thoroughly. Combine Five Roses Flour, sugar, tumeric and mustard seed. Gradually add 1 cup water, stirring until smooth. Stir in vinegar and dry mustard. Cook until sauce coats spoon and mixture thickens, stirring constantly. Add vegetables; simmer 15 minutes. Pack hot into sterilized jars, leaving ¼" head space. Adjust caps; seal. If desired, process jars 10 minutes in boiling water bath to insure against spoilage.

Yield: 8 to 9 (16 oz.) jars.

Note: The flavour of Mustard Pickles mellows with age. Allow at least 1 to 2 months storage before using.

PICKLED RED CABBAGE

1 head red cabbage	8 cups white vinegar
½ cup salt	4 tablespoons whole pickling spice
1 cup sugar	

Remove all dark, outer leaves from cabbage; slice ¼-inch thick or put through food chopper. Place in large pan or crock and sprinkle with salt; cover with water and let stand over night. Drain thoroughly and pack cabbage loosely in sterilized jars. Bring vinegar, sugar and whole pickling spice (tied in muslin bag) to boiling point, stirring until sugar is dissolved. Remove pickling spice and pour scalded vinegar over cabbage to cover; seal immediately. If vinegar is strong, dilute with a little water.

Yield: About 4 (16 oz.) jars.

WATERMELON PICKLES

16 cups watermelon pieces*	2 pieces ginger root
1 cup salt	1 lemon, thinly sliced
Cold water	8 cups granulated sugar
2 tablespoons whole cloves	4 cups white vinegar
3 cinnamon sticks	4 cups water

Use the firm light pink watermelon flesh; cut in 1-inch pieces. Dissolve salt thoroughly in 8 cups cold water, pour over watermelon pieces—add more water if needed to cover watermelon. Let stand 6 hours; drain, rinse well and cover with fresh cold water. Cook until just tender; drain. Tie spices in a cheesecloth bag and combine with remaining ingredients; simmer 10 minutes. Add watermelon pieces and simmer until clear; remove spice bag. (Add boiling water to syrup if it becomes too thick before the watermelon pieces are clear.) Pack, boiling hot, into hot sterilized jars, leaving ⅛-inch head space; seal.

Yield: 6 (8 oz.) jars.

*Approximately ½ a large watermelon.

Note: Good with pork or turkey.

N O T E S

CANDY

An extra special treat when made yourself! Read these few tips so that you can turn out perfect candy every time.

Prevent crystals from forming by buttering the sides of the saucepan before adding ingredients. When mixture bubbles up, grains of sugar can't cling.

Select a heavy saucepan that has high sides and inside is smooth.

Always stir until sugar is dissolved. One sugar crystal can cause whole mixture to be grainy.

Beating can be made easier by first cooling cooked mixture without stirring to lukewarm (110°F.). Use buttered pan or platter. Always have pan ready before making candy.

TO TEST CANDY

Use a candy thermometer, if possible. If not, follow the cold water test.

COLD WATER TEST

Drop a few drops of syrup into a small bowl of very cold water (not ice-cold). Form drops into a ball. The firmness indicates temperature of syrup.

TEST	TEMPERATURE	COLD WATER TEST
Thread	230°F. - 234°F.	Syrup forms 2″ thread when dropped from spoon
Soft Ball	234°F. - 240°F.	Syrup forms a soft ball which flattens on removal
Firm Ball	244°F. - 248°F.	Syrup forms a firm ball which does not flatten on removal
Hard Ball	250°F. - 266°F.	Syrup forms a ball, hard enough to hold its shape, yet plastic
Soft Crack	270°F. - 290°F.	Syrup separates into threads which are hard but not brittle
Hard Crack	300°F. - 310°F.	Syrup separates into threads which are hard and brittle

THERMOMETER TEST

Clip candy thermometer to pan after syrup boils. The bulb of the thermometer must be covered with boiling liquid. Read thermometer at eye level. Check accuracy of thermometer by placing it in hot water. When water boils, thermometer should register 212°F. If it is above or below, add or subtract degrees to make allowance in recipe.

BROWN SUGAR FUDGE

1½ cups granulated sugar
1 cup brown sugar
⅓ cup light cream
⅓ cup milk

2 tablespoons butter
1 teaspoon vanilla
½ cup chopped nuts (optional)

Combine sugars, cream, milk and butter in heavy 3 quart saucepan. Cook over medium heat, stirring constantly, until sugar dissolves and mixture comes to a boil. Cook to soft ball stage (238°F.) without stirring. Remove from heat and let cool to lukewarm (110°F.) by placing pan in cold water. Add vanilla; beat vigorously until mixture thickens and begins to lose its gloss. Stir in chopped nuts and quickly spread into buttered pan or platter; cut in squares.

Yield: 18 to 20 pieces.

CHOCOLATE FUDGE

3 cups granulated sugar
1 cup milk
3 squares unsweetened chocolate
Pinch of salt

2 teaspoons corn syrup
3 tablespoons butter
1½ teaspoons vanilla
Walnut halves (optional)

Combine sugar, milk, chocolate, salt and corn syrup in a heavy 3 quart saucepan. Cook over medium heat stirring constantly until sugar is dissolved, chocolate melts and mixture comes to a boil. Cook to soft ball stage (236°F.) without stirring. Remove from heat immediately; add butter and let cool to lukewarm (110°F.) by placing pan in cold water. Add vanilla. Beat vigorously until mixture thickens and starts to lose its gloss. Stir in nuts. Spread quickly into buttered pan or platter. Cut in squares. Top each square with a walnut half, if desired.

Yield: 18 to 20 pieces.

MOLASSES PULL TAFFY

2 cups granulated sugar
1 cup molasses
½ cup water
1 tablespoon white vinegar

¼ teaspoon cream of tartar
⅛ teaspoon baking soda
2 tablespoons butter

Combine sugar, molasses, water and vinegar in heavy 3 quart saucepan. Cook over medium heat, stirring constantly until sugar dissolves and mixture comes to a boil. Add cream of tartar and cook to very hard ball stage (260°F.). Remove from heat; stir in baking soda and butter. Pour into buttered shallow dish. When cool enough to handle, pull it with the hands, until it is porous and light coloured— takes about 20 to 30 minutes. Cut in 1" lengths and chill for a few minutes to harden. Wrap individual pieces in waxed paper, if desired.

Yield: 10 dozen 1" pieces.

DIVINITY FUDGE

1½ cups brown sugar
½ cup water
1 teaspoon white vinegar

1 egg white, stiffly beaten
½ teaspoon vanilla
½ cup chopped nuts

Combine brown sugar, water and vinegar in heavy 2 quart saucepan. Cook over medium heat, stirring constantly until sugar dissolves and mixture begins to boil. Cook to hard ball stage (250°F.) without stirring. Remove from heat immediately and gradually pour over stiffly beaten egg white, beating until thick and mixture holds its shape. Fold in nuts and vanilla. Drop by teaspoonfuls onto waxed paper or spread on buttered pan and cut in squares.

Yield: 2 dozen pieces.

MAPLE CREAM

3 cups brown sugar
⅔ cup light cream

½ cup chopped nuts
¼ teaspoon maple flavouring

Combine brown sugar and cream in heavy 3 quart saucepan. Cook over medium heat, stirring constantly until sugar is dissolved and mixture begins to boil. Cook to soft ball stage (238°F.) without stirring. Let cool to lukewarm (110°F.) by placing pan in cold water. Beat until creamy; add nuts and flavouring. Continue beating until mixture thickens and begins to lose its gloss. Spread on buttered pan or platter; cut in squares.

Yield: 2 dozen pieces.

CANDY APPLES

4 cups granulated sugar
2 cups boiling water
½ teaspoon cream of tartar

Few drops red food colouring
18-20 medium-size apples

Mix sugar, boiling water and cream of tartar in top of double boiler. Bring slowly to boiling point over medium heat, stirring constantly. Boil without stirring until syrup reaches hard crack stage (310°F.) or changes to a yellow colour; **watch carefully.** Wash off any sugar which may adhere to sides of saucepan, using a wet cloth wrapped around handle of wooden spoon or index finger. Remove from heat and place in pan of hot water during dipping. Stir in red food colouring. Use firm, clean, medium-size apples; insert a wooden skewer in stem end of each. Dip in hot syrup to cover apples; hold over pan until dripping stops. Place on waxed paper until set.

Yield: Enough syrup for 18-20 apples.

POTATO CANDY

1 medium-size potato
3-3½ cups icing sugar, sifted
1-1½ cups shredded coconut

1 teaspoon vanilla
2 squares unsweetened chocolate, melted

Cook potato in unsalted boiling water until soft; drain and mash with a fork. Work in sifted icing sugar with a wooden spoon. (Amount of icing sugar will depend on size of potato.) Blend in coconut and vanilla. Mixture will look like a thick icing. Shape into 2 rolls, 1″ in diameter. Wrap in waxed paper and chill until firm—about 2 hours. Pour melted chocolate over rolls to coat completely. Cool and rewrap. Store in refrigerator until ready to use. Serve in thin slices.

Yield: Approximately 2½ dozen slices.

TAFFY FRUIT AND NUTS

Make candy apple syrup, omitting the red food colouring. When syrup is ready for dipping, take fruits and nuts separately on a long skewer; dip in syrup to cover, remove and drain on waxed paper. Any kind of nuts, dates, figs, orange sections, candied cherries, candied pineapple, etc., may be used. This makes a very popular Christmas sweetmeat.

POPCORN BALLS

½ cup corn syrup
½ cup molasses
¼ teaspoon salt

1 teaspoon white vinegar
2 tablespoons butter
8 cups popped corn

Combine syrup, molasses, salt and vinegar in heavy 3 quart saucepan. Cook to hard ball stage (256°F.), stirring carefully to prevent burning. Remove from heat; add butter, stirring just enough to mix. Slowly pour the cooked syrup over the popped corn; mix well. Butter hands lightly and **quickly** shape mixture into balls.

Yield: About 1 dozen medium-size balls.

PEANUT BRITTLE

3 cups granulated sugar
½ teaspoon salt

2 cups unsalted peanuts
2 tablespoons butter

Combine sugar and salt in large heavy skillet. Heat over high heat until sugar lumps. Lower heat and continue cooking, stirring constantly until sugar is completely melted—will be a rich brown colour. Stir in nuts and butter. Pour immediately on greased jelly-roll pan and spread thinly. Cool and crack into pieces.

Yield: About 2 dozen pieces.

Note: If salted nuts are used, omit salt in recipe.

UNCOOKED CHOCOLATE FUDGE

1 egg white, unbeaten
2 tablespoons milk
2⅓ cups sifted icing sugar

2 squares unsweetened chocolate
½ teaspoon vanilla
⅓ cup chopped nuts

Mix egg white with milk. Gradually stir in icing sugar. Melt chocolate and add to sugar mixture with vanilla; beat until well blended. Stir in nuts. Spread on buttered pan or platter. Chill until firm; cut in squares.

Yield: 18 to 20 pieces.

We appreciate the fact that from time to time certain problems may arise with regard to home cooking and baking. For this reason we are pleased to remind you that our Five Roses Kitchens will always be most pleased to help you. Address all inquiries to:

PAULINE HARVEY, *Director*
FIVE ROSES KITCHENS
BOX 6089
MONTREAL, P.Q.

FOREIGN FARE

Would you like to try a Scandinavian Smörgåsbord or a tantalizing French dish—or even an exotic dish from the Far East? To help you entertain your guests, we have selected a few menus from around the world and included the recipes to go with them.

FRANCE

MENU

Prize Onion Soup (page 117)

Boeuf Bourguignon

Green Salad   *French Dressing (page 185)*

French Bread (page 18)   *Butter*

Crêpes Suzettes

BOEUF BOURGUIGNON

1 cup bouillon	1½ cups chopped onion
3 tablespoons Five Roses All-purpose Flour	1 cup burgundy wine
	1 bay leaf
1 tablespoon tomato paste	¼ teaspoon thyme
2 lbs. lean beef, round or chuck	1 teaspoon chopped fresh parsley
3 tablespoons bacon drippings	1 cup mushrooms
2 tablespoons sherry	¼ cup butter

Blend bouillon, Five Roses Flour and tomato paste to make a smooth paste; set aside. Cut beef into 1″ pieces. Heat bacon drippings in a heavy kettle or Dutch oven. Add meat and brown on all sides; remove from fat and set aside. Add the sherry and onions; cook until onions are transparent, stirring occasionally. Blend in tomato paste mixture. Bring quickly to boil, stirring constantly; stir in burgundy wine and seasonings. Add beef; cover and simmer 2½ to 3 hours or until meat is tender. Meanwhile, slice mushrooms and sauté in butter. Add to meat about 15 minutes before serving.

Yield: 4 servings. Recipe may be doubled.

CRÊPES SUZETTES

½ cup Five Roses All-purpose Flour	¾ cup milk
2 tablespoons sugar	1 tablespoon melted butter
Pinch of salt	1 tablespoon cognac or brandy
1 egg, beaten	1 tablespoon butter

Make crêpes first. Stir Five Roses Flour, sugar and salt together. Combine beaten egg and milk; add all-at-once to dry ingredients and beat until smooth. Add melted butter and cognac; strain. Let stand for 2 hours to develop the cognac flavour. In a small frying pan or skillet (about 5″ to 5½″ in diameter), heat 1 tablespoon butter. Pour 1 tablespoon batter onto hot butter and rotate pan quickly to spread batter. Cook 1 minute on each side. Set aside and repeat, cooking one at a time. Pile cooked crêpes on top of each other.

Sauce

½ cup sifted icing sugar	1 tablespoon lemon rind
½ cup butter	2 tablespoons sherry
Juice and rind of 1 orange	3 tablespoons cognac
Juice of 1 lemon	

Melt icing sugar and butter in a skillet over low heat or in a chafing dish, stirring constantly. Strain orange juice and add with lemon juice, rinds and sherry; bring to a boil. Heat crêpes, one at a time, in sauce and fold them in half, then in quarters; place around edge of skillet. When all crêpes are done, sprinkle with cognac. As soon as cognac is warm, ignite. Serve while sauce is flaming.

Yield: 20 crêpes (4 to 6 servings).

ITALY

MENU

Chilled Tomato Juice

Lasagne

Tossed Almond Salad (page 180)　　　　　　*Italian Dressing (page 185)*

Garlic Bread (page 21)　　　　　　*Butter*

Strawberry Meringue

STRAWBERRY MERINGUE

1 recipe Hard Meringues (page 71)	⅓ cup sugar
2 cups fresh strawberries	1 teaspoon vanilla
2 cups whipping cream	

Prepare recipe for Hard Meringues. Shape into 8 individual nests with a spoon or with a decorating cone filled with the meringue mixture onto a paper lined cookie sheet. Bake in a slow oven (250°F.) for 2 hours. Turn oven off and leave to dry in oven for 1 hour. Slice the strawberries, setting 8 whole ones aside for decorating. Whip the cream; add the sugar and vanilla and beat until cream holds its shape. Fold the strawberries into the cream; chill. Just before serving, spoon mixture into shells. Top each with a whole strawberry. If desired, sprinkle a few drops of cognac on each meringue shell before filling.

Yield: 8 servings.

LASAGNE

1 medium onion, finely chopped
1 clove garlic, minced
2 tablespoons olive oil
1 lb. ground beef
1 can (10 oz.) sliced mushrooms
1 can (7½ oz.) tomato sauce
1 can (5½ oz.) tomato paste
2 teaspoons salt
1 teaspoon dried oregano
¾ cup water

2 eggs
1 package (10 oz.) frozen chopped
  spinach (optional)
1 cup creamed cottage cheese
⅓ cup grated Parmesan cheese
1 lb. lasagne noodles, cooked and
  drained
1 package (12 oz.) Mozzarella
  cheese, thinly sliced

Sauté onion and garlic in 1 tablespoon of olive oil; add ground beef and break apart; cook until brown. Blend in mushrooms (including mushroom liquid), tomato sauce, tomato paste, 1 teaspoon of the salt, oregano and water; simmer 15 minutes. Mix 1 of the eggs with the thawed spinach, cottage cheese, Parmesan cheese, remaining olive oil and salt. Beat the second egg slightly and toss with the cooked noodles. Pour half of the meat sauce in an oblong baking pan (9″ x 13″) and cover with a layer of half of the noodles. Spread all the cottage cheese mixture over the noodles; then cover this with the remaining noodles. Top with remaining meat sauce. Bake in a moderate oven (350°F.) 45 minutes; arrange strips of Mozzarella cheese on top and bake 15 minutes longer. Serve hot.

Yield: 8 servings.

To double recipe: Repeat procedure twice. Use 2 smaller pans if another 9″ x 13″ pan is not available.

Note: This recipe may be made the night before. Prepare Lasagne, but do not bake it. Cover and store in refrigerator until ready to bake.

SWITZERLAND

MENU

Chilled Juice
Fondue Bourguignonne

Onion Sauce   *Sauce Piquante*

Russian Sauce   *Sauce Béarnaise*

Tomato Aspic (page 183) on Lettuce

Crusty Rolls (page 26)   *Butter*

Fresh Fruit Cocktail
Cheese and Crackers

FONDUE BOURGUIGNONNE

Allow ½ lb. fillet mignon or sirloin steak per person and cut into 1″ pieces. Heap, uncooked, into individual serving bowls. Put 1½″ of cooking oil into electric saucepan or chafing dish with a good heating element. Keep fat hot. Fat should be hot enough to brown a 1″ cube of bread in 1 minute. Arrange meat, skewers or fondue forks and a selection of sauces (recipes follow) on table. Have each guest cook their own meat in the fat (takes only a few minutes) and then dip the cooked meat into the sauce of their choice. Allow about 2 to 3 tablespoons of each sauce per guest. Serve with a salad and hard rolls.

ONION SAUCE

Combine ¾ cup finely chopped onion with 1 cup mayonnaise.

RUSSIAN SAUCE

Combine ¼ cup chili sauce with 1 cup mayonnaise.

SAUCE PIQUANTE

Combine 1 teaspoon dry mustard, ½ cup finely minced shallots, 1 cup commercial sour cream and ½ cup whipping cream. Add salt to taste. Makes about 2 cups.

SAUCE BÉARNAISE

Add 1 teaspoon tarragon leaves to 1 cup Hollondaise Sauce (page 120).

FRESH FRUIT COCKTAIL

Combine fresh diced apples, orange sections, melon balls, fresh pineapple chunks and fresh strawberries. Sprinkle a few drops of kirsch, brandy or cognac before serving.

CHINA

MENU

Melon Soup

Egg Foo Yoong

Chicken Chop Suey   *Sweet and Sour Spareribs*

Rice

Fortune Cookies

MELON SOUP
(DONG GWAH JONG)

1 small watermelon	1 tablespoon sugar
3 cups watermelon cubes	2½ teaspoons salt
6 cups chicken stock	Dash of pepper
½ cup bamboo shoots	¼ teaspoon monosodium glutamate
1¾ cups sliced mushrooms	¾ cup slivered blanched almonds,
¾ cup diced smoked ham	toasted
¾ cup diced cooked chicken	1 teaspoon chopped shallots
1 whole preserved ginger, thinly	2 tablespoons finely chopped parsley
sliced	

Remove top of watermelon. Scoop out enough watermelon to measure 3 cups cubes. Discard seeds. Scallop edges of watermelon and refrigerate until ready to use. Heat stock in a large saucepan; add bamboo shoots, mushrooms, ham, chicken, ginger, sugar, salt, pepper and monosodium glutamate. Add watermelon cubes and pour all into watermelon shell; sprinkle with almonds, shallots and parsley. Serve at once.

Yield: 8 cups (10 to 12 servings).

EGG FOO YOONG

¼ cup chopped shallots
1 stalk celery, cut in thin strips
½ cup sliced mushrooms
¼ cup sliced water chestnuts
½ cup bamboo shoots

3 tablespoons fat
6 eggs
½ teaspoon salt
¼ teaspoon pepper
1 teaspoon soya sauce

Sauté shallots, celery, mushrooms, water chestnuts and bamboo shoots in the fat for 1 or 2 minutes. Mix eggs, salt and pepper with a fork and add to the vegetables. Cover and cook over medium heat until mixture is golden brown on bottom—about 15 minutes. Remove from pan and cut in long, narrow strips. Sprinkle with soya sauce.

Yield: 6 to 8 servings.

CHICKEN CHOP SUEY

½ cup chopped onions
¼ cup sliced celery
3 tablespoons vegetable oil
1½ cups chopped, cooked chicken
1 teaspoon salt
Few grains pepper
½ teaspoon monosodium glutamate
1 cup hot water

1 can (14 oz.) bean sprouts
1 can (4½ oz.) water chestnuts, sliced
2 tablespoons soya sauce
1 tablespoon Five Roses All-purpose Flour
2 tablespoons cold water

Sauté onions and celery in oil until golden. Add chicken and seasonings, mix well. Add hot water; cover and cook 5 minutes. Add bean sprouts, water chestnuts and soya sauce mixed with Five Roses Flour and cold water. Cook, stirring constantly, for 5 minutes. Serve immediately with hot rice. Drain off sauce, if desired.

Yield: 4 to 6 servings. Recipe may be doubled.

SWEET AND SOUR SPARERIBS

3 lbs. spareribs
2 teaspoons soya sauce
1 tablespoon vegetable oil
2 tablespoons cornstarch
½ cup sugar
½ cup white vinegar

1 tablespoon soya sauce
¼ teaspoon monosodium glutamate
1 green pepper, chopped
1 can (19 oz.) pineapple chunks and juice
½ cup chopped onion

Cut spareribs in small serving pieces; trim off excess fat. Mix the 2 teaspoons soya sauce with vegetable oil and rub over spareribs. Place spareribs on a rack in shallow roasting pan; broil until well browned. Drain off excess fat; remove rack and leave spareribs in pan. Combine cornstarch, sugar, vinegar, soya sauce and monosodium glutamate. Cook over medium heat, stirring constantly, until clear. Add green pepper, pineapple and juice; cook 30 minutes longer, stirring frequently. Add onions and pour over spareribs. Bake in a moderate oven (350°F.) 25 to 30 minutes.

Yield: 4 to 5 large servings or 8 appetizer servings.

FORTUNE COOKIES

Make Sugar Cookie dough (page 65). Roll ¼″ thick and cut with round cookie cutter. Place folded fortune paper in centre; fold dough over and press down edges to seal. Bake in a moderate oven (350°F.) 5 to 8 minutes.

Makes about 3 dozen.

JAPAN

MENU

Shrimp Salad

Sukiyaki   *Rice*

Mandarin Oranges

SHRIMP SALAD

1 large cucumber, thinly sliced	¼ teaspoon salt
6 cooked fresh shrimp	¼ teaspoon monosodium glutamate
½ cup wine vinegar	Dash of celery salt
2 tablespoons sugar	Lettuce leaves

Peel cucumber if desired. Arrange cucumber slices and shrimp on bed of lettuce in serving dish or individual salad bowls. Combine remaining ingredients in a jar and shake well; pour over cucumber and shrimp.

Yield: 6 servings.

SUKIYAKI

1½ lbs. beef tenderloin or sirloin	½ cup sugar
1 cup bamboo shoots	½ cup apple juice or sauterne wine
2 medium-size onions, coarsely	½ cup water
chopped	½ cup soya sauce
1 cup fresh mushrooms, sliced	2″ square of suet
6 green onion tops, cut in 1″ pieces	½ cup salted cashews
2 cups Chinese cabbage, cut in ½″	
x 2″ strips	

Slice meat into paper-thin strips (across the grain). Arrange meat and vegetables attractively on a large platter or tray, keeping each item separate. Have a small container of sugar, apple juice, water and soya sauce handy. Preheat large skillet or chafing dish; add suet and heat until fat is melted, then remove suet. Add beef and sauté until brown. Stir in vegetables except green onion tops; cook for 10 minutes, tossing gently to prevent sticking. Add apple juice mixture, green onion tops and cashews; stir well and serve immediately on a bed of rice.

Yield: 4 servings. Recipe may be doubled.

SCANDINAVIAN SMÖRGÅSBORD

A true Scandinavian Smörgåsbord is only the introduction to a main meal. However, it can be adapted into a main course. Whatever the number of dishes, it must be eaten in courses like any other meal. Begin with the herring and anchovies. Then take a clean plate so that entire meal will not have a herring flavour. Proceed through the fish dishes and cold cuts and then on to the warm dishes. Follow with a salad and of course cheese on wafers or bread. Dessert should be delicate and the coffee strong. It is far better to make several visits to the table than to fill the plate with foods that don't blend. Here are a list of foods to fill your smörgåsbord —the asterisks (*) indicate recipe is given.

FISH
Herring in Sour Cream *
Anchovies
Smoked Salmon
Sardines
Shrimp with Dill *
Fish Balls *

MEAT
Assorted Cold Cuts
Liver Pâté
Ginger Sausages *
Swedish Meat Balls *

SALADS AND VEGETABLES
Pickled Beets *
Stuffed Celery
Tossed Salad
Tomato Aspic (page 183)

CHEESE
Roquefort
Norwegian Goat Cheese
Cheddar
Edam
Swiss

BREADS
Swedish Rye
Lumpa
Pumpernickel
Rye Wafers

DESSERTS
Assorted Fresh Fruit
Spiced Peaches *
Mandelformar * (Almond Tarts)
Morkakor * (Crisp Cookies)

FISH BALLS

2 tablespoons butter
¼ cup Five Roses All-purpose Flour
¾ teaspoon salt
¼ teaspoon white pepper
1 cup light cream
3 cups cooked flaked fish, well
    drained
1 egg yolk, slightly beaten

Few sprigs of dill
¼ teaspoon chopped chervil or
    parsley
Few drops Worcestershire Sauce
2 eggs, beaten
1 cup fine dry bread crumbs
1 qt. vegetable oil

Melt butter in saucepan over medium heat. Blend in Five Roses Flour, salt and pepper. Heat until mixture bubbles, stirring constantly. Gradually stir in cream and cook until thickened, stirring constantly. Let cool. When sauce has cooled, blend in flaked fish, egg yolk, dill, chervil and Worcestershire Sauce; chill 1½ hours. Shape into 1″ balls and dip into beaten eggs; roll in bread crumbs. Heat vegetable oil to 375°F. in deep fryer; add a few fish balls at a time and fry until golden brown. Serve with Hollandaise Sauce, Tartar Sauce or Seafood Cocktail Sauce (pages 120-123).

Yield: 4 to 5 dozen fish balls.

HERRING IN SOUR CREAM

4 salt herring
Water

2 tablespoons chopped shallots
¾ cup commercial sour cream

Soak the herring overnight in enough water to cover. Change the water twice; drain. Skin and bone the herring and chop finely, removing as many bones as possible. Combine the chopped shallots and sour cream and mix with the herring. Chill until ready to serve. Serve on canapés or on crackers or serve as a dip.
Yield: 1¼ cups.
Note: Prepared canned herrings may be used. Do not soak in water.

SHRIMP WITH DILL

2 lbs. fresh or frozen shrimp in shells
8 cups water
6 slices lemon

2 tablespoons salt
5 to 6 sprigs fresh dill

Clean but do not shell shrimp. Combine remaining ingredients and bring to a boil. Add shrimp and simmer 15 minutes. Remove from heat and let cool. Pour off the juice and chill shrimp in refrigerator for at least 2 hours. Serve shrimp in their shells and let guests do their own shelling.
Yield: Enough for 8 persons.

SWEDISH MEAT BALLS

1½ lbs. ground beef
½ lb. ground pork
1 small onion, minced
2 boiled potatoes, mashed
2 cups soft bread crumbs
2 teaspoons salt

Dash of pepper, cloves and
cinnamon
½ bay leaf, crushed
2 eggs
¼ cup Five Roses All-purpose Flour
¼ cup butter

Gravy

¼ cup butter
¼ cup Five Roses All-purpose Flour
3 cups stock
1 cup light cream

Salt and pepper to taste
Few drops commercial gravy
colouring

Sauté onion; combine with meat, mashed potatoes, bread crumbs, seasonings and eggs. Mix well until you have a spongy, smooth mass; shape into 1″ balls. Roll in Five Roses Flour. Brown evenly in butter, shaking pan during the process to keep round shape. Keep warm while preparing gravy. To make gravy: Melt butter over medium heat. Blend in Five Roses Flour and stir to a golden paste. Gradually add stock, stirring constantly. Stir in cream and season to taste. Add gravy colouring to give a rich dark brown colour. Simmer sauce 4 to 5 minutes. Pour sauce over meat balls and cook over low heat, 40 to 50 minutes. Serve warm.
Yield: 6 to 7 dozen meat balls.

GINGER SAUSAGES

2 egg yolks
1 lb. pork sausage meat
½ cup chopped dill pickle

1 teaspoon ginger
2 tablespoons Five Roses All-purpose
Flour

Beat egg yolks; mix with sausage meat, pickles and ginger, blending well. Chill 2 to 3 hours. Shape into very small sausages and roll in Five Roses Flour. Fry in frying pan or in a deep fryer at 375°F. Serve warm.
Yield: 4 to 5 dozen.

PICKLED BEETS

1 cup brown sugar
1½ cups white vinegar
½ cup apple cider (optional)

10 whole cloves
Pinch of salt and pepper
4 cups sliced cooked or canned beets

Combine brown sugar, vinegar, apple cider and seasonings; stir until sugar is dissolved. Pour this brine over the beets and let stand in refrigerator overnight.

SPICED PEACHES

4 lbs. fresh peaches
Whole cloves
2 cups white vinegar

4½ cups sugar
4 cinnamon sticks

Select firm ripe peaches; remove skins. Stud each peach with 3 whole cloves. Pour vinegar into a saucepan; add sugar and 2 cinnamon sticks. Bring to a boil and boil 5 minutes. Drop peaches, a few at a time, into boiling syrup. Let boil 5 minutes until peaches are tender and transparent. Discard cinnamon sticks. Place peaches, syrup and 2 fresh cinnamon sticks in a large bowl; cover and refrigerate until ready to serve. If peaches are not to be used for some time, pack in sterilized jars and place a fresh cinnamon stick in each jar. Pour hot syrup over peaches and seal jars.

Yield: 12 to 15 peaches.

MANDELFORMAR
(Almond Tarts)

⅔ cup butter
⅓ cup sugar
1 egg yolk
½ cup ground, blanched almonds

1½ cups Five Roses All-purpose
Flour
¼ teaspoon almond flavouring
Sweetened whipped cream
Loganberries (optional)

Cream butter; add sugar and cream until light. Mix in egg yolk and ground almonds. Add Five Roses Flour and almond flavouring; blend well. Shape into 2 rolls, 1″ in diameter. Wrap in waxed paper and chill thoroughly—about 1 hour. Slice in ¾″ thick slices; press into small tart pans so that entire shell is ¼″ thick. Bake in a moderate oven (325°F.) 10-12 minutes until golden brown. Cool. Fill with sweetened whipped cream and loganberries.

Yield: About 2 dozen small tarts.

MORKAKOR
(Crisp Cookies)

½ cup butter
¼ cup sugar

1 cup Five Roses All-purpose Flour
¼ teaspoon almond flavouring

Topping

1 egg white
6 tablespoons sugar

2 tablespoons finely chopped
almonds

Cream butter and sugar until light and fluffy. Blend in Five Roses Flour and almond flavouring. Roll out dough ⅛″ thick, between 2 pieces of waxed paper. If dough is hard to roll, place in refrigerator for a little while. Cut dough into fancy shapes with floured cookie cutters. Place on a greased cookie sheet. To prepare topping: Beat egg white until soft peaks form. Gradually add sugar and beat until stiff. Spoon meringue over cookies; sprinkle with chopped almonds. Bake in a moderate oven (350°F.) 8 to 10 minutes or until golden brown on top.

Yield: About 2 dozen, depending on size of cookie cutters.

INDEX